KU-715-766

Book No. **04186563**

30121 0 04186563

≺ ≻

RECONSTRUCTING WOMEN'S THOUGHTS: THE WOMEN'S INTERNATIONAL LEAGUE FOR PEACE AND FREEDOM BEFORE WORLD WAR II

MODERN AMERICA

A series edited by Barton J. Bernstein

RECONSTRUCTING
WOMEN'S THOUGHTS

THE WOMEN'S INTERNATIONAL LEAGUE
FOR PEACE AND FREEDOM BEFORE
WORLD WAR II

≺ ≻

Linda K. Schott

STANFORD UNIVERSITY PRESS
STANFORD, CALIFORNIA
1997

STAFFORDSHIRE
UNIVERSITY
LIBRARY

Stanford University Press
Stanford, California
© 1997 by the Board of Trustees of the Leland Stanford Junior University
Printed in the United States of America

CIP data are at the back of the book

Stanford University Press publications are distributed exclusively by Stanford University Press within the United States, Canada, Mexico, and Central America; they are distributed exclusively by Cambridge University Press throughout the rest of the world.

UNIVERSITY
LIBRARY

SITE: Thompson

-1 DEC 1997
(mk)

CLASS No.
307. 178082

≺ ≻

For Elizabeth Spilman Rosenfield
and in memory of Elsie Boehle Schott

STAFFORDSHIRE
UNIVERSITY
LIBRARY

04186563

≺ ≻

Acknowledgments

Early in my education, several teachers—Michael Stehling, Shirley Stages, Charles Hundley, and Patti Hundley—were essential to my decision to continue my education; in college, two historians—Stanley Campbell and James Vardaman—taught me well and urged me to pursue graduate education. When I began this project, I received indispensable advice from David Kennedy and Estelle Freedman; both have continued to offer invaluable insights in the ensuing years. I also received comments and advice from the members of the Women's History Dissertation Writing Group: Sue Cobble, Yukiko Hanawa, Susan Johnson, Sue Lynn, Valerie Matsumoto, Peggy Pascoe, and Frances Taylor Anton. In the last stages of this project, Peggy Pascoe again took time away from her own work to provide astute comments on mine. Thanks also go to Ann Lane for commenting on the entire manuscript.

At the University of Texas at San Antonio, Woodruff Smith (now at the University of Massachusetts at Boston) and Gena Dagel Caponi provided comments on several stages of this book; and the members of the Faculty Research Committee provided me with a research grant at a critical juncture. My dean, Dwight Henderson, expressed confidence in my abilities and strongly supported women's issues on campus. My colleague Linda Pritchard was all that a faculty mentor should be. Linda has also done more than anyone else to improve the environment for women on our campus; her work made my work easier and more pleasant.

Staff and administrative assistants at both Stanford and the University of Texas at San Antonio have been crucial to my work as a scholar, a teacher, and an administrator; my thanks to Loraine Sinclair, Monica Moore, and Betty Eldon at Stanford and Karen Casto, Elisa Jimenez, Martha LaRoque, Mary McNair, and Ayse Tobey at UTSA. When I became director of the Center for the Study of

STAFFORDSHIRE
UNIVERSITY
LIBRARY

Women and Gender, Bettie Karter and Jan Kruse in the dean's office of the College of Social and Behavioral Sciences kept me from stepping on toes or violating regulations; and the center's graduate assistant during 1993–94, Chris McDade, increased my productivity through her efficiency, skill, and good humor. Especially helpful during the last year of work on this book were graduate assistants Gabriela Gonzalez, Will Guthrie, Robert Kinnally, and Sandra Rubenstein.

Library staff at several institutions also deserve my thanks: Green Library at Stanford, the Minnesota Historical Society, the Wisconsin State Historical Society, the Bentley Library at the University of Michigan at Ann Arbor, the Sophia Smith Collection at Smith College, the Schlesinger Library at Radcliffe College, the New York Public Library, the Library of Congress, and the University of Texas at San Antonio. Special thanks go to Edith Wynner of the New York Public Library, to Wendy Chmielewski and other staff members at the Swarthmore College Peace Collection, and to Sue Mc-Cray at UTSA.

Several friends and relatives have read not a single word of what I have written, yet have contributed enormously through their support and friendship. My longtime friends Loraina O'Neill and Kelly Rogers relieved the pressures of publishing, professing, and parenting with trips shopping and camping; they have also shared my concerns about balancing our lives as professionals and parents. The unconditional love of my father, Rudolph Schott, and my brother, Randy Schott, has always accompanied me and made me stronger. My husband, Jack Noonan, and my sons, Gabriel and Decker, have also given me such love. Decker has grown up with this book, learning at an early age to come to the computer to tell me, "I need some attention now, Momma." As I finished this book and he finished kindergarten, he told his teacher that what his mom liked most was "peace." I would like to think he said this because of my work on this book, but I suspect his comment really stemmed from my repeated requests for "peace and quiet." The response to my work by my older son Gabriel, in true teenage fashion, was more complex; he jokingly threatened to destroy my computer but then excelled in his history classes at school. My husband resolved numerous computer problems, asked about the book's progress when things were going well, and stayed wisely silent when they were not. He also assumed his share of parenting and household responsibilities and graciously accommodated my out-of-town trips and evening administrative responsibilities. After meeting him, historian Anne Scott responded to my complaints about academic life by saying, "But surely having such a lovely husband makes it all easier." It does, and I thank her for pointing it out and him for all that he has done.

Finally, I dedicate this book to two women: Elizabeth Spilman Rosenfield and Elsie Boehle Schott. Elizabeth Rosenfield provided me with pleasant living quarters and expert editorial assistance while I was in graduate school; more important, she provided an unsurpassed example of a lifetime of achievement and personal elegance as well as a model of intellectual curiosity and critical engagement with the world. Elsie Schott, my mother, passed away in 1989, and I have never stopped missing her. As a full partner with my father on our family ranch, she taught me early to resist traditional roles. She provided a model of how to love and nurture. Both women are appropriately honored, I believe, by a book on women who did likewise.

Contents

A photo section follows p. 156.

STAFFORDSHIRE
UNIVERSITY
LIBRARY

<>

RECONSTRUCTING WOMEN'S THOUGHTS: THE WOMEN'S INTERNATIONAL LEAGUE FOR PEACE AND FREEDOM BEFORE WORLD WAR II

STAFFORDSHIRE
UNIVERSITY
LIBRARY

<≺ ≻

Introduction

INTELLECTUAL HISTORIANS have paid too little attention to the
thinking done by women. Since the early 1970s, when feminist
historians began a sustained examination of women's lives, even
fields once assumed to be bereft of women, such as political history
and the history of foreign relations, have been reinterpreted to include the activities of women.[1] But the same has not been done with
intellectual history.

Some feminist historians, of course, have examined the past to
understand the history of feminism and other movements for the advancement of women or have written biographies of a handful of intellectually prominent women. Furthermore, feminist philosophers
are working to understand the ways in which philosophy was and is
engendered.[2] But those who identify themselves as intellectual historians have only rarely written on women or women's ideas. Consider the results of an examination of the journal of record for intellectual history, the *Journal of the History of Ideas*. Between 1981
and 1992 this journal published 453 substantive articles or com-
mentaries; of these, nine, not even 2 percent, were about women or
mentioned women in the title.[3]

Several factors account for this neglect of women and their ideas.
First, many intellectual historians have assumed that their subjects
should be those who "specialized" in thinking or were "expected by
groups within their society to take the lead in doing it."[4] This assumption excludes the vast majority of women in spite of the reality
that some women have thought deeply and systematically. The different life patterns of women have made it unlikely that the opportunity to devote their lives to abstract thought would be theirs; and
sexist assumptions about women's character and intelligence have
made it virtually certain that women would not be expected to take
the lead in thinking.

Second, many intellectual historians have also assumed that a core of "great ideas" exists and that the people who have written about them are the proper subjects for intellectual history. The scholar Jane Arscott, among others, has criticized this view, noting that traditional historians of political thought have focused only on "the biggest and brightest intellectual buoys marking the deepest intellectual channels." This narrow focus leads to what Arscott evaluates as the "fundamental problem with the canon": "the penchant for studying only a very limited cross-section of all that it encompasses, thereby limiting the history of political thought to an excessively narrow range of concepts and themes."[5] Scholars who follow this approach neglect other concepts and themes as well as the thinkers who advanced them.

Third, the ideas that have been considered "great" may very well have been only peripherally important to women's lives. Historians have spent a great deal of time and effort, for example, trying to understand the development of the ideas of democracy and individualism; but these concepts were much more important to enfranchised men than they were to women (or to the enslaved and those whose way of life was more communitarian). Historians have also analyzed changing concepts of human nature; but as feminist scholarship has helped us realize, "human" was usually understood as male, and whether women perceived human nature differently from men was rarely considered.[6] If we look at the past through women's eyes, we must ask if there are ideas that women have identified as important but that men have devalued or ignored. We cannot know the answer to this question until we study what women have written and done.

Fourth, the sources most commonly used by intellectual historians are books and articles, for these are the forms through which those considered important thinkers have traditionally best explained their ideas. But because of the distinctive historical realities of women's lives, women have been less likely to write books and articles, and what they did write was less likely to be preserved. Until the mid-nineteenth century most women were denied access to educational institutions, where they could have responded to men's ideas and developed their own. When they were finally admitted to these institutions, the hostile environment and male-dominated discourse constructed a powerful paradigm of "intellectual importance" that often caused women to stifle their own views and interpretations; and if they did dare to express them, men typically dismissed them as unimportant.[7]

Furthermore, few women have had the leisure time for uninterrupted thought and writing. Instead, women ordinarily have performed the caretaking duties that have allowed men to work without interruption. As historian Gerda Lerner puts it:

> For many centuries the talents of women were directed not toward self-development but toward realizing themselves through the development of a man. Women, conditioned for millennia to accept the patriarchal definition of their role, have sexually and emotionally serviced men and nurtured them in a way that allowed men of talent a fuller development and a more intensive degree of specialization than women have ever had. . . . Women have had less spare time and above all less uninterrupted time in which to reflect, to think and to write.[8]

Relying on books and articles as the central sources for historical investigation is also problematic because doing so privileges those who expressed their ideas in written form over those who expressed their ideas in other ways. As philosopher Elizabeth Karmarck Minnich notes, this makes it appear "as if all Important Ideas are in texts, and only in texts." By relying on books and articles, Minnich writes, scholars "inaccurately and unfairly privilege those who write over those who think, talk, act, and teach with such involvement that they do not pause to produce the texts that, in a text-dominated culture, confer that peculiar thing, ownership of ideas."[9] In short, women have often been too busy—with caretaking, social activism, wage earning—to record and analyze the ideas behind these activities; but the ideas are there and are important, albeit expressed differently.

Because women have tended to express their ideas differently than men, historians who seek to reconstruct and evaluate those ideas fairly must examine the forms women have used: short pieces, such as diary entries, poems, and letters; the records of organizations in which women were active; and the recorded actions of women.[10] In doing so, historians will challenge the intellectual authority granted by authorship of a book or an article and begin to retrieve the ideas of those for whom the separation of thought and action was undesirable because of their philosophical perspectives or unattainable because of their personal circumstances.

In this book, I examine the ideas and activities of a group of edu-

cated women: the most constant and involved national leaders of
the U.S. section of the Women's International League for Peace and
Freedom. Established in 1919, the Women's International League for
Peace and Freedom (WILPF) was an international organization that
grew out of women's opposition to World War I. In the United
States, women had united in opposition to the war in the Woman's
Peace Party in 1915; what was left of this organization reformed in
1919 as the U.S. branch of the WILPF.[11]

Although this book focuses on a peace organization, it is not a
study of women's role in the peace movement or an organizational
history of the WILPF; other scholars have completed or are currently
at work on these much-needed projects.[12] Rather, this book exam-
ines the ideas that brought the leaders of the WIL into the organization and that shaped WIL policy throughout the period between
World War I and World War II.

Some of the leaders of the WIL wrote books and articles, but
most did not. On the whole, their ideas were expressed most eloquently in organizational records, statements of principle and policy, and personal correspondence between leaders. With the exception of statements of principle, these documents were not intended
by their authors to convey a systematic philosophy. Nonetheless,
when combined with an understanding of the personal backgrounds
of the WIL leaders and placed in the context of early-twentieth-cen-
tury America, these documents tell us what these women thought
was important and why.

Only after reconstructing the thoughts of the WIL leaders can we
and should we analyze how their ideas affected our intellectual heritage. Thus the first six chapters of this book focus on rebuilding the
worldview of the WIL leaders. Because ideas do not confine themselves to our chronological markers, the first three chapters cover
material that predates the establishment of the WIL. Chapter 1 ex-
amines the early ideas of Jane Addams and Emily Greene Balch, two
women who provided constant and influential leadership to the
WIL. Chapters 2 and 3 examine the organization and development
of the Woman's Peace Party; although formally separate organizations, the WPP and the WIL shared many leaders, members, and
philosophical perspectives. Chapters 4, 5, and 6 examine the actions
taken by the WIL during the decades between the wars and the ideas
on which those actions were based. Finally, in Chapter 7, I explain

how the ideas of the WIL are reflected in our current understanding of intellectual life in the early twentieth century and suggest how the reconstruction of women's thoughts changes our understanding of our intellectual heritage.

The WIL Leaders

The women who led the WIL during the interwar years can be divided into two categories: those who were active more or less constantly throughout the 1920s and 1930s and those whose involvement was more episodic. In the second group were women who held national leadership positions for several years or who served repeatedly as delegates to national and international conventions: Heloise Brainerd, Gertrude Carmen Bussey, Eleanor Fowler, Ruth Gage-Colby, Dorothy Hommel, Addie Waites Hunton, Lucy Biddle Lewis, Faith Ward Libby, Lola Maverick Lloyd, Bertha McNeill, Anne Martin, Jeannette Rankin, Florence Taussig, Mary Church Terrell, Mabel Vernon, and Amy Woods.[13] Many of these women divided their time among several causes: peace (with the WIL and other peace organizations), feminism, the organization of labor, and other social reforms. Some were younger women who became important WIL leaders only late in the 1930s; still others served as leaders in name but lived too far from Washington for constant involvement. Three of these women—Lola Maverick Lloyd, Anne Martin, and Mabel Vernon—were often at odds with the others, but they continued their affiliation with the WIL for many years despite their differences.

The women whose ideas are clearly presented, either through their own writings or through organizational records, constituted the backbone of the WIL during the interwar years—they gave the WIL their constant allegiance and devoted most of their lives to its work. This smaller group included Jane Addams, Emily Greene Balch, Katherine Devereaux Blake, Dorothy Detzer, Hannah Clothier Hull, and Mildred Scott Olmsted. Of this group, the two who best fit the conventional notion of an intellectual are Addams and Balch. Addams wrote numerous highly acclaimed books and articles and associated with the leading intellectual figures of her time. Her contemporaries thought highly of her work, and historians have also recognized her as a significant thinker.[14] After reading her book *Democracy and Social Ethics* (1902), William James told her he considered it "one of the great books of our time" and acknowledged that he had "learned a lot from your pages."[15] He felt similarly about her book *Newer Ideals of Peace* (1907) and commented that hers "was a deeply original mind, and all so quiet and harmless! Yet revolutionary in the extreme."[16]

Emily Greene Balch was also respected in her time as an intellectual of importance, not only by her female colleagues but also by the men whom historians have identified as significant thinkers of the period. A professor of economics and social science at Wellesley College for twenty years, Balch wrote a groundbreaking study of Slavic immigration to the United States and numerous articles on pacifist theory and international relations. She also shared organizational memberships and discussed international politics with men such as Roger Baldwin, Franz Boas, John Dewey, W.E.B. Du Bois, Paul Kellogg, Reinhold Niebuhr, Norman Thomas, Oswald Garrison Villard, and Stephen Wise. Late in her life, when she was awarded the Nobel Prize for Peace, John Dewey praised her "constructive statesmanship—her intellectual leadership in the understanding and solution of the complicated concrete problems of organizing the affairs of a dynamically peaceful world." Balch, Dewey wrote, had "a gift amounting to genius for discovering new approaches to political and economic problems of international importance."[17]

The other members of the inner circle of WIL leaders—Detzer, Hull, Blake, and Olmsted—did not participate in traditionally defined intellectual activity to the same extent as Balch and Addams. They did devote their lives to the WIL, however, and played a major role in the development of principles and policies during the 1920s and 1930s. Their comments appear frequently in organizational records, and they often expressed their views in correspondence with each other. By expanding our notion of "intellectual activity," as we have expanded our notion of "political activity," we can include the thoughts expressed by these women, however fragmentary and fleeting.

The women who led the WIL were a homogeneous group. Of the women listed above, three were African Americans—Hunton, McNeill, and Terrell—but the rest were European American. They were all middle or upper class. Most of them were born between 1860 and

1900. Blake, Addams, Balch, Lewis, and Terrell were among the oldest, having been born between 1858 and 1867; Detzer, Bussey, Fowler, Gage-Colby, Libby, McNeill, and Olmsted were among the youngest, born between 1887 and 1908. Most of these women were well educated, and several had graduate degrees. Only one, Lucy Biddle Lewis, never attended college. The majority used their education professionally, often in social work or teaching, or eventually made work with the WIL their profession (see Appendix).

Most WIL leaders combined their careers with reform activity. Usually they had been active in the suffrage campaign, and after the vote was won they affiliated with either the National Woman's Party or the League of Women Voters. They also worked with the Young Women's Christian Association, the Women's Christian Temperance Union, the Women's Trade Union League, the National Association for the Advancement of Colored People, the Consumers' League, and of course, other peace organizations such as the Fellowship of Reconciliation, the American Friends Service Committee, the War Resisters League, the National Council for Prevention of War, and the National Committee on the Cause and Cure of War.

In surveying 170 state and national leaders of the WIL, historian Anne Marie Pois found that most WIL leaders married. In the inner circle, however, over half were unmarried: Jane Addams shared a lifelong friendship with a woman, Emily Greene Balch lived with family members or alone, Katherine Devereaux Blake never married, and Dorothy Detzer married only late in life and after she left her leadership position with the WIL.[18] Those who were married throughout the time they worked with the WIL—Hannah Clothier Hull and Mildred Scott Olmsted—shared their commitment to peace work with their husbands. In general, the women who helped lead the WIL either had supportive husbands, partners, or family members or had enough money to hire people to help with household and family responsibilities. Although most WIL leaders had significant relationships with men during some portion of their lives, most selected careers in which they usually worked with other women. Their day-to-day contact with other women produced strong friendships, which in turn often influenced their organizational affiliations.[19]

Unlike the other major pacifist organizations in this period—especially the Fellowship of Reconciliation and the American Friends

STAFFORDSHIRE
UNIVERSITY
LIBRARY

Service Committee—the WIL was a secular organization. Its records indicate that its policies were never based explicitly on Christian principles; rather, most were based on an understanding of what the leaders believed to be women's distinctive moral priorities. This understanding was often, but not always, clearly articulated.

The shared life experiences and political orientation of these WIL leaders did not, of course, mean that they always agreed about matters of principle and policy. But they did share a commitment to making decisions through consensus building: they were willing to work together until they developed a policy statement that expressed the commonly held fundamentals of their ideologies.[20] Statements of policy and principles, then, can be taken as a philosophical stance with which all the leaders would concur, even if each of them might have given it a slightly different emphasis individually. Through the principles, policies, and activities of the WIL, these women expressed their views on contemporary social and political issues. The issues of greatest concern to them fell into two categories: those relating to women and those relating to world peace.

Pacifism and the Movement for World Peace

The cause that initially brought the national leaders of the WIL together was world peace. They were not the first to work for this cause—a nonsectarian peace movement had existed in the United States since 1815.[21] Before the Civil War the organizations leading this movement were the American Peace Society, the New England Non-Resistance Society, and the League of Universal Brotherhood, whose leaders—men such as Elihu Burritt, William Lloyd Garrison, and William Ladd—were also the leaders of other reform efforts, especially the movement for the abolition of slavery. Women also played major roles in this movement, drawing connections between violence, slavery, and the subjugation of women.[22]

This movement ended as the country moved toward civil war in the 1850s. After the war, the older reform-oriented leaders and organizations never regained their prominence, and most peace activity in the post–Civil War era concentrated on the abolition of international war through the establishment of international law and arbitration treaties. An exception was the Universal Peace Union, founded by James and Lucretia Mott and Albert Love. This tiny organization criticized all violence and supported reforms such as temperance, industrial arbitration, improved relations with American Indians and African Americans, and the women's rights movement. Women's organizations, such as the Women's Christian Temperance Union, the National Council of Women, and the National American Woman Suffrage Association, also established separate departments and committees to work for peace.

It took the Spanish-American War to fully revitalize peace activity; at its end, the peace movement grew tremendously, with 45 new peace organizations appearing between 1901 and 1914. These new organizations, however, were usually led by lawyers and businessmen, members of the economic elite. Just as these men believed they were bringing order to the American economic system, so they tried to bring order and rationality to the peace movement. Support for arbitration treaties, international law, and international trade agreements reached new heights.

During the nineteenth century, peace activity had spanned the spectrum from nonresistants such as William Lloyd Garrison on the left to internationalists and arbitrationists on the right. The gradations of peace activity and pacifist commitment were numerous, and they remained so throughout the twentieth century. When women organized during World War I, the variety of their experiences and beliefs caused controversy over the exact extent of their pacifist commitment, eventually prompting the Woman's Peace Party to clarify its position as one of "nonresistance." This term, with a proud heritage in the nineteenth-century work of William Lloyd Garrison, was commonly used by pacifists at the time. As used by the WPP, it meant that the WPP would not commit or condone violence, even in self-defense. This position put the WPP on the far left of the spectrum of peace advocates. Not all members of the organization, of course, agreed with such an extreme position, but it continued to be the official position of the organization.

When the WPP reorganized as the WIL in 1919, it continued to advocate nonresistance, although the term used to describe this position became "nonviolent resistance" or "nonviolence," perhaps because of the influence of Mohandas Gandhi. A subtle shift in meaning also occurred. Unlike "nonresistance," the terms "nonviolent resistance" and "nonviolence" no longer meant only the refusal to commit or sanction violence; they included a commitment to eradicate the underlying causes of violence—political, economic, and social inequalities of all kinds. The WIL leaders did not spend much time precisely defining their philosophical position, but their commitment to equality and justice as well as their abhorrence of violence qualify them as advocates of nonviolence.

The WIL's advocacy of nonviolence sometimes conflicted with its distinctive emphasis on nurturing. In her 1907 book, *Newer Ideals of Peace,* Jane Addams discussed the importance of nurturing others, which became a fundamental belief of the WIL throughout the interwar years. By nurturing, Addams and the other WIL leaders meant providing their fellows with a decent and relatively equal quality of life; a fundamental part of this commitment was the provision of adequate food. But there were times, especially in the 1930s, when the goal of a decent quality of life for all people conflicted with the goal of practicing nonviolence. If a nation was mistreating its own citizens and warring with surrounding nations, it was degrading the quality of life for those people; and if all nonviolent techniques did not deter its actions, advocates of nonviolence began to look like unsympathetic observers or even collaborators. The WIL leaders found no completely satisfactory answer to this dilemma, but their conversations and actions do help illuminate the contours of their philosophy.

Feminism and the Importance of Women's Caretaking Work

The leaders of the WIL were greatly concerned about the role of women in society. Although they did not call themselves feminists—largely because they associated the term with advocates of the Equal Rights Amendment, which they opposed—they held beliefs now commonly accepted as feminist. They perceived women as a disadvantaged social group, believed that women's condition was socially constructed, opposed hierarchies based on sex, and worked to abolish such hierarchies.[23]

The feminism of the WIL leaders grew partially from the gender role prescribed for them by virtue of their social status and the age in which they lived. They had been thoroughly exposed to the rhetoric of "separate spheres" and the idea of complementarity. Men and women were not the same, they had been told; rather, each had characteristics that suited them for particular roles in society. Because men were more rational and aggressive, they were suited for public activities such as politics, business, and war; because women were more emotional and nurturing, they were suited for private activities such as caring for the home, the children, the infirm, and the elderly.[24]

However inaccurately this conception of gender roles may have described the lives of real women and men, and however limited it may seem today, it was used by some women to expand their opportunities. Beginning with the so-called Republican mother who argued that if she were responsible for educating the sons of the republic, she herself needed further education, women effectively argued that their characteristics gave them special knowledge and authority. Thus in the nineteenth century, women demanded and acquired the right to teach school, practice medicine, march for temperance, speak in public, and become missionaries, to mention only a few of women's many activities.[25]

This is not to deny, however, that some women (and probably some men) chafed at the restrictions put upon them. If they were such moral citizens, some women wondered, why were they not allowed to vote? And some discovered that nurturing did not come naturally to them: Charlotte Perkins Gilman, told by her doctor that the only cure for her nervousness was a completely domestic life, nearly lost her sanity before she fled her husband and child. Other women fulfilled the role of mother but resented the amount of time they spent taking care of their families; Elizabeth Cady Stanton, for example, often yearned to exchange diapers and the nursery for campaigning on behalf of women's rights.

Women's and men's lives throughout the nineteenth century only partially reflected the rhetoric of separate spheres, and by the last third of that century the discrepancy between reality and rhetoric was becoming increasingly obvious to middle- and upper-class women. As the future leaders of the WIL grew up, they observed and experienced the strength of women's friendships, but they also acquired educations equal to those of the men their age. They fulfilled their traditional responsibility of nurturing their family members, but they also looked outside the home for others who needed assis-

STAFFORDSHIRE
UNIVERSITY
LIBRARY

tance and care. In doing so, they stretched the boundaries of their sphere until it encompassed much more than their homes. They became not just the moral guardians of their families but the caretakers and nurturers of the nation. Some went to work in professions such as teaching, nursing, and social reform. Others worked largely through voluntary associations, caring for those neglected by government and organizing on behalf of causes that had been considered unimportant or simply overlooked by male political and business leaders.

This caretaking work, whether professional or volunteer, was influenced by and then itself influenced the way these women understood their world. Working with other women far more than they worked with men made it likely that they would perceive gender differences more than similarities and that they would identify women as a group with distinctive interests and values. And spending their lives caring for others while they observed most men of their class pursuing wealth and power made it likely that they would identify nurturing as one of women's distinctive characteristics. The ideology of complementary roles for men and women made sense of the daily pattern of their lives, even if the rhetoric of separate spheres no longer rang completely true. Furthermore, the idea of complementarity gave them justification for doing work that they believed men had wrongfully neglected and caused them to value the work traditionally done by women. It also dictated that they oppose the notion that either men or women were superior. At least theoretically, there could be no hierarchy based on a person's sex in this scheme; women and men were different but not unequal.

The disjuncture between these beliefs and their personal experiences of unequal treatment and opportunities must have been confusing and sometimes painful, an irritant to which they sought a healing solution. The balm they eventually found was the developing scientific consensus that the differences between women and men were socially constructed, not biologically ordained. The women who would later lead the WIL were exposed to this view in their interactions with leading scientists and social scientists, especially at the University of Chicago and Wellesley College. By the time they began organizing for peace, the elements of a feminist consciousness were firmly in place.

This feminist consciousness was also intimately linked to their pacifism. The leaders of the WIL not only eschewed the use of violence (in their own mission and in general) but believed that abstinence from violence had to be accompanied by a positive commitment to nurturing. This commitment developed into a strong program for social justice. The eradication of violence was not enough; equally important was getting rid of racism, sexism, class inequality, and the exploitation of human and natural resources. As the WIL leaders would eventually phrase it, violence was inherent in inequality. For them, feminism and pacifism were inseparable.

The Accepted Intellectual Context:
Victorianism and Modernism

The era during which the leaders of the WIL worked and matured, the late nineteenth century and the early twentieth, is often pictured as a time of transition. What was rural became urban; what was simple became complex; what was uniform became diverse. Behind these generalizations were concrete changes in everyday life. Cities grew as migrants from depressed rural areas and immigrants from Europe sought employment in steadily growing businesses and factories. Those cities could be wondrous places, with the glow of electric lights, the increasingly familiar sputter of automobiles, and an alluring array of consumer goods. But they could also be frightening and confusing. The pace was fast, the goods were out of the economic reach of many workers, and the electric lights often illuminated only dirt, disorder, and corruption.

In the rural areas of the nation parents watched their children move away to seek their fortunes in the cities, and farmers struggled to pay creditors and secure fair shipping rates from the railroads. At the same time, farm life became less isolated as telephones and automobiles shortened the distances between neighbors and communities; and the advent of mail order catalogues brought the consumer goods of the city straight to the rural mailbox.

Intellectual historians interpret this era as one in which a Victorian mindset gave way to a modernist one. They characterize Victorianism as grounded in a set of firm philosophical assumptions: that the universe was predictable and governed by unchangeable natural laws, that human beings were able to ascertain immutable truths about all areas of life, and that absolute moral principles could be determined. Fundamental to these assumptions was a worldview that assumed a moral dichotomy between civilization and savagery. This worldview in turn caused Victorians to view the world oppositionally: right and wrong, white and black, superior and inferior, male and female. These opposites, they believed, were inherent and must therefore be kept distinct and separated.[26]

Ironically, historians portray the fundamental impulse of modernism as just the opposite. Daniel Singal writes in his recent reassessment of modernism, "The quintessential aim of Modernists has been to reconnect all that the Victorian moral dichotomy tore asunder—to integrate once more the human and the animal, the civilized and the savage, and to heal the sharp divisions established in the nineteenth century in areas such as class, race, and gender." Only this, modernists believed, would make it "possible to combat the fundamentally dishonest conception of existence that the Victorians had propagated, liberate the natural human instincts and emotions that the nineteenth century had bottled up, and so restore vitality to modern life." This "integrative mode," as Singal calls it, explains the modernist fondness for paradox, ambivalence, and placing concepts and observations along a spectrum instead of in clearly separate categories, as well as the movements to eliminate racial segregation and separate spheres for men and women. It also accounts for the modernist desire to reunify the human mind, fusing the conscious with the unconscious and the emotional with the rational into a truly "authentic" self.

Modernists could never be certain that they would achieve the integration they sought, however, for they believed the universe was constantly changing and that human knowledge would thus remain partial and transitory. In such a situation, humans had to resign themselves to moral uncertainty and be willing to readjust constantly to changing situations. This atmosphere of change and uncertainty meant that the modernist goal of integration would itself remain unattainable. Modernists would live in a state of constant tension, striving for a goal that they believed was ultimately unreachable.

These generalizations about Victorianism and modernism are based largely on men's writings. In his analysis of the transition from Victorian to modernist thought in the American South, for example, Singal analyzed the thoughts of nine men and one woman. George Cotkin, in a recent analysis of late-nineteenth-century American thought and culture that sincerely tries to integrate women, lists in his index 36 women's names and 173 men's names. Furthermore, the structure of Cotkin's book implies that women's ideas are vital only to the discussion of women. His mentions of women are confined almost entirely to the chapter that discusses women; only five women are mentioned in chapters exploring religion, philosophy, anthropology, and consumerism.[27]

Since our current understanding of Victorianism and modernism is based largely on the ideas of men, are these interpretive constructs helpful to understanding the ideas of women? Did the women who organized the Woman's Peace Party, for example, base their decision to organize separately from men on a Victorian conviction of women's moral superiority, as many historians have argued?[28] Or can their work for integration be seen as modernist, even though they sought to achieve it through separatist action? Did their emphasis on the importance of nurturing betray Victorian sentimentality, out of place in an age of increasing professionalism and rationalization? These questions and others are addressed in the last chapter, in which I argue that the ideas of women fit only partially and uncomfortably into the largely male-defined categories of traditional intellectual history. To understand and appreciate women's thoughts, we must dissolve the old constructs and let new, multifaceted ones replace them.

Philosophical Foundations

The Early Ideas of Jane Addams and
Emily Greene Balch

THE DECADES IMMEDIATELY preceding World War I were years of intense debate about the nature of the political and economic systems of the United States. Businesses had grown larger than ever before, and the economy struggled to recover from the depression of the 1890s. To most people it was clear that the economy, or at least the largest corporations, would have to be controlled or regulated in some way. Politics also seemed to have gotten out of hand, especially in the growing cities. Corruption was widespread, and here too most people believed that something had to change.

In the social realm, the need for change was also apparent. Immigrants continued to pour into the United States, landing first in the large cities along the coastlines and waterways. There most stayed, unable or unwilling to move into the far less populated regions of the West, the Midwest, and the South. With backgrounds in agriculture or skill in trades for which there was little demand in the rapidly industrializing United States, these people usually ended up working for low wages and living in crowded, unhealthful conditions. Some eventually returned to their native countries, but for those who stayed the climb out of poverty and squalor was usually slow, hard, and uncertain.

The international situation was similarly unsettled. The men who most influenced the foreign policies of the United States had been encouraging the expansion of its economic and political influence abroad. As a result, the United States worked to consolidate its influence in Latin America and the Pacific; it risked war with Great Britain over a border dispute in Venezuela in 1896 and annexed the Hawaiian Islands in 1898. This last act came in the middle of the

U.S. conflict with Spain over Cuba and the Philippines, a conflict that ended with the United States formally acquiring colonies for the first time. That acquisition did not pass unchallenged, however, and a great deal of discussion arose over the wisdom of becoming an imperial power. Taking part in that discussion was Jane Addams.

Jane Addams and the Substitution of Nurture for Warfare

Jane Addams was born in 1860 in northern Illinois. Her father, John Addams, was a wealthy businessman, banker, and state senator; her mother, Sarah Addams, ran the family and reared the children until her death in 1863. Addams was then reared by her aunt and a nurse until her father remarried in 1868. She attended a one-room school with the other children in the community, but as she got older, set her heart on going to college at Smith. Her father refused to allow her to do so, sending her instead to the Rockford Female Seminary in Rockford, Illinois, a school he had patronized for many years. Addams soon became a leader at Rockford and attracted many friends, the closest of whom was Ellen Gates Starr, with whom Addams later founded Hull House.[1]

After graduating from Rockford, Addams returned to her family home in Cedarville, Illinois, with plans to renew her studies at Smith College in the fall. But when her father died suddenly from a ruptured appendix, Addams began a steady spiral downward into sickness and despondency. Following a pattern that was common in the late nineteenth century for women and men of the upper-middle and upper classes, Addams languished, unable to chart a course for her life. She attempted medical school in the fall of 1881 but soon withdrew because of health problems. In 1883 she went on a two-year tour of Europe with her stepmother and other family members and friends. In the summer of 1885 she returned to the United States and resumed her role as occasional companion to her stepmother and other family members. Still dissatisfied with her lack of purpose, Addams planned another trip to Europe, this time with friends Ellen Starr and Sarah Anderson. It was on this trip that Addams finally decided on her life's work. Influenced by the example of Toynbee House in London as well as by other social reform institutions, Addams decided to open a social settlement house in the United States.

Addams and Ellen Starr moved to Chicago in January 1889 and began publicizing their plans for a social settlement. They successfully attracted financial support from many of the city's prominent citizens and opened Hull House in September. The venture became famous quickly, often being reported as a selfless effort by the wealthy to help the less fortunate. Addams herself, however, always reminded audiences and readers that Hull House was founded not just to help the poor. There was an entire generation of women who had been taught, by both parents and institutions of higher learning, that they should do something meaningful with their lives; but when they graduated, most often the dominant expectation was that they would either return to their families or marry and begin families of their own. If neither choice appealed to them, their other options were limited. Addams realized that she and many of her friends were in this situation. As she later phrased it, the decision to open a social settlement arose not only from the obvious need for such an institution but also from the "subjective necessity" of finding meaningful work and wider experience for educated women like herself.

Hull House flourished in the years that followed. It attracted a remarkable group of women, many of whom would lead social and political reform groups in the decades to come. They included Julia Lathrop, Florence Kelley, Grace Abbott, Edith Abbott, Alice Hamilton, Charlotte Perkins Gilman, and Emily Greene Balch. Some men also worked there, and others visited, did research, and gave guest lectures. Among the latter were several University of Chicago professors who developed close ties to Hull House and its residents. Addams remained the undisputed leader of the venture, however, and her fame grew; by the end of the century she was a prominent national figure.

Like many people of her generation, Addams had a deep faith that the human race was gradually becoming more civilized and less capable of barbaric acts such as war. The United States' war with Spain and its repression of the Filipino independence movement, however, challenged this faith and forced her to examine and develop her beliefs more thoroughly. From 1898 until 1907 she occasionally wrote articles and gave speeches outlining her views, and in 1907 she published *Newer Ideals of Peace*. Although not her last publication on this issue, this book was the most systematic statement of her views, views that did not change significantly during the rest of her lifetime.

In this book as well as in her other works, Addams endeavored to show how problems that most people considered totally unrelated were actually closely connected. The woman's movement, the labor movement, the struggle against the unfair and violent treatment of African Americans, the movement for mediation of international conflicts, the efforts to clean up the cities, both physically and politically: all of these were part of the peace movement, as Addams conceived of it. For to Addams, peace was not simply the absence of war; it was actively caring for all people.

Addams based her views largely on her experiences at Hull House. As she noted in the preface to *Newer Ideals of Peace*, "These studies in the gradual development of the moral substitutes for war have been made in the industrial quarter of a cosmopolitan city where the morality exhibits marked social and international aspects."[2] It was living and working among peoples of diverse backgrounds, within Hull House itself and in its neighborhood, that had convinced Addams that nurturing others could provide a peaceful alternative to war.

But defining her understanding of peace for an audience that had not shared her experiences was difficult. Critics accused her of advocating nonresistance, a philosophy that they incorrectly associated with passivity. Addams disputed this accusation but also struggled to find terms that would better define her position. Addams wanted to convey a sense of dynamism; words such as " 'overcoming,' 'substituting,' 're-creating,' 'readjusting moral values,' 'forming new centres of spiritual energy,'" she wrote, "carry much more of the meaning implied."[3] She wanted not only more active descriptors but also a more active approach to creating peace. International treaties and the arbitration of conflicts, the most commonly proposed methods for achieving a peaceful world during the period before World War I, did nothing to solve the underlying causes of conflict. Far more important, Addams believed, was "the nourishing of human life."[4] Addams devoted much of the rest of her book to giving examples of what she meant, how it could be accomplished, and by whom.

To gain a sympathetic audience, Addams needed to make clear that abolishing war would not weaken the nation. Some of her contemporaries worried that, because of industrialization and urbanization, American citizens were growing too accustomed to comfort, security, and leisure. Theodore Roosevelt, for example, believed that a degree of militarism and violent conflict was essential to ensure nobility, hardiness, and courage within a nation's citizenry.[5] Addams rejected this position outright. The proponents of war, she wrote, argue that war is "interwoven with every fibre of human growth and is at the root of all that is noble and courageous in human life, that struggle is the basis of all progress." Addams argued in response that to continue to believe that war "stirs the nobler blood and the higher imagination of the nation, and thus frees it from moral stagnation and the bonds of commercialism" was "to borrow our virtues from a former age and to fail to utilize our own." She could still find admirable the courageous acts committed by warriors in the past but thought it was "stupid" to think that only war could elicit that kind of courage. "Let us by all means acknowledge and preserve that which has been good in warfare and in the spirit of warfare," she wrote; "let us, however, not be guilty for a moment of shutting our eyes to that which for many centuries must have been disquieting to the moral sense." War, she continued, is "an implement too clumsy and barbaric to serve our purpose." Certainly, there were "other methods" of getting people to sympathize with each other and share a common purpose.[6]

Addams's position was similar to that advanced by William James, the Harvard philosopher and psychologist who formulated many of the tenets of pragmatism. Since the late 1880s James had toyed with the notion of an alternative to war that would still elicit the personal traits desired by Roosevelt and others. In 1904 James and Addams both spoke to the Universal Peace Conference on this topic, and in 1910, shortly before his death, James published an essay in which he outlined his "moral equivalent" of war. He proposed a program of civilian service to the state, in which the young men of the nation would struggle against nature instead of against each other or the youth of other nations. This period of required service would induce selflessness and physical strength in a group perceived as lacking those characteristics.[7]

Addams tended to agree with James, at least that an alternative to war could stir the same selflessness and nobility that war supposedly stirred. Her "moral substitute" for war, however, was both more general and more inclusive than James's. First, she had no clear-cut proposal like James's for a civilian service program. Rather, Addams believed that a widespread concern for social welfare could provide the moral substitute for war. Occasionally she gave specific examples of the kind of concern she thought necessary—such as the "determination to abolish poverty and disease"—but most of the time she wrote more generally about "the nourishing of human life" and "pushing forward social justice."[8] These general phrases described the types of social reform in which she and her colleagues at Hull House took part: cleaning up the physical environment, improving the conditions in which people worked, making the political system less corrupt, providing child care and education. More and more people around the nation were pursuing these reforms, she believed; thus more and more people were experiencing the rewards of working for others.

Addams probably overstated the general commitment to these activities. Many people, of course, never took part in social welfare work and did not even agree that it was important. At the same time, because her work at Hull House had attracted both national and international attention and praise, it was understandable that she would interpret that response as widespread support for her aims and programs. Certainly there must have been plenty of people who praised what she did without any intention of doing it themselves. If that thought occurred to Addams, as it must have, she chose to ignore it, focusing instead on the general approval of her program. This choice was necessary politically, for if she did not have faith in her own program, neither would others. But this choice also reflected her own hope that humanity would gradually progress away from barbarism and violence and toward humanitarianism and peace.

Her view of the progressive development of humanity was a common one at the turn of the century. What was different about Addams's position was her belief that women and members of the working class had important roles to play in this development. Addams had formulated her view of women's role early in her life. While still at Rockford Female Seminary she had written that "the impervious will of man is at last forced to admit that woman like himself possesses an intellect [and] that she exerts a potent influence in the age in which she lives." She and other young women like her wanted "the same right to independent thought and action" that men had; but, she added, they also wanted to "retain the old ideal of womanhood—the saxon lady whose mission it was to give bread unto her household."[9] Addams thus summarized the prescribed nineteenth-century gender roles in which she, as a member of the upper class, had been schooled: men were independent and active while women were nurturing. But she did not simply accept those roles as they had been taught her and place herself in the woman's role. Instead, she claimed both the male and female roles. She refused to abandon the important work traditionally associated with women in order to claim the rights traditionally ascribed to men.

Addams developed this position further in *Newer Ideals of Peace*. The separation of men and women and the division of characteristics accordingly, Addams wrote, were the roots of the problems of the modern city. American cities were in trouble on the one hand "because office holders have carried with them the predatory instinct learned in competitive business," and on the other hand "because women, the traditional housekeepers, have not been consulted as to its multiform activities."[10] Because men had been taught by a competitive economic system to do whatever was necessary to serve their own interests, they could not be expected to work selflessly for social welfare. And women, who had been taught to care for others, were not allowed to participate in the running of businesses and cities.

This was a seriously flawed division of responsibilities and rights, and in it, women lost even more than men. Addams pointed out that women were "losing what they have always had." She believed that "most of the departments in a modern city can be traced to woman's traditional activity"—concern for health and cleanliness, for example. But she also made clear that as "so soon as these old affairs were turned over to the care of the city, they slipped from women's hands, apparently because they then became matters for collective action and implied the use of the franchise." And women, taught to leave the affairs of government to men, had generally not resisted this transfer of responsibilities, even when the responsibility in question was one closely associated with women's traditional role. Addams found this situation appalling. "Are we going to lose ourselves in the old circle of convention and add to that sum of wrong-doing which is continually committed in the world because we do not look at things as they really are?" she asked. "Old-fashioned ways which no longer apply to changed conditions," she wrote, "are a snare in which the feet of women have always become readily entangled."[11]

One remedy for this situation was to extend the vote to women. Debate on this issue had begun officially in 1848, subsided during the Civil War, and then resumed during the debate over extending the vote to freed male slaves. Suffragists split over whether to support that cause or to work for its defeat if the vote for women were not included. They finally reunited in 1890 with the formation of the National American Woman Suffrage Association (NAWSA), which led the struggle for the next twenty years. Suffragists generally made two arguments for their cause. They argued that it was only fair to extend to female citizens this right of citizenship and that giving the vote to women would improve government by bringing women's distinctive concerns into it.

Addams agreed with these reasons for giving the vote to women, but she also believed that getting the vote would help to educate women about public affairs. "As we believe that woman has no right to allow what really belongs to her to drop away from her," she wrote, "so we contend that ability to perform an obligation comes very largely in proportion as that obligation is conscientiously assumed."[12] She wanted to bring what she considered to be women's traditional concerns and abilities into the public realm while also helping more women to see the importance of participating in that realm.

Addams's alternative to war, her "moral substitute," demanded that women assume their equal share of responsibilities and rights in public affairs. She based this demand on her belief that caring for people's welfare had been neglected by the men who had run the government so far, and this neglect had led to the poor state of American cities. One part of the solution was to allow women to bring into public affairs the concerns they had cultivated as caretakers of children, the sick, and the elderly. Yet she also made clear that women's concerns, much less their abilities, did not stop there. She did not want to confine women to the role of nurturer, but she did want to convince the larger population that nurturing was important work.

Addams also believed that people from the working class had an important role to play in the development of a peaceful, humanitarian world. She believed that workers shared some of the qualities that she identified with women's traditional role: they produced rather than destroyed, and they nourished the nation through their labor. As early as 1904 she had asked, "Who should band together for preserving human life, for keeping the fields free from the trampling of soldiers, from the destruction of the precious bread that men love to have?" Her answer was "the workers, who year after year nourish and bring up the bulk of the nation." It was the workers, "those who produce," who should lead the peace movement.[13]

The workers to whom Addams looked were generally immigrants living in the poor, crowded sections of major American cities. Life was hard there, and Addams believed that the residents responded to their difficulties not by struggling against each other but by supporting each other. Equally important was that the residents of the inner city came from many different nations. Leaving their native lands had forced these immigrants to seek companionship among strangers, ignoring their superficial differences and emphasizing their common plight. "Because of their difference in all external matters, in all of the non-essentials of life," Addams wrote, "the people in a cosmopolitan city are forced to found their community of interests upon the basic and essential likenesses of their common human nature; for, after all, the things that make men alike are stronger and more primitive than the things that separate them." It was not that these people were naturally kinder or more cooperative; such a belief would have undermined Addams's argument. What made her position convincing, she believed, was that this kind of harmony grew out of a real situation. The immigrant worker had to cooperate with his neighbors "not only to avoid crushing the little folk about him, but in order to save himself from death by crushing." It was this "irresistible coalescing of the altruistic and egoistic impulse" Addams suggested, that was the "strength of social morality."[14]

For Addams, then, the inner-city neighborhoods in which she lived and worked offered great hope for a peaceful world. "It is possible," she wrote, "that we will be saved from warfare by the 'fighting rabble' itself, by the 'quarrelsome mob' turned into kindly citizens of the world through the pressure of a cosmopolitan neighborhood." Addams did not think this transformation would happen quickly; in fact, she acknowledged that inner-city residents would continue to be overtly supportive of war. But she believed that their daily experiences would gradually force them to overlook superficial differences and acknowledge their similarities until eventually they and others in the United States would "find it as difficult to make war upon a nation at the other side of the globe as upon our next-door neighbor."[15]

This belief seems idealistic. Certainly, looking backward from the late twentieth century, the inner cities look more like battle-grounds than the cradles of a peaceful world. But did today's urban problems evolve inevitably from the circumstances Addams described? Was Addams's vision of the inner cities so inaccurate, or did the nation pursue policies that sidetracked the developments Addams foresaw? The suburban development that grew steadily throughout the twentieth century undeniably contributed to the decline of inner-city communities; cities became places to work, not to live—at least for those who could afford to move elsewhere. Businesses developed with little concern for their impact on the neighborhoods in which they operated or the workers they employed. Some workers prospered through long hours of hard work and were able to move out of the inner city; others stagnated, mired by poverty and the racial biases of the European Americans who dominated the society and the economy. These developments bear little resemblance to the "nourishing of human life" advocated by Addams. There was, she noted, an "undoubted tendency to barbarism and degeneracy when the better human qualities are not nourished."[16] In other words, Addams believed that the environment in which people lived and worked greatly affected their behavior. Exploit people and they would exploit each other in turn; nurture people and they would nurture others.

Thus, although Addams's beliefs and hopes may have been idealistic, because they were never tested, judging them is difficult. What can be said with certainty is that Addams's alternative to war—the active nurturing of people led by those she believed had the most experience with nurturing and producing, women and workers—included groups that peace organizations at the time usually excluded. The most prominent peace organizations before World War I tended to be elitist and focused on relations among nation-states, not among individuals.[17] And even those peace activists who accepted Addams's belief that war had to be stopped at the individual level tended to be exclusionary and elitist.

A dramatic case in point is the alternative to war posed by William James. James did not believe that war could be stopped through international treaties and arbitration agreements, for he believed that individuals often found war exciting, an alluring relief from an otherwise routine life lacking in opportunities for heroism. His proposed alternative to war, however, was tailored to fit the needs of wealthy men, not men and women of all classes. He claimed that his civilian service program would recruit "the whole youthful population." But among the benefits of his program, he said, were that it would make the participants "better fathers" and "make the women value them more highly." Furthermore, he claimed that this civilian service program was needed because people had lost contact with "the permanently sour and hard foundations" of life and with hard physical labor. Surely the workers in factories and fields around the nation hardly needed more of this kind of contact; it was only those of the privileged class, such as James himself, who had lost contact with the reality of life for most people.[18]

Addams, of course, was also from the privileged class, but she had chosen work that thrust her into the middle of working-class life. Furthermore, as a woman she had experienced exclusion in various ways, and unlike many others of her class, she had been sensitized to the pain of exclusion and economic need. Most important, she recognized that people's differences could be sources of strength. She incorporated this insight into her proposed alternative to war: a diverse, pluralistic society in which citizens and the government made the nurturing of human life a top priority. It almost went without saying that such a society would be one in which all people would be equally valued, regardless of race, ethnicity, class, or gender.

The society envisioned by Addams would also be a nation at peace and without colonies. Addams abhorred violence and believed that it resulted from failing to regard other people as valuable and equal human beings. "Class and group divisions with their divergent moralities," she noted, "become most dangerous when their members believe that the inferior group or class cannot be appealed to by reason and fair dealing, but must be treated upon a lower plane." Addams believed that people with this attitude "inevitably revert to the use of brute force—to the methods of warfare."[19] Violence by employers against striking workers, unionists against nonunionists, and European Americans against African Americans was the result.

The same attitude of condescension led to imperialism, in Addams's view. Developed nations, such as the United States, that tried to impose their political and economic systems upon others did not acknowledge the merits of different cultures and values. Indeed, Addams believed they were showing that they were not truly democratic. Instead of trying to impose on other nations "old and possibly worn out ideas," Addams wanted Americans to trust the people of other nations, "although they are of a different color, although they are of a different tradition from ours." This trust might then "nourish them into another type of government, not Anglo-Saxon even," and, she mused, "prove that some things that are not Anglo-Saxon are of great value, of great beauty."[20]

Addams's anti-imperialism had other roots as well. Like most other Americans of her generation, Addams believed that the democratic traditions of the United States made it exceptional among nations. In her view, however, this exceptionality was fading as the United States pursued economic opportunities in other countries. "Had our American ideals of patriotism and morality in international relations kept pace with our experience, had we followed up our wide commercial relations with an adequate ethical code," Addams believed, Americans would have declined "commercial advantages founded upon forced military occupation." If America was to remain true to the ideas that made it exceptional, it would have to "employ something more active and virile, more inventive, more in line with our temperament and tradition, than the mere desire to increase commercial relations by armed occupation as other governments have done."[21]

Well before the beginning of World War I, Addams warned of the dangers of imperialism and the unrelenting pursuit of economic gain; a far better goal, she believed, was developing a respect for different cultural traditions that would make intervention in other nations' affairs and the exploitation of their citizens and resources unthinkable. Addams also emphasized the ways in which groups that had been ignored by or excluded from the dominant culture could contribute to the attainment of a fair society at home and a peaceful

STAFFORDSHIRE
UNIVERSITY
LIBRARY

world abroad; in fact, she suggested that these groups were more likely than the traditional leaders of society to eventually bring the most essential change to American society, the substitution of nurture for warfare.

Many of Addams's ideas—and her future work in the peace movement—were shared by Emily Greene Balch, a woman with whom Addams had worked and corresponded since the early 1890s. Balch's ideas, however, developed not from working in a social settlement but from her academic training and research in economics and sociology.

Emily Greene Balch: "To Do All I Can as Well as I Can for the Best Purpose I Can See"

Emily Greene Balch was born in 1867 in Jamaica Plains, Massachusetts, into a family whose roots in New England went back to the colonial period. Her father was a graduate of Harvard and a practicing attorney in Boston; her mother, a teacher before her marriage, bore six children before her premature death in 1884. Emily was the second child and played a major role in the care of her younger siblings after her mother's death. The family was loving and supportive, with the relationship between Emily and her father being especially close.[22]

As a youth, Emily Balch attended a private school for girls in Boston. She then planned to attend the Harvard Annex, now Radcliffe, with her good friend Alice Gould. Gould's father, however, was a Harvard professor, and he balked at the idea of his daughter's attending college so close to home. It was bad enough to have her going to college; it would be much worse to have his Cambridge friends know of this disgrace. Gould and Balch then settled on Bryn Mawr and entered there in 1886.

Balch realized that for a woman to attend college was to set herself apart from the mainstream. She believed that her decision would make her a "marked character in the neighborhood" and feared that people would tease that they "were afraid to talk to me, I was so learned." She noted, however, that these same people seemed to have little trouble talking to young men with college educations and "could not see why my very modest undergraduate studies should be more of a barrier" than that of the men.[23]

Yet Balch was neither an advocate of women's rights nor a suffragist when she entered Bryn Mawr. She did eventually decide to support the struggle for women's suffrage but recorded in her journal that this was a "change to an opinion which was wholly against my taste and associations."[24] She neglected to explain why. Perhaps she disliked appearing to support the rights of any one group over those of others, or perhaps she simply meant that her support for suffrage flew in the face of her traditional upbringing and the views of her family and friends. Regardless, this decision began her connection with women's rights movements, a connection that would last throughout her life, although it never became her primary cause.

Another connection she forged at Bryn Mawr was with the Society of Friends, or Quakers. This group had founded Bryn Mawr to provide women with an education equal to men's, and their influence at the school was strong. Balch began attending Quaker meetings and found herself drawn to the Quaker way of worship and their strong witness for peace. Much later in her life she would make this connection a formal one.

Academics demanded most of Balch's time and attention, of course, and she excelled in her studies. Although she was initially attracted to literature, by her last year Balch had switched to economics. She had begun to study the conditions of workers in England and the United States and was particularly affected by Jacob Riis's *How the Other Half Lives*.[25]

Balch got the chance to pursue such topics when she was awarded a fellowship for study in Europe the year after her graduation in 1889. In Paris she conducted historical research on France's program of public assistance for the poor. She was dissatisfied with this work, however, because she was relying on secondary sources instead of observing firsthand the conditions of the poor and the operations of the public assistance program.[26] Balch shared the desire for experience, instead of abstract study, that had prompted her future colleague Jane Addams to found Hull House.

After her year of study in Paris, Balch returned to the United States determined "to see something of things for myself." She first worked with the Children's Aid Society of Boston. Then, in the summer of 1892, Balch attended the Summer School of Applied Ethics conducted by Dr. Felix Adler. There she met people who were to influence the rest of her life, including Jane Addams, Helena Dudley, and Julia Lathrop, all social reformers involved in the settlement house movement. She also met Katherine Coman and Vida Scudder, who would later be colleagues at Wellesley College. As a result of their experiences that summer, Balch, Dudley, and Balch's friend Helen Cheever started the settlement Denison House in Boston the next winter. Balch directed this operation, although she never made the settlement house her primary residence, and began to see firsthand the problems of the working class. She became involved in labor unionism as well as with the Consumers' League.

Balch took a special interest in the problems of working women while she was at Denison House. She and the other residents worked to improve the conditions of women tobacco strippers and telephone operators in particular. Balch also participated in the "Working Girls' Club," in which women workers and wealthier women such as Balch met together. The ideal of this club, according to Balch, was "to bring rich and poor together not in the one demoralizing relation of benefactor and beneficiary but as far as may be naturally and simply, in all true kindliness and goodwill, to learn of one another."[27]

Balch's characterization of this club seems naive; it is likely that no matter how much she tried to deny the class differences between herself and the women workers she met, the workers at least were still quite aware of them. There is no reason to suspect, however, that Balch was being deliberately disingenuous. Her statements before this time, as well as her activities later, show that she was genuinely interested in learning about the lives of the working class and in trying to help the workers improve their conditions. Her statements also illustrate her early commitment to breaking down artificial barriers among women in the interest of further integration.

Balch obtained more settlement house experience in the following years by spending time at Hull House with Jane Addams.[28] During this time, her acquaintance with Addams no doubt blossomed into the deep friendship that endured throughout their lives and their work for peace. Unlike Addams, however, Balch could not commit herself to a career in social work. "I gradually became dissatisfied with my philanthropic efforts," she recalled, and decided that she could have more impact as a teacher: "If I could awaken the desire of women students to work for social betterment and could help them to find the best methods worked out at that time, my efforts however feeble would at least mean getting hold of the long arm of the lever." Thus she decided to leave settlement work and continue her education, first at the Harvard Annex, then at the University of Chicago, and finally at the University of Berlin.[29]

Because the University of Berlin was not open to women, Balch—and her fellow student Mary Kingsbury [Simkovitch]—had to secure permission to study there from administrators as well as from each of their professors. Balch was conscious of her responsibility as a pioneer; she wrote her father that she "should be awfully sorry to make women *personae non grata* in the university now they are just being let in."[30] This sense of responsibility surely curtailed Balch's activities to some extent, but it did not prevent her and Kingsbury from participating in the meetings of a social science association whose members were all men. At the first meeting Balch, Kingsbury, and a few other women sat in the gallery while the male students sat on the floor below and drank beer; at the second meeting Balch was somewhat disturbed to find an open room with no gallery. The men did not turn the women away on that account, however, but seated them at the head table. The men also stopped smoking, for which, Balch wrote, she and Kingsbury were sorry. On the whole, Balch concluded, "the students behave very well, simply take no notice of us for the most part. No one ever opens a door for you or says excuse me if he bumps into you."[31]

These experiences at the University of Berlin influenced Balch's understanding of gender roles. In an almost exclusively male institution for the first time, she had to puzzle out a sort of personal code of behavior. She believed that she was participating as an equal—whether her male colleagues felt the same is open to question—and found that participation intellectually stimulating and socially liberating. In general, then, Balch seemed comfortable moving in the world of the German students and only challenged traditional roles by her mere presence and force of mind. She did not make evident a sense that women brought a particular set of concerns or values to the university, as her friend Jane Addams might have, but seemed secure in her sense that women could fit into this male world with few problems.

While in Berlin, Balch wrote long, descriptive letters to her family members. The content varied depending on whom she was addressing but usually focused on the social and academic events she attended and the short trips into the countryside she occasionally made. She rarely commented on political affairs, but she did mention the Venezuelan-British border crisis. She had been following the affair in the English newspapers and had found the prospect of war disturbing. "I could not believe war possible," she wrote her father, "but for a short time the prospect looked really threatening, did it not?" She also told her father that she found the Germans to be "a most peaceable folk, in spite of their enforced militarism."[32] Balch had not yet become a pacifist, but issues of war and peace were clearly beginning to occupy her mind.

Balch's mind was also occupied with concern about her future. Although she had earlier decided to pursue teaching, she began to consider working with her father's law firm. He responded supportively, although he did not understand her motivation. He did not think she wanted simply to "be a pioneer opening the way to women in this field," and he certainly did not want her to do it to be a comfort to him. He told her "it would be anything but a comfort if I felt you were being taken away from your true work" and that "it would be a pure waste if you were put to some clerical work." Her father seems to have understood Balch's mixed motivations even better than she did, and it was doubtlessly very important to her that he thought "it would be a mistake to give up on what you are doing unless it becomes very irksome." He believed that she could make a fine contribution as a teacher and that she had a "high order of ability and a kindly and equable spirit."[33]

Not long after receiving this advice, Balch decided to return to the United States to pursue her doctorate. On the passage home, however, she found herself on the same ship as her acquaintance Katherine Coman, who was teaching economics at Wellesley. When Coman invited her to take a half-time position at Wellesley, Balch could not refuse. She wanted to earn her own income and cease being an expense to her father; she also wanted to fulfill his wish that she live at home. This job would allow her to do both. Balch accepted Coman's offer and began her career as a college professor.

Balch was a successful professor, although she was not at all conventional in that role. She demanded that her students master economic and sociological theory, but she also encouraged them to see how these theories meshed with reality by getting involved in social reforms. Balch herself served on numerous state commissions, helped organize and lead the Boston Women's Trade Union League, joined the Socialist Party, and supported striking workers. While doing all of this, she also conducted research for her first major book, *Our Slavic Fellow Citizens*, published in 1910.

In this book Balch expressed the pluralistic perspective she had developed during her travels and years of study. For this exhaustive study of the immigration of Slavs to the United States, Balch committed herself to conducting firsthand research. In an era when intensive fieldwork was still the exception among sociologists and anthropologists, Balch traveled to Austria-Hungary, the home of most of the immigrants, as well as to the communities they had settled around the United States. The resulting lengthy, detailed description of the life and customs of the Slavs in both Europe and the United States was timely, for immigration had become a volatile political issue. The United States had long been a preferred destination for European immigrants, but before 1880 most had come from northern and western Europe. This began to change in the 1880s, as more and more people began coming to the United States from southern and eastern Europe. Because these "new" immigrants tended to be Catholic or Jewish instead of Protestant, many native-born Americans worried that it would be impossible to assimilate them. Scholars of the era often provided evidence for this worry, arguing that white American culture was distinctively different from—and superior to—other cultures. The view of sociologist Edward A. Ross, for example, that the increasing number of immigrants from southern and eastern Europe was causing a decline in the quality of the U.S. population, was held by many other sociologists, anthropologists, and psychologists.[34]

It was not, however, held by Balch, for she apparently shared Addams's belief that environment or culture shaped people more than their genetic structure. Rather than predicting decline in the quality of American culture, Balch argued that immigrants were neither better nor worse than American citizens; and rather than predicting a conflict of cultures, she argued that both the native-born Americans and the immigrants would change significantly, biologically and culturally. Biological change, she predicted, would occur when the new immigrants eventually intermarried with each other and with native-born Americans to form "a fused and welded people," "a new race of mankind." Balch termed this biological change "fusion."

Balch also predicted that both native-born Americans and immigrants would undergo cultural changes due to assimilation. Too many people, Balch wrote, saw assimilation as a "one-sided" process, "a form of conquest and extirpation." But this was not accurate in Balch's view: "As a matter of fact, men grow alike in intercourse as inevitably as two communicating bodies of water reach the same level. But the level reached is a new one, not that of either one before the interchange began." Most people perceived assimilation, as occurring only to immigrants because the changes and adaptations they made were greater than those of native-born Americans. Because often the only culture or customs immigrants shared were those they acquired in the United States, they necessarily had to emphasize those things American if they wanted to communicate outside their own ethnic groups. To lessen the immigrants' sense that their culture was being taken away from them and the sense of superiority of the native-born citizens, Balch believed it was vital to remember that "each immigrant group exerts a certain influence on the community into which it comes."[35]

Balch also stated strongly that assimilation should not be coerced. She did believe that immigrant children should be required to learn English, but not at the expense of their native tongue; being bilingual, she believed, would provide immigrant children with an economic advantage in American society. In all matters other than language, Balch made it clear that pluralism should be tolerated, even encouraged. The correct attitude toward cultural assimilation, Balch wrote, was "a confident faith in freedom, a candid recognition of the right of all to be as different as they please, with no reserves and no jealousies." Any other response would simply cause ill will.[36]

If native-born Americans were not expected to "Americanize" the new immigrants, what were their obligations? Balch wrote that at first glance it seemed obvious that it was the "plain duty" of native-born Americans "to give the immigrant (and every one else) fair treatment and honest government, and to maintain conditions making wholesome, decent living possible." In fact, however, this was neither necessary nor possible. Instead, Balch wrote, "We can and must do what in the end will be a better thing. We must get our new neighbors to work with us for these things." Native-born Americans should not simply offer the immigrants material inducements to abandon their heritage. Rather, native-born Americans had to "work together with them for justice, for humane conditions of living, for beauty and for true, not merely formal, liberty." The result of this approach, Balch believed, would be a society "in which we may preserve every difference to which men cling with affection, without feeling ourselves any the less fellow citizens and comrades."[37]

Balch's studies of immigration had convinced her of the importance of pluralism. Much like Jane Addams, Balch believed that cultural differences should be appreciated, not eliminated. Balch had also pointed out the futility of trying to coerce changes within people. If not forced, assimilation of both the immigrant and the native born would occur more or less naturally; if the dominant population tried to force the process, however, the immigrants would only cling more tightly to their old ways and become resentful of their native-born neighbors.

Balch's research had led her to a position consistent with that advocated by other leading social scientists of her time such as Franz Boas and William I. Thomas. She conceptualized humans as essentially similar, with observable differences caused by differences in cultures. If a person's culture changed—because of either immigration or emigration—then that person would also be slowly changed. Humanity was essentially a unity with multitudinous and diverse variations.[38]

Balch carried this appreciation of pluralism with her in the years that followed. And when World War I began she interpreted it as a breach of pluralism. Why should nations go to war, she wondered, when it was clear "to any scientifically minded person that it is desireable to have all types of mankind, and especially all types of culture, develop each to the fullness of its inner capacity and flourish side by side?"[39] What was clear to Balch, however, was evidently not clear to others, and she had to watch in despair as nation after nation joined the fray.

Balch had not yet committed herself to working in the peace movement, although she had followed the reports of peace conferences with interest and had occasionally discussed international problems with her students. She had also read the works of the paci-

STAFFORDSHIRE
UNIVERSITY
LIBRARY

fist Leo Tolstoy. She was not totally convinced by his condemnation of any use of physical force, but she was inspired by his example. Like her friend Jane Addams, Balch admired Tolstoy's renunciation of his wealth and social position and toyed with the same idea, but again like Addams, Balch decided that she did not have to follow his example exactly. If Tolstoy's example was "not the literal example for us today," Balch wrote, "it is not that we are called to do less, love less, or to less completely make our whole life and all its circumstances instruments of our love." Fully aware of her own limitations, Balch resolved "now and tonight, tomorrow morning and every morning, and all day and every day to keep on trying to see how I can be of use, how I can live nearer to God, nearer to other people, not in puritanical self-discipline but trying honestly and hard to learn, to curb, and to spur, to feel after the light, to do all I can as well as I can for the best purpose I can see." She then added laconically, "This is not an easy job."[40]

The job of living up to her ideals was hard enough in peacetime; it would get even harder when the world went to war. Her personal principles and the belief in pluralism that arose from her scholarly work would compel her to oppose that war; and her custom of working with women and for women would lead her to do so in their company.

The early lives of Addams and Balch were similar in many respects, and the ideas they developed were also similar. Both women grew up in privileged families, sustained close friendships with other women, spent time in Europe, received some degree of advanced education, and selected careers in which they worked with both immigrants and women. During the period preceding World War I, Addams and Balch only occasionally interacted, but their ideas were nonetheless developing along parallel tracks.

By the time World War I began, Addams and Balch had already formulated the ideas that would undergird their work with the peace movement in the following decades. First, both women valued the differences among people and advocated a pluralistic society. Differences among people, they believed, were shaped largely by the cultures in which they lived, and cultural differences, among people living in the United States and among nations, were sources of strength, not weakness. People should be allowed to maintain their particular cultural traditions if they desired to do so; this was true both for old and new immigrants to the United States and for other nations. The forced "Americanization" of immigrants and of other nations was wrong.

Second, both Addams and Balch condemned forced change, especially when the force employed was violent. Both women had read Tolstoy and thought long and hard about his condemnation of physical force. Neither completely adopted his views, but both were influenced by both his ideas and the life he led. In addition, Addams had already enacted her philosophical opposition to violent change through her protest against the Spanish-American War. Balch had not yet taken the step of direct protest, but the ideas that would compel her to do so were firmly in place.

Third, Addams had clearly articulated, in her book *Newer Ideals of Peace*, the importance of nurturing one's fellow human beings. People were more likely to live peacefully, she believed, when they had a satisfactory quality of life—adequate food, shelter, clothing, and employment. Balch shared this belief but did not articulate her views as clearly as Addams. Rather, Balch enacted her belief in nurturing through her work in social settlements and labor unions.

Finally, both Addams and Balch spent most of their time working with women on behalf of other women. They did not ignore the problems of men, but custom and ideology turned their eyes most often to women's problems and made them most comfortable working with women.

Unity Among Women, 1915

As ONE COUNTRY after another marched to war during the opening days of August 1914, people around the world watched in
horror. Here in the United States, Emily Greene Balch shared that
horror: "We can only trust it will be both short and final."[1] She gave
no indication that she was planning to be involved in a movement
to make the war "both short and final," but she and many other
women would in fact do just that. Prepared by decades of public activism—in groups ranging from the Socialist Party to the General
Federation of Women's Clubs—a wide variety of women would decide that stopping this world war was their next goal.

To achieve this goal, they decided to form a new organization, a
peace society for women only. This organization, the Woman's Peace
Party, brought Jane Addams and Emily Greene Balch into sustained
contact and began the work that would eventually result in the formation of the Women's International League for Peace and Freedom.
This work would be shaped by the ideas that Addams and Balch had
developed separately in the years before World War I: a commitment
to pluralism, the condemnation of violently enforced change, the necessity of helping people live in dignity and good health, and the importance of women working on behalf of other women. This last
idea was developed first because the formation of the Woman's
Peace Party caused Addams, Balch, and all its new members to thoroughly examine their reasons for organizing separately from men.
Their discussions reveal a great deal about the understanding of gender differences and the feminist consciousness with which these
women operated.

The Decision to Organize

Women's protest against World War I began in late August 1914, when 1,500 women marched through the streets of New York City carrying a large white peace banner and accompanied by the mournful beat of muffled drums. Later that fall, two European activists, Rosika Schwimmer of Hungary and Emmeline Pethick-Lawrence of England, traveled to the United States. In speeches on the East Coast and in the Midwest, their message was always the same: it was the responsibility of women in the United States to do whatever they could to stop the war.

The message eventually took hold, and probably the two best-known women in the United States, Carrie Chapman Catt and Jane Addams, began discussing how to organize the efforts of American women. Catt was a leader of the National American Woman Suffrage Association (NAWSA); Addams was widely known for her work at Hull House. Neither had yet committed herself primarily to peace work—although Addams had written on the subject—and neither one of them particularly wanted to lead the movement. But women around the nation kept turning to them until they could no longer ignore their pleas.

It would have been logical for women who wanted to protest the war to turn instead to the leaders of the established peace societies, but most of these organizations had sunk into inactivity with the beginning of the war. In addition, their male leaders were perceived by some of the most prominent women in the country as hostile to women. Anna Garlin Spencer, a professor of sociology and ethics at Meadville Theological College, told Carrie Chapman Catt that the national peace organizations with which she was familiar, like the military, did not value women's points of view.[2]

Spencer also told Catt that she had already conferred with Lucia Ames Mead about a women's demonstration for peace. Mead had been a national leader in the peace movement since the Spanish-American War when she, like Addams, condemned the action of the United States in the Philippines as imperialism. Mead and her husband, Edwin Doak Mead, became full-time peace activists in 1901. In 1908 Mead had helped found the American School Peace League, an organization that promoted peace education in the schools.[3] Mead had a great deal of experience in the peace movement, but be-

cause she was personally unpopular neither Catt nor Spencer wanted
her to call a women's peace meeting. Furthermore, Catt believed
that "the fact that the Meads who are so conspicuous in the peace
movement in this country have made no move in the present crisis
up to this time, is sufficient reason why others must take up the
work. . . . You are the one woman in the nation who ought to call
such demonstrations if they are to be held."[4] Addams, who had recently helped organize men and women into the Emergency Peace
Committee in Chicago, responded by saying, "While I believe that
men and women work best together on these public measures, there
is no doubt that at this crisis the women are the most eager for action."[5] With that admission, Addams agreed to invite several
women's groups to a meeting to be held in Washington, D.C., in January 1915.

As for Catt, she would help when she could, but, she wrote, "I
think it most advisable that the suffragists should not be the prime
mover in this step."[6] Catt did not clarify this statement, but it seems
likely that it was motivated by her unwillingness to work with
members of the Congressional Union. A group of more militant suffragists who had split from the NAWSA in 1913, the Congressional
Union was particularly active in Washington, D.C., where its members were burning copies of President Woodrow Wilson's speeches
and openly defying the police. Catt feared that these tactics would
injure the entire suffrage movement and did not want to be associated with those who were perpetrating them. Furthermore, the existence of the Congressional Union showed that the suffrage movement was not completely united.[7] Catt herself was already aware
that it was easier to talk about women working together for women
than it was to keep them working together. Her comment to Addams foreshadowed the difficulties that the Woman's Peace Party
would face as it tried to unite women behind the cause of peace.

Why a *Woman's* Peace Party?

When Jane Addams called the women's peace meeting in January
1915, she invited all women's organizations that had standing peace
committees. Three thousand women responded to her call, reflecting the tremendous amount of activism and organization among

women during this era. Both the International Woman Suffrage Alliance and the National American Woman Suffrage Association sent representatives, as did more broad-based women's organizations such as the National Council of Women and the General Federation of Women's Clubs. Also participating were groups defined by religion—the National Council of Jewish Women and the National Conference of Catholic Charities—and groups defined by occupation—the Women's Trade Union League, the International Congress of Farm Women, the National League of Teachers, and the League of American Pen Women. Women came representing the National Federation of Settlements, the Women's Christian Temperance Union, and the National Association of Colored Women. Peace advocates of long standing came from the American School Peace League, the World Peace Foundation, and the American Peace Society. Even the Daughters of the American Revolution and the Society of Spanish-American War Nurses sent representatives.[8]

This diverse group assembled at the New Willard Hotel in Washington, D.C. Many of the women knew each other from previous reform efforts and this familiarity must have facilitated the organizing process. Still, forming a new national organization was a daunting task, and the women spent two days discussing why they were meeting and what action they could take. Several of the most prominent women in the United States spoke, sounding variations on three general themes: the inviolability of human life, women's unique responsibility to oppose war, and women's need for the vote in order to oppose war effectively.

These themes reverberated most loudly because the assembled women were trying to justify their decision to organize separately from men and the established peace organizations. In the early to mid-nineteenth century, separate organizations for women were, of course, the norm. During the late nineteenth century, however, as historian Lori Ginzberg argues, younger women began eschewing women's organizations in an effort to meet a professional standard.[9] By the early twentieth century, there were conflicting tendencies: women's organizations flourished, but most women reformers also worked frequently with men and in male-dominated organizations. Women organizing separately no longer went without notice, especially when they were organizing around an issue not traditionally considered solely within their sphere.

One of the first speakers at the conference was Fanny Garrison Villard. Seventy-one years old, Villard had participated in charity work in the late nineteenth century and then become politically active; in 1906 she had begun working for women's suffrage. She also had an abiding interest in the peace movement, an interest that had been fostered by her nonresistant father, William Lloyd Garrison. His voice seemed to echo through hers when she first took the podium to exhort the audience to hold human life sacred and inviolable. Her own voice grew gradually louder, however, as she emphasized her belief that, in fact, men had not adequately respected human life. It was now up to women to organize in support of the principle of the inviolability of human life.[10]

This theme was elaborated upon the next day by the English activist Emmeline Pethick-Lawrence, who had been touring the United States speaking on the need for a women's peace meeting. Pethick-Lawrence reminded the conferees of Villard's words and echoed them herself: "It is the supreme duty of women, who give birth to human life, to stand for this truth against the whole world, and to band themselves together to insist upon its recognition as a fundamental moral law. Human life is sacred and inviolable." She went on to illustrate her belief that women had a unique responsibility to ensure the inviolability of life. Pethick-Lawrence asked her listeners to

Think of those battle fields sodden with the blood of our human fellow beings . . . ; think of those shelterless and fugitive women, bearing in their violated bodies the unborn children of the next generation; think of those mothers stifling the wailing of their children in their arms, hiding in the woods and ditches of those desolated villages; think of those trains bearing back to their homes the dead to be buried on the refuse heaps. . . . If men can tolerate it, women cannot![11]

Jane Addams sounded a similar theme. In a long and complicated speech, Addams tried to explain her understanding of the war and why women were obliged to oppose it. She stated that she previously had conceptualized human history as a progression from a less civilized era when human life was not respected to the modern era when increasing numbers of people, both women and men, were becoming convinced of the "sanctity of human life." Unfortunately, she continued, the current war had almost obliterated this belief, and humanity found itself again "at the foot of the ladder, beginning again to build up this belief in the value of human life above all else that the planet contains." The work of women was central to this rebuilding process. It was the women, Addams stated, who "must start the work of preventing war." She believed that there were plenty of men who thought that war was unnecessary, but they were not speaking out. The women, in the United States and then in the belligerent nations themselves, had to voice their protest. Addams believed that this protest was "grounded in the soul of women all over the world" and that once women voiced it men would be thankful and ask why they had not done so earlier.[12]

This belief that it was women's responsibility to end war needed some explanation, which Addams and others attempted to provide. Generally, the speakers agreed that women were more sensitive to the value of human life than men were, but their opinions on why this was so varied. Jane Addams and Anna Howard Shaw held the most commonly voiced, though slightly divergent, opinions. Addams stated her views directly: "I do not believe women are better than men—even in the suffrage societies and suffrage debates I have never maintained this—, but there are things upon which women are more sensitive than men, and one of these is the treasuring of human life."[13]

Addams went on to explain that women valued human life more than men did because they usually spent their lives nurturing others. "It is women," she told her listeners, "that have been responsible for the care of children and the aged and all that class which needed especial care." Furthermore, it was women who cared for future soldiers when they were children and when they were ill, and who taught them in schools. And when a soldier died in combat, the work of those women died with him. When women opposed war, Addams believed, they were also opposing the wanton destruction of their life's work.[14]

Anna Howard Shaw, a prominent leader in the women's suffrage movement, agreed that women protested war because war destroyed their life's work; but Shaw also believed that it was relevant that most women gave birth to children. "Today we weeping women have dried our eyes," Shaw told the conferees, "and instead of submitting tamely to the destruction of our life's work and of the whole purpose of our being, we refuse to weep and insist on being heard in our own defense and in the defense of the things in which we are vitally interested." A woman who decided to bear children risked death in childbirth, Shaw noted; and if she lived, she set aside her own ambitions and aspirations to devote herself to the raising of her infant. If that infant grew to be a soldier who was later killed in battle, Shaw believed that not one but two lives—his and his mother's—were lost. Men had asked Shaw what women knew about war, and she responded, "What, what, friends, in the face of a tragedy like that, in the face of a crime like that, what does a man know about war!"[15]

Addams carefully separated nurturing from mothering, while Shaw conflated the two roles.[16] Both women agreed, however, that women's greater sensitivity to the value of human life and their special responsibility for ending war were tied closely to their traditional role as nurturers. Whether as mothers or teachers or nurses or social settlement workers, women usually devoted themselves to taking care of others, Addams and Shaw believed; they were understandably concerned about preserving the lives they nurtured.[17]

The other theme that resounded in the meeting hall was that women needed the vote in order to fulfill their responsibility. Shaw had already explained how women suffered from war. "Because of that," she said, "we women have a right to demand that in the councils of the nations the mothers of men shall have a voice in regard to their lives and the lives of their children." She did acknowledge that some of the conferees had questioned this demand for the vote, but in her mind the answer was clear. "A woman who does not want to have anything to say in regard to her nation going into war has no right to have anything to say in regard to her nation coming out of war."[18] Similarly, the historian and suffragist Anne Martin suggested that the women recommend to Congress that the women's suffrage amendment be submitted to a vote of the legislature as an immediate step toward constructive peace. Her feelings were shared by Rosika Schwimmer, the Hungarian activist who had accompanied Pethick-Lawrence to the United States. Too many American women, she said, were not yet full citizens, "only daughters or wives of citizens," and thus had little control over decisions that affected them greatly. Schwimmer believed that by organizing for peace the women of the United States had proven to their political leaders that they were indeed qualified to vote.[19]

With these strong statements about women's responsibility for peace ringing in their ears, the women at the conference decided to organize themselves as the Woman's Peace Party and to enact a platform. Building on the statements made by Addams more than those made by Shaw, the party platform and its preamble declared women's equality to men and stressed their different moral priorities. The preamble began by emphasizing the common ground shared by both male and female opponents of the war. "Equally with men pacifists," it stated, women understood that "planned-for, legalized, wholesale, human slaughter" was the "sum of all villainies." But, the preamble continued, there were also significant ways in which women's hatred of war differed from men's. Women's opposition to war was based on a "peculiar moral passion of revolt against both the cruelty and the waste of war." Women were the "custodians of the life of the ages" and would no longer consent to "its reckless destruction." Women had always been "particularly charged with the future of childhood and with the care of the helpless and the unfortunate" and would no longer silently accept "that added burden of maimed and invalid men and poverty-stricken widows and orphans which war places upon us." Women had always worked to establish homes and "peaceful industry" and would no longer endure "that hoary evil which in an hour destroys the social structure that centuries of toil have reared." Women were charged with teaching morals and ideals to each new generation and would no longer tolerate "that denial of the sovereignty of reason and justice by which war and all that makes for war today render impotent the idealism of the race."[20]

The language used in the preamble emphasized the role of society and culture rather than biology in women's opposition to war. Its authors depicted women as the "custodians" rather than the bearers of life and as having been charged—by society, one infers— with the care of others and the teaching of morals and ideals. Women, they said, were tired of seeing their contributions to society and industry destroyed, and their anger at this destruction gave rise to their opposition to war.

Having clarified why women opposed war, the preamble then stated what the women organizing the Woman's Peace Party wanted. "As human beings and as the mother half of humanity," the organizers demanded "that our right to be consulted in the settlement of questions concerning not alone the life of individuals but of nations be recognized and respected." They also demanded "that women be given a share in deciding between war and peace in all the courts of high debate—within the home, the school, the church, the industrial order, and the state."[21]

Throughout the preamble, most of the roles ascribed to women were widely accepted as appropriate: bearing, rearing, and educating children; caring for the infirm and indigent members of society; and establishing homes and social institutions such as churches and schools. This conceptualization of women's roles was, of course, shaped by the experiences of the assembled women, most of whom were members of the upper and middle classes. These women had been taught that these were women's proper roles, and their economic standing had ensured that most of them had not stepped outside these roles into the paid workforce. Some had worked among the poor, however; they knew that most poor women struggled for economic survival, often working long hours outside the home, yet were still expected to care for the family and the household. Women of every economic class, they believed, were charged with nurturing others. This common responsibility united women and made clear that all women were particularly disadvantaged by war.[22]

The preamble did not, however, portray women only as traditional nurturers. It also made clear that women were human beings and deserved larger, nontraditional roles, that women needed a public voice and the power to make changes in the public realm, and that women needed access to all the sources of power that men had. The preamble thus used the notion of women's differences from men to justify women's inclusion in all realms of activity. This was not a new strategy; it had been used, albeit usually to a more limited extent, by women throughout the nineteenth century. What was new in the arguments of the preamble was the notion that the responsibilities assigned to women by society, not their innate nature, made them oppose war. Women's abhorrence of war, it argued, was primarily shaped by their cultural experiences, not by their biology. This argument modified the nineteenth-century understanding of women's differences from men and put the ideas expressed in the preamble and by WPP leaders in line with the most recent scientific and social scientific research.

Scientific Theories on Sex Differences

Scientific explanations of sex differences underwent significant changes during the nineteenth and twentieth centuries. During the early nineteenth century, such explanations had emphasized the commonalities of humans, but by the middle of the nineteenth century the emphasis was on differentiation and hierarchy. As historian Cynthia Eagle Russett states, "Environmentalism lost favor; categories hardened and were made permanent. Physical attributes were construed to be the determinants of character. . . . According to the new doctrines a glance might suffice to read an individual's character and destiny." Furthermore, the scientists promulgating these new doctrines were "claiming, and in large measure being granted, decisive authority in matters social as well as strictly scientific."[23]

As scientists expanded their realm of authority, so too did some women want to expand theirs. When more women became involved in social reforms such as temperance, moral reform, and abolition, their leaders began to challenge the limits traditionally placed on women's public activities. They first articulated their views publicly at the Seneca Falls convention on women's rights in 1848.

The statements made there drew a great deal of attention to the "woman problem," and scientists rushed to illuminate the issue with the supposedly objective light of science. Leading this rush were some of the most influential scientists and popularizers of science in the nineteenth century: Herbert Spencer, Walter Bagehot, Frank Fernseed, Patrick Geddes, and William I. Thomas. On the whole, these men agreed that secondary sex differences between men and women had evolved naturally. Males were more intelligent, more adventurous, and more aggressive than females; correspondingly, females were gentle, inoffensive, and less able to reason.[24]

The earliest studies of secondary sex differences tended to conclude that the existence of such differences proved that women were inferior to men. Herbert Spencer, for example, argued that women were a case of arrested evolutionary development, and Frank Fernseed wrote that civilization had evolved from a primitive matriarchy to sophisticated patriarchy. Given what he considered proof of male superiority, Fernseed could not resist a gibe at advocates of the movement for sexual equality: "These results, I fear, will not be

STAFFORDSHIRE
UNIVERSITY
LIBRARY

welcome to the successors of John Stuart Mill. But when did a 're-former' stoop to consider such trifles as biological facts?"[25]

These conclusions were not undisputed, however. Other scientists were less certain that the existence of secondary differences between the sexes necessarily meant that one sex was superior to the other. The ideas of Patrick Geddes exemplified this position. Geddes began his scientific education under Thomas Huxley, the controversial Darwinist, but he later moved out of the natural sciences and into sociology and economics, focusing on city planning and the problem of world peace. It was likely his interest in these subjects that brought him together with Jane Addams and her fellow social reformer and settlement house leader, Lillian Wald, as well as with William James and John Dewey.[26]

Also of interest to these people would have been Geddes's work on sex differences, *The Evolution of Sex*, written with his younger colleague, J. Arthur Thomson in 1889. Geddes and Thomson argued that sex differences could be explained by looking at the primary sex cells—the egg and the sperm. The egg was large and passive, they noted, but the sperm was small and active; these characteristics, they posited, reflected opposite metabolic processes: "It is generally true that the males are more active, energetic, eager, passionate, and variable; the females more passive, conservative, sluggish, and stable." Males, therefore, were katabolic (energy using) while females were anabolic (energy storing). These opposite metabolic processes, Geddes and Thomson continued, determined the behavior of the sexes. Males were more variable and thus tended to lead evolutionary progress; females tended to preserve the "constancy and integrity" of the human species. Yet females did have their time of glory. Geddes and Thomson wrote that "along paths where the reproductive sacrifice was one of the determinants of progress," females deserved credit for "leading the way." Males, with a larger range of experience, "may have bigger brains and more intelligence, but the females, especially as mothers, have indubitably a larger and more habitual share of the altruistic emotions. The males, being usually stronger, have greater independence and courage; the females excel in constancy of affection and in sympathy."[27]

The metabolic differences between males and females also dictated that the sexes would have different types of intelligence. Geddes and Thomson wrote, "That men should have greater cerebral variability and therefore more originality, while women have greater stability and therefore more 'common sense,' are facts both consistent with the general theory of sex and verifiable in common experience." Thus women had "greater integrating intelligence" while men were stronger in "differentiation." Female anabolism dictated that women had "greater patience, more openmindedness, greater appreciation of subtle details, and consequently . . . more rapid intuition." On the other hand, male katabolism determined that men had "a greater power of maximum effort, of scientific insight" and exhibited a "stronger grasp of generalities." In short, Geddes and Thomson summarized, "man thinks more, woman feels more."[28]

As certain as they were that the sexes differed in important ways, Geddes and Thomson did not argue that women were inferior. Rather, they wrote, "the two sexes are complementary and mutually dependent." In fact, the dominance of one sex over the other would retard the evolution of the human species. "The actual path of progress," Geddes and Thomson wrote, "is represented by action and reaction between the two complementary functions," and the ideal for which humans should strive was "a more harmonious blending of the two streams."[29]

The theory of sexual complementarity had triumphed in western Europe in the late eighteenth and early nineteenth centuries and had become common in the United States as well. Because women and men were equal but different, the theory postulated, the roles they played in society were equally valuable although necessarily different. Women were suited to the private, emotional world of the home, while men were suited to the public, rational world of the state; but both the public and the private were equally necessary.[30] However limited it seems today, this theory was a decided improvement over the previous theories that postulated women's inferiority. According to the theory of complementarity, and especially in the work of Geddes and Thomson, biology proved only that men and women were different, not that women were inferior to men. In addition, the suggestion by Geddes and Thomson that progress would occur only through the "harmonious blending" of male and female functions implied the necessity of increased interaction between the sexes—perhaps even their integration.

William I. Thomas, a young sociologist at the University of Chicago, expanded on this implication. In his 1897 doctoral thesis,

Thomas relied heavily on the work of Geddes and Thomson. He argued that all social phenomena originated in biological conditions. Men's katabolic nature, he believed, had led gradually to the industrial development occurring in the United States and also, less fortunately, to the social and economic dislocation that plagued Chicago and other large cities. But the solution to these problems was obvious. Women's anabolic nature determined that women nurtured the weak and helped the unfortunate; thus social equilibrium could be restored by encouraging women to play an active role in social reform.[31]

Thomas quickly began to modify these early ideas. Influenced by his friendships with functionalist psychologists—especially James R. Angell, John Dewey, and George Herbert Mead, all of whom spent some time at Chicago—as well as by contact with female graduate students and with the immigrants whose neighborhoods he observed, Thomas gradually rejected the biological determinism that underlay his previous work. He came to believe that mental differences between the sexes, as well as among races, developed not because of an individual's cell structure but because of the individual's experiences and group relationships.[32]

One of the graduate students whose work most influenced Thomas was Helen Bradford Thompson, a student of psychology under James Angell. For her doctoral thesis, Thompson studied the motor skills and sensory abilities of equal numbers of men and women selected from Chicago undergraduates of the same age and background. She looked especially for indications of sexual differences, designing her study to test current theories about these differences. Thompson concluded that, superficially, at least, her results fit well with the prevailing theory posited by Geddes and Thomson. Men did seem to have "better-developed motor ability and more ingenuity," and women seemed to have "keener senses and better memory." She had not found confirmation of the belief that women were more influenced by emotion than men, but she agreed that women's "greater tendency toward religious faith" and the "greater number of superstitions among them" pointed toward "their conservative nature—their function of preserving established beliefs and institutions." Yet Thompson could not accept Geddes and Thomson's biological determinism. In her view, their theory rested on "far-fetched analogies only." She admitted that the sex differences Geddes and Thomson had identified might be correct, but she argued that their methods were not particularly sound or their conclusions consistent. Acknowledging the effect social opinion could have on supposedly objective science, Thompson concluded that if Geddes and Thomson's own beliefs about the mental differences between the sexes had been different, they might well have reached different conclusions.[33]

If "nature" did not explain mental differences between the sexes, what did? Thompson answered "nurture." Her study, she believed, showed that the "psychological differences of sex seem to be largely due . . . to differences in the social influences brought to bear on the developing individual from early infancy to adult years." And in answer to the men who had rushed to shine the objective light of science on the "woman problem," Thompson wrote that her study led her to conclusions different from theirs. If social forces, not biological structures, accounted for psychological differences between the sexes, the "question of the future development of the intellectual life of women is one of social necessities and ideals, rather than of the inborn psychological characteristic of sex."[34] In other words, the controversy over women's place in society could be solved only by analyzing society's ideals and goals, not through scientific confirmation of the theory of complementarity or male superiority.[35]

Scholars at Wellesley College were also challenging the notion of biologically determined mental differences between women and men. In 1895 a student, Cordelia C. Nevers, challenged a study by a prominent psychologist, Joseph Jastrow. In a word association test, Jastrow had found that women responded to words by naming concrete objects while men responded to the same words with remote, general, and abstract terms. Jastrow said this proved that men were more variable than women. Because variability was considered desirable—it produced a greater number of geniuses and a wider array of personalities—Jastrow's work suggested that men were superior to women. But in conducting a similar study at Wellesley, Nevers found that women did not exhibit a lack of variability. Jastrow, probably angered by having his work criticized by an undergraduate, denied that Nevers's work weakened his case.[36]

The argument was then joined by Nevers's teacher, Mary W.

Calkins, who had completed the work for a doctorate in psychology at Harvard but had been denied the degree because she was a woman. Although Calkins admitted that Nevers's evidence had not been conclusive, she argued that there was a greater weakness with Jastrow's research: he had disregarded the impact of the environment on women and men. Calkins argued that, from infancy on, women and men were treated differently, and thus it was impossible to eliminate the influence of environment on tests such as the one administered by Jastrow.[37] The importance of the environment in shaping observable mental differences between women and men was made even clearer by the last voice to join this scholarly debate. Amy Tanner, a graduate student at the University of Chicago, criticized both Jastrow and Calkins and proposed a new standard for psychological research. The existence of inherent differences between women and men, she argued, "can not be demonstrated until men and women are not only nominally but actually free to enter any profession." Because many professions were closed to women, the "real tendencies" of women could not be tested.[38]

The work done at the University of Chicago by Amy Tanner, Helen Thompson, and William I. Thomas, and at Wellesley by Cordelia Nevers and Mary Calkins, signals a change in the scientific understanding of the causes of mental differences between the sexes. First, supposed proof of biologically determined male superiority had given way to proof of biologically determined complementary differences only; then biological determinism was challenged by new evidence that environmental forces were more influential than biological ones. In 1910 Helen Thompson Woolley characterized the change: "The very small amount of difference between the sexes in those functions open to experimentation, the contradictory results obtained from different series of investigations, and the nature of the differences which prove to be most constant, have led to the belief that the psychological differences of sex are of sociological rather than of biological origin."[39]

What had not changed for most scientists was the belief that the men and women living in the early twentieth century exhibited mental differences distinguishable by sex. No one was certain of their cause; no one knew how long they would last. Yet almost every scientist believed they existed.[40]

Different and Equal, Separate and Integrated

Given this scientific consensus, it was not surprising that the organizers of the Woman's Peace Party based their decision to create a women's peace organization on the argument that women were different from men. Their belief that women had a special regard for the value of human life was similar to the scientific theory that women were less aggressive and more altruistic than men. Furthermore, their belief that men's and women's characteristics complemented each other led to their position that women should work in the public sphere as well as the private. Finally, these women did not believe that the differences between men and women were immutable or biologically determined. Consistent with the findings of Helen Thompson and other scholars at the University of Chicago and Wellesley, the organizers of the Woman's Peace Party tended to emphasize that women had been shaped by their environments to be more nurturing and caring than men. The existence of a feminist consciousness among these women in 1915 is clear. Although they believed women were different from men, they also believed that those differences had been socially constructed and that those differences mandated that women have access to all the sources of power held by men.

The party's leaders were closely connected to the people and institutions conducting the newest scientific research on differences between the sexes. Jane Addams, for example, had ties to the University of Chicago and knew Patrick Geddes and John Dewey personally. Likewise, Emily Greene Balch began her tenure at Wellesley just as the Jastrow-Nevers-Calkins debate reached a climax.[41] And University of Chicago researcher William I. Thomas was married to Harriet Thomas, who served as the executive secretary of the Woman's Peace Party in 1915.

The belief that differences between the sexes were due to socialization or environment more than to biology was crucial to the work the women of the WPP planned to do and the way in which they planned to do it. They wanted women to continue moving into the public sphere, taking their belief in the importance of nurturing and caretaking with them; only this movement, they believed, could humanize a nation that had overvalued the work done by men. Simultaneously, however, these women were accustomed to working with other women and identified strongly with them. They had all lived or worked with men and would continue to do so, but they also knew the importance of having women's organizations, free from the involvement of men, where women could run their own show in their own way. The theory on which they built the Woman's Peace Party, then, gave women the right to move into the public realm and to do so in the company of other women; it supported separatist action at the same time that it demanded the integration of women.

The emphasis on the role of socialization or environment would also be important to the leaders of the Woman's Peace Party in another way: it helped them reject the notion of inherent differences between races. Most of the scientists working on sex differences understood that their work had implications for ideas of race as well.[42] If research demonstrated that visible sex differences did not dictate innate differences in ability, would not similar research suggest that visible racial differences likewise did not dictate innate differences? It is not surprising, then, that the organizational conference of the WPP issued a statement condemning racial prejudice and calling for the creation of "a democracy that when it has done its perfect work will know no limitations of race, color, class or sex."[43]

The organizers of the Woman's Peace Party had thought deeply about women's role in society, and their ideas on sex differences were consistent with the latest scientific theories. Their understanding of the differences between men and women led them to begin their new organization with the goal of using women's common characteristics to unite all women against World War I, and eventually against all wars. That goal was elusive, however, and was gradually balanced by an acceptance of the differences among women.

Differences Among Women, 1915–1919

THE ORGANIZATIONAL conference of the Woman's Peace Party ended with enthusiasm and confidence on January 11, 1915. Women from across the political spectrum had agreed on statements of principle and policy, united by their belief that women had a "peculiar moral passion" for peace. It must have been an inspiring and empowering occasion, and most of the women likely returned to their homes with renewed hopes for peace. Peace did not come, however, and as the war ground on in Europe, the apparent unity of the Woman's Peace Party began to shatter. Three issues were particularly divisive: women's suffrage, the precise nature of the party's pacifism, and the performance of war relief work.

The debates that occurred over these issues illustrate how the ideas central to Jane Addams and Emily Greene Balch became central to the WPP as well. The WPP endorsed the condemnation of violent force only one year after its founding, and the commitment to nurturing shaped the attitude of most WPP members toward war relief work. Finally, the organization embodied a commitment to women working with and on behalf of other women. The debates within the organization over women's suffrage, however, show that WPP leaders and members struggled to enact this commitment, especially when they radically disagreed with the actions of some of their colleagues.

An analysis of the debate over all of these issues provides yet another crucial insight: that the leaders of the WPP were willing to tolerate a range of opinions on crucial issues. Just as Addams and Balch had come to value differences among peoples and cultures, so the leaders of the WPP came to value differences of opinion among WPP members. Core moral principles such as those expressed at the organizational conference had to be maintained, the leaders of the WPP believed, but they also realized that there would be discussion and disagreement about how to enact those principles. Women shared common perspectives, but they did not all think alike.

Supporting Suffrage, Opposing War

Although the organizational meeting focused on the opposition to war that united its members, it was clear even then that there would be some disagreements. The first arose over whether to link women's work for peace with women's work for the vote. Several speakers hailed women's suffrage as a great aid to the peace movement, but not all felt the same way. Some did not favor suffrage for women, and among those who did, some believed that it was wisest to keep the two issues separate. The plank in the party platform that asked for the vote for women was one of the most controversial.

This plank was also the main reason for the statement, incorporated into the preamble to the party's platform, that all were welcome to join "who are in substantial sympathy with the fundamental purpose of our organization, whether or not they can accept in full our detailed statement of principles."[1] The leaders of the WPP knew that not all women would accept the WPP's principles unconditionally, but they continued to believe that women would unite behind the fundamental principles—the inviolability of human life and the necessity of women's work to ensure that inviolability. To put it another way, the inviolability of human life was a moral principle that they saw as universal; but on other issues, they were willing to allow a spectrum of beliefs.

The "substantial agreement" clause became the loophole that allowed those individuals or state branches that did not want to support women's suffrage but did want to work for peace to participate in the WPP. For example, only two weeks after the organizational conference a member complained to Addams that the suffrage plank was causing problems. Addams apologized but added that she believed that "anyone who attended the meeting at Washington would realize that it was absolutely fundamental to the undertaking" because the platform was directed to "humanizing" the conception of government. For people who could not see that connection, however, Addams suggested dealing with the problem by emphasizing "that we do not require an agreement to the letter of the platform."[2]

Several groups took advantage of this flexible policy. The New Jersey and Maryland branches chose not to include suffrage in their state platforms, and in Connecticut the WPP included in its statement of purpose that it was not organized for suffrage propaganda. The Connecticut branch added, "It was felt by many who are intensely interested in the principle of suffrage, as well as by those who oppose it, that the subject can be handled best by those societies organized primarily for that purpose."[3]

This policy of asking only "substantial sympathy" of its members allowed the WPP to encompass, rather than exclude, differing positions. One conflict occurred when the Washington, D.C., branch offered to extend its summer campaign into Maryland. The leader of the Maryland branch consented but asked the Washington branch to avoid any discussion of suffrage at the meetings in Maryland and to "keep to the main object—Peace." In response, the Washington branch decided to forgo its Maryland campaign, for it did not wish to restrict its speakers. Both branches, however, remained within the national WPP.[4]

The same issue surfaced again at the annual meeting of the WPP in 1916, when the members were to decide whether to affiliate with the International Committee of Women for Permanent Peace (ICWPP). This group had formed in April 1915, when women from Europe and the United States met at the Hague Congress of Women. There, one of the main topics had been how women could organize for peace, and many of the WPP leaders attended and played leading roles. The assembled women established the ICWPP and required that its members support women's work for both peace and the vote. Some WPP members worried that if their organization affiliated with this group the WPP would have to eliminate its flexible policy of requiring only substantial agreement with its platform. But Addams did not interpret the ICWPP as requiring that its members support women's suffrage. "What they mean," Addams suggested, "is to stand for the two things together—woman's body working for woman's voice in government, believing that in that way Peace will be more easily attained." After considerable discussion, the WPP voted both to maintain its flexible policy and to become the U.S. section of the ICWPP.[5]

WPP members who had not been active in the suffrage movement but who had been active in the women's club movement or in

social or political reform at the local level worried that linking suffrage to women's work for peace would hinder their recruitment of
other women like themselves. Strong supporters of women's suffrage
had exactly the opposite worry; they feared that allying themselves
with the women working for peace, specifically the WPP, would
lessen the support for women's suffrage. For example, Josepha Whitney, a suffragist and WPP member from Connecticut, worried about
being linked to the more radical WPP branches through membership
in the national organization. She confided to WPP executive board
member Lucia Ames Mead, "I do not want to do anything just now
to hamper my usefulness for the Federal Suffrage Amendment, the
greatest aid to an intellectual awakening among women."[6]

Likewise, suffrage leader Carrie Chapman Catt did not want to
be linked with the women coordinating the WPP organizational conference in Washington because they were members of the Congressional Union, which had recently split from Catt's National American Woman Suffrage Association in a dispute over tactics. Catt told
Addams that she and other NAWSA leaders believed the Congressional Union was injuring the suffrage movement and could injure
the peace movement as well by committing "untactical" blunders.[7]
Catt also hesitated to become closely associated with the peace
movement because of her role as a leader of the International
Woman Suffrage Alliance (IWSA). The IWSA was divided over tactics for winning the franchise and had to cope with the tensions created by the European war as well. As its leader, Catt prayed that she
"might walk so straight a path that I could help pull that body together again at the end of the war."[8]

Catt maintained this stance throughout 1915, declining Addams's request to represent the United States on the International
Committee of Women for Permanent Peace: "My mission . . . will
not be a little impaired if I ally myself too much with the peace activities." She told Addams that "the guarantee of permanent peace is
the most important question in all the world" but excused her non-
participation on the ground that her own "feeble efforts" would not
make any difference. As long as the European war raged, Catt believed, any attempt to educate the public about the necessity of
peace was "like throwing a violet at a stone wall." She pragmatically
resigned herself to wait until the war ended, predicting that public
opinion would then again support the cause of peace.[9]

Up to this point, Catt's refusal to become involved in the peace movement was understandable, and the WPP leaders did not openly criticize her decision. As it became increasingly certain that the United States would enter World War I, however, Catt began to abandon her stance as the neutral leader of the suffrage movement and became convinced that the success of the suffrage movement depended on what action the NAWSA took at that point. Catt called a meeting of the NAWSA council for February 23 and 24, 1917. Knowing what Catt had in mind, the WPP leaders wrote to Catt expressing their hope that the NAWSA would "take no action concerning service to our government anticipatory of war since many women suffragists hope such a calamity may be averted, and feel that this is a time when patriotism may be effectively shown by refraining from any action tending to increase the war spirit."[10]

But the WPP failed to change Catt's course, and the executive council of the NAWSA passed a resolution to support the government if the country went to war. The council also emphasized, however, that "the first object of the association *should continue to be the submission of the Federal Amendment, and that war activities should not interfere with the purpose of the organization, which was Votes for Women*."[11] Catt was pleased with the actions of the council, especially because they were supported by Americans who favored entering the war and by high government officials.[12]

This resolution caused controversy among both peace activists and suffragists. The New York branch of the WPP dropped Catt as a member, and hard feelings developed between Catt and the leaders of the national WPP.[13] Individual members of the WPP also protested. For example, Gwyneth Roe was a strong supporter of both the WPP and the suffrage movement, and she felt that Catt had betrayed both. Roe reminded Catt that many women in the suffrage movement were, as she was, also committed to the peace movement. Arguing ardently that the causes of peace and suffrage must be kept separate, Roe told Catt that she was "not merely shocked by being handed over to the Governor and President for war service" but was "particularly humiliated by what I have done to other women." Roe had persuaded several women to join the suffrage movement by assuring them that suffragists worked only for votes for women. Roe challenged Catt to "justify turning the women of this organization [NAWSA] over to any other purpose than that of equal suffrage under any circumstances whatever, but especially to war service when there are among its members large numbers of women opposed to any act that can possibly be construed by anyone as the slightest aid to precipitating war."[14]

Catt justified the NAWSA's position by arguing that it would increase women's chances of winning the franchise. For Catt, pledging suffragists to do war work was not delivering them to another purpose, as Roe and others charged, but was another tactic, albeit a bit more indirect than others, to win the vote and advance women. Choosing this tactic split Catt from the peace movement, to which she would not return until 1924 when she founded the National Committee on the Cause and Cure of War. Although it is not certain to what degree her position increased support for women's suffrage, it did anger women like Roe, who even ten years later wrote of Catt, "When it comes to talking peace CCC should add another C to her name for Camelion."[15]

Another woman who was forced by the war to choose between her desire for world peace and for women's suffrage was Jeannette Rankin, the first woman elected to the U.S. Congress. Born in 1880, Rankin earned a bachelor of science degree from the University of Montana in 1902 and studied briefly at the New York School of Philanthropy and the University of Washington. In 1910 she entered politics by participating in the campaign for women's suffrage in the state of Washington. In 1913 she became a field secretary for the NAWSA, and in 1916 she was elected to represent the people of Montana in the House of Representatives.

Because she was the first woman to hold national political office, Rankin's vote on whether the United States should enter World War I was seen as especially important. Many suffragists told Rankin that she would destroy the suffrage movement if she voted against the war; such a vote would strengthen the antisuffrage argument that enfranchising women would weaken the nation's defense.[16] On the other hand, women who had argued that enfranchising women would help to eliminate war obviously wanted Rankin to vote against the declaration of war. The leader of the National Woman's Party, Alice Paul, told Rankin that "it would be a tragedy for the first woman ever in Congress to vote for war."[17] And when Rankin did vote against entering the war, congratulations from WPP members poured in. The Pennsylvania branch wrote to her to express its satisfaction with her vote and its admiration of her courage.[18] Margaret Lane of the New York branch shared those feelings. She believed that Rankin, "pledged to 'suffrage first' as she was and almost persuaded by the suffragists that she would be a traitor to the cause of suffrage if she voted against war," had shown great courage.[19]

Despite such support, that vote helped defeat Rankin when she stood for reelection in 1918. She then began working for the peace movement, moving from one organization to another throughout the 1920s and 1930s. Deprived of her promising political career, Rankin must have wondered about the wisdom of her vote against entering World War I. Looking back on her life, however, she showed no regret. Being the first woman elected to the U.S. Congress had been important, she believed, but "there was even more significance in the fact that the first woman who was ever asked what she thought about war said 'NO.'"[20]

The controversy stirred by Rankin's vote, by the NAWSA resolution in support of the war, and by the WPP's endorsement of women's suffrage shows some of the fissures that plagued activist women during the war years. Although many of these women had worked together in the past and shared the belief that women had a special responsibility to promote peace, they were frequently divided over tactics and strategies. Women working together with other women was easier said than done.

Defining Pacifism

Divisions among WPP members became more apparent as the organization defined its pacifism and policies more precisely. Since the early nineteenth century, peace activists in the United States had differed about the proper way to establish and maintain peace. Some considered themselves "nonresistants." Usually members of the historic peace churches such as the Mennonites and the Society of Friends (Quakers), these people believed that true Christians should refuse to take part in violence. They did not believe that they were obligated to try to resolve conflicts or abolish injustice without violence, only to keep themselves free from violence.[21] Some Quakers did work for particular causes such as the abolition of slavery; but on the whole, religious nonresistants submitted to the existence of violence but refused to participate in it.

Another variety of nonresistance came from William Lloyd Garrison, a founder of the New England Non-Resistance Society in 1838. Garrisonian nonresistants opposed any violence and worked to correct social injustices such as slavery and the unequal treatment of women. Furthermore, because governments relied on the threat of violent force to keep their citizens behaving properly and to keep other nations at bay, the Garrisonian nonresistants also rejected allegiance to governments; they acknowledged only Jesus Christ as the ultimate lawgiver.[22]

The Civil War, of course, stopped most peace activity. When it resumed after the war, its leaders and its goals had changed, with nonresistance being far less common. In the late nineteenth century, the leaders of the peace organizations tended to assume, as did many Americans, that war had become anachronistic and that conflicts would be peacefully resolved through existing laws and arbitration. During World War I, however, many peace organizations were willing to support the use of violent force if international law and arbitration failed, and especially if it were for a virtuous cause such as the triumph of democracy.

By the early twentieth century, the spectrum of peace activity ran from complete nonresistance on the left to support for virtuous wars on the right. Where the WPP would stand on this spectrum was not immediately decided. At the organizational conference, the assembled women spent more time explaining why they had felt it necessary to organize for peace separately from men than they did explaining their position on peace-related issues. The positions supported in the WPP platform, such as reliance on international law and democratic control of foreign policy, were not new to the peace movement, and they placed the WPP somewhere in the middle of the spectrum of peace organizations. Its plank calling for an international police force, however, pushed the WPP farther to the right.

Within months, the national leaders of the WPP began to reconsider these planks, particularly the one calling for an international police force to replace national armed forces. A similar position was supported by a new organization, the League to Enforce Peace (LEP). Founded in June 1915, the LEP wanted the major nations of the world to unite in an international league that would both require its members to submit disputes to the judgment of an international tribunal and demand that its members form a joint military force in order to prevent any one member from going to war. It simultaneously supported campaigns for preparedness as well as peace and argued that Germany had to be defeated before peace could thrive.[23]

At a meeting of the WPP national executive board and the chairs of state branches in November 1915, opinion was divided on whether it should continue to support the formation of an international police force. The central issue was whether peace could be enforced: could people and nations be forced to be peaceful, or did that constitute a contradiction in principles? Lucia Ames Mead, who had been active in several peace organizations before World War I, stated that she still believed in "coercion as a last resort," but Lucy Biddle Lewis, a member of the Society of Friends, disapproved of the LEP and wanted the WPP to "stand for the higher ideals." Fannie Fern Andrews, who was a member of the LEP, spoke in favor of it, arguing that more important than the LEP's ultimate reliance on violent force was its emphasis on internationalism. Jane Addams and Anna Garlin Spencer shared Andrews's appreciation of the LEP's effort to foster internationalism, but did not want the WPP to endorse the LEP.[24]

Disagreement over this issue surfaced again at the first annual meeting of the WPP in January 1916. Fanny Garrison Villard urged the members to define the organization's position more clearly by differentiating it from that of "ordinary" peace parties. She suggested that the WPP put itself "on record as unalterably opposed to war or preparations for war as a means of settling disputes between nations." Suffrage leader Janet Richards suggested that the WPP add to its platform a plank that would urge nations to use economic pressure and boycotts to deter war. After discussing the issue, the convention delegates voted unanimously to replace the plank calling for an international police force with Richards's suggested plank.[25]

This change of opinion became even more evident at the next session of the meeting. In that session, Villard offered a resolution that opposed the use of violent force for any reason, even self-defense. WPP members Agnes Wambold and Laura Clay objected to this proposal, arguing that self-defense should not be considered part of "the war spirit." Villard answered, with a tone of certainty that rang with the authority of her family's long history of leadership in the peace movement, "On the ground of self-defense we have no more right to do wrong than on any other ground. If it is wrong to kill for one purpose, it is wrong to kill for another." The WPP platform had stated that one purpose of the organization was to arouse people and nations "to respect the sacredness of human life"; Villard now stated that it was apparent that not all WPP members shared that opinion. Whether Villard's tone of disillusionment was genuine or only a rhetorical tactic, she was reminded by WPP president Jane Addams that almost none of the WPP members had supported such a thoroughly nonresistant position over the previous year. Addams was correct, but she evidently did not express the current belief of most WPP members, for her statement was met with shouts of objection. Hannah Clothier Hull, a Quaker and a leader of the Pennsylvania branch of the WPP, then stepped into the discussion, thanking Villard for testing the WPP's position. She then suggested that the WPP should support Villard's resolution, arguing that "if we do not stand for the highest, there is no use for the Woman's Peace Party." The other delegates applauded Hull's comments, and Villard's resolution passed.[26]

With the passage of this resolution, the WPP put itself on record as opposing the use of all violent force, even in self-defense. It would not support an international police force, and it would stand for a completely nonresistant approach to establishing and maintaining peace. But how would this principle translate into policy? On the whole, it seems likely that the WPP leaders were not overly concerned about policy at this point. The environment in which the WPP leaders lived and worked was extremely hostile and made any real accomplishments virtually impossible. More important to the WPP leaders was to stand for a principle, a principle that might serve as a beacon in the postwar world.

But if the nonresistant principle of the WPP was to serve in this manner, it needed to be more clearly explained. That task was taken up by Emily Greene Balch in 1917, probably in response to recent articles written by John Dewey. Dewey—philosopher, educator, social reformer, and longtime friend of Jane Addams—had previously advocated peaceful means to resolve conflicts but gradually became convinced of the need to use force in the cause of democracy. In 1916 he wrote two articles, "Force, Violence and Law" and "Force and Coercion," in which he tried to sort out when the use of force was justifiable and in which he criticized the stance of pacifists who refused to support World War I, saying that they did not distinguish force from violence.[27] Balch addressed this point in her article "The Great Solution," although she did not refer to Dewey's criticism explicitly. To explain what nonresistance was and how it could work in the real world, Balch began by distinguishing among force, violence, and coercion. She implicitly agreed with Dewey's assertion that to oppose all force was absurd. "The use of force has in and of itself no moral color," Balch wrote, and thus force could not be used to determine "whether or not an act is morally justifiable."

The criterion for determining moral and effective action, Balch argued, should be "the element of coercion." Although she admitted that coercion might be justifiable in some circumstances, she said that its use was "always subject to the gravest possible question" because it violated human free will and thereby took away a person's chance to be a moral being. In addition, she wrote, the use of coercion was also ineffective. "It is a primitive illusion to suppose that force employed will have its simple direct effect and that only, that to try to mould, to break, to smash, will evoke no vigorous explosion of force in reaction. The opposite is true. Contrariness, self-justification, red-hot anger with its literal madness, may easily more than offset the attempted pressure." Finally, Balch admitted that in some exceptional cases, forcible coercion could achieve the subjugation of its object. Even then, however, it produced the "broken will, the forced submission, the hated task, the humiliation of defeat, the sullenness of the beaten."[28]

How then did she propose to respond to aggression and injustice? Instead of trying to coerce an opponent, Balch believed the only genuine solution was "the overcoming of evil by a fresh welling forth of good," a "kindliness so contagious that ill-will is not merely melted, but attracted into harmony; reason so clarified, so uncontroversial, so appealing, that the opponent becomes the auxiliary; will-to-good so strong that it does not merely annul that of the 'enemy,' but irresistibly draws him onto cooperation."[29]

These were the characteristics that Balch associated with nonresistance, although she noted that both nonresistance and the alternative term, "super resistance," were "too negative" to convey accurately this philosophical position. Ten years earlier in her book

Newer Ideals of Peace, Addams too had found the term nonresistance inadequate and had struggled to more accurately express her belief in the importance of nurturing. In neither case did the language adequately represent the positive activism that these women wanted to convey.

Balch's argument did, however, advance an important insight, an insight that would become central to the philosophy of the Women's International League for Peace and Freedom and to pacifist theory in the following decades. Balch realized that forcible coercion—violent, economic, or moral force—violated free will, but more important, it caused negative psychological effects in both its object and its perpetrator. She believed that the means used to achieve an end would influence the end itself.

In this respect Balch's analysis differed crucially from the wartime analysis of John Dewey. Although initially reluctant to support World War I, Dewey became an advocate of U.S. involvement because he believed the war could be the means to a desired end— the reorganization of American society through applied intelligence and the furtherance of democracy at home and abroad. As the war progressed, however, Dewey had to admit that the ideals of worldwide democracy and a peace without victory had surrendered to government propaganda, suppression of civil liberties, and the concentration of economic and political power in the hands of an ever smaller group of wealthy individuals and nations. By the war's end, Dewey came to believe that his endorsement of the war had been a mistake; after 1918 he became a firm advocate of nonviolent methods of resolving conflicts. The means used to achieve an end, he argued in the following years, had to be consistent with the desired end.[30]

The pacifist minister John Haynes Holmes also struggled with these concepts. He argued in 1918 that even "the most idealistic reliance on force invariably creates opposing force and ends in violent contest." Like Balch and Dewey, he concluded that the means determined the ends and that alternatives to the use of violence for settling conflicts must be found. He also agreed with Balch that the only effective alternatives to the use of violence were reason, love, and example.[31]

Whether Dewey's change of mind or Holmes's analysis was related to Balch's article is unknown.[32] Because her article was published in a Quaker publication, it probably reached a small audience, and one that was largely sympathetic to its position. The originality of her ideas is clear, however, and for those who read her article, her discussion must have significantly advanced their understanding of nonresistance. Earlier than others in the pacifist movement, Balch had begun to clarify terminology and to build a logical, persuasive argument against the use of forcible coercion and in favor of consistency between means and ends. Just as important, writing this article served to clarify Balch's own thinking, and she took that clearer understanding with her as she worked for peace in the 1920s and 1930s.

But Balch's article did not affect the opinions of most Americans or even many WPP members. The Massachusetts branch of the WPP, for example, disagreed with the acceptance of nonresistance by the national WPP and only a couple of months after the 1916 annual meeting put out literature advocating a "newer preparedness." And the first step toward achieving this preparedness was to form a league to enforce the peace, precisely what the national WPP had abandoned at its annual meeting.[33]

The Massachusetts branch took an even more conservative stance after the United States entered the war, committing itself to "constructive internationalism" and the removal of "the menace of Prussian Military domination." It also asked its members to unite behind President Wilson and to work for the goals he had articulated,[34] actions that placed the Massachusetts branch among the more conservative peace organizations, such as the American Peace Society and the Carnegie Endowment for Peace, that had supported Wilson's policies from the beginning.[35] It also put the Massachusetts branch in direct conflict with the national WPP.

The national WPP apparently simply chose to ignore that conflict. It still accepted members who were in substantial sympathy with its policies; perhaps it excused the position of the Massachusetts branch on those grounds. Or the national WPP may not have felt strongly enough to protest. Once the United States entered the war, maintaining a strong pacifist stance became far more difficult, and Addams and other WPP national leaders were strongly criticized by both the government and the press. One way for them to counter

STAFFORDSHIRE
UNIVERSITY
LIBRARY

that criticism was to engage in war relief work—but what looked like a place of refuge only became another point of controversy within the WPP.

The Ethics of War Relief Work

Soon after the Woman's Peace Party organized in 1915, controversy began over whether its members should participate in "war work"— volunteer activities such as food preservation, nursing, and bandage preparation. For some WPP members, the answer to this question was an unqualified no. For a larger number of members, however, war relief work could be construed as nurturing, and nurturing was work with which these women readily identified.

Before the United States entered World War I, the leaders of the national WPP did not sanction war work. First, and fundamentally, they believed that any energy spent on war work was also energy no longer available for the positive work of fostering mediation and internationalism. (After it became clear that mediation would not end the war, this argument carried less weight.) Second, the WPP suspected that as international affairs became more pressing the government would give less attention to domestic problems. In lieu of governmental concern, the WPP believed that it should do all it could to alleviate these problems. Third, many WPP members had worked to organize labor and refused to engage in volunteer work that they believed would lessen the amount of work available to paid workers. Finally, and most generally, the WPP was opposed to "aiding war, any war, by either direct or indirect service."[36]

This position was problematic both ethically and personally. How did one determine whether an action that was intended to ease domestic suffering actually worked indirectly to aid the war? Nursing a wounded soldier back to health, for example, could be construed as a simple humanitarian act, but it could also be interpreted as replenishing the fuel for the war machine. When looked at in this way, nursing and other forms of nurturing relief work seemed in opposition to pacifism.

Even more ambiguous was assuming a job that had been vacated by a soldier. Rebecca Shelley, a young pacifist from Michigan, confronted this issue when her sister wrote her that, with so many men at war, she hoped to be able to find work as a chemist. The letter made Shelley aware of her own "doctrinaire conflict." At first she wished her sister success in finding a position as a chemist, but on second thought, she found herself against her sister's taking a job that would allow a man to go to war. Shelley then added that it was impossible "to keep out of the sweep of the war," and that the best one could do was "to keep one's conscience clear of willful participation in the terrible gain of slaughter."[37]

Emily Greene Balch was also bothered by the ethical dilemma posed by the issue of war work, but unlike Shelley she reconciled herself to it. Balch worked hard to stop the war, attending the Hague Congress of Women in 1915, meeting with European leaders to try to begin the process of mediation, and working in the United States with several peace organizations. And she did all this at the expense of her professorship at Wellesley College. After several leaves of absence, the Wellesley trustees declined to rehire someone who had been so actively and visibly opposed to the policies of the United States government. Balch wrote in her defense that she believed that "any effort to obstruct the war"was "not only inexpedient and silly, as well as unlawful, but also morally wrong." And, she added, "In all such activities as food conservation and relief reconstruction work of all kinds I can of course take part gladly to the limit of my ability."[38]

Balch's choice was also the choice of most of the WPP members and leaders. Once the United States entered the war, the WPP leadership modified its opposition to war work. Representing the national WPP, Lucia Ames Mead advised the chairs of state branches that "it seems eminently fitting that some part of our work should now be diverted to channels of relief." She suggested that each state branch perform some type of public service, thus letting critics of the WPP "perceive our readiness to serve our country."[39] This was a practical step by the national WPP because most of its members would have done relief work anyway. Most had done volunteer and nurturing work for years to try to improve their society. When the national WPP asked them to give up this kind of activity, it placed them in an ethical dilemma. They had become involved in the WPP in the belief that women had a special sensitivity to the value of human life and thus a special responsibility to prevent war. To have expected them to abandon this kind of work just when their society seemed in greatest need would have been futile, and had the national WPP maintained an uncompromising position against war work it would have lost members even more quickly. In fact, the women who did comply with the WPP's request often were accused of being inhumane for not helping the American soldiers. For women who were used to receiving esteem and respect for their services, that was a bitter pill to swallow.[40]

As the national WPP modified its opposition to war work, so did individual members. In order to maintain their ethical opposition to the war without seeming hard-hearted, some WPP members ingeniously modified their war work. One New York member decided that instead of knitting for soldiers she would knit for those who daily stood in the breadlines in New York City. She organized what she called the Black Cross Society, with the motto, "Feed America First: Knit for Our Own Bread Line; Charity Begins at Home." By emphasizing the domestic costs of the war, she could protest the war while still demonstrating her ethical commitment to her fellow citizens.[41]

Others made only slight modifications in their work. The Massachusetts branch advocated what Rose Dabney (Mrs. J. Malcolm) Forbes called an antiwar knitting circle, whose members would knit for soldiers while listening to someone read a war play or pamphlet. This activity allowed women to gain "very valuable peace ideas" and answered charges that they were inhumane.[42] In practice, however, it was little more than an effective rationalization for performing work that full-fledged war supporters also performed.

The Massachusetts branch also made its headquarters "an agency for Volunteer activity in certain established lines of humanitarian effort." It chose to concentrate on education and civil welfare because the war would cause a decrease in the resources available for those services. It coordinated offers of volunteer service, provided building space for organizations—such as the State Department of Agriculture—that were engaged in immediate, constructive national service, and allowed individuals to use its headquarters to assist other organizations such as the Friends' War Victims Relief Committee and the Red Cross Emergency Relief Committee.[43]

Some WPP branches and members, of course, were appalled when the WPP modified its opposition to war work. The New York branch, for example, continued its strong stance against such work throughout the war. Crystal Eastman, an attorney and a leader of the suffrage movement, remembered that its members had been "pacifists in war-time as well as pacifists in peace-time" and had refused to perform war work.[44] Similarly, Ada Lois James, a suffragist, socialist, and pacifist from Wisconsin, could not understand "the psychology of women who respond to war work when they never are interested in other forms of patriotic service." The honor conferred upon women for performing volunteer work for the Red Cross, James wrote in her diary, "makes me actually sick. I cannot sleep often."[45] The novelist and journalist Zona Gale shared James's dislike of war work and urged Jane Addams to try to keep the WPP from performing such work. "It seems to me," she wrote, "far worse than the suffrage party, as a party, rolling bandages. It is intensely important that a strong anti-war party should persist, and if the woman's branch of the anti-war party slips into woman's ancient work of relief and conservation as now invited by war, surely it will lose some great indefinable strength and spirit."[46]

Jane Addams herself felt the ethical dilemma posed by war work as strongly as any member of the WPP. Perhaps hardest of all for Addams, as for so many WPP members, was the sense that she was not being useful or helpful. In her heart she believed that she was doing what was best for her country, that she was standing for the values that were necessary for a peaceful world, but it was hard to keep that in mind as her speaking engagements declined and the requests for articles dwindled. What a relief it must have been when the opportunity came in early 1918 for her to work with Herbert Hoover's Department of Food Administration; this was work that conformed to her commitment to nurturing. Since college, she had written and spoken on the physical and spiritual importance of providing all people with adequate food. She could speak around the country once again, and although she would not get the adoration she had received in earlier years, she would at least not be heckled and ridiculed. Performing this kind of war work provided Addams with a niche, albeit a compromised one, in which she could be useful for the remaining months of the war.[47]

The responses of WPP members and leaders to the war were as diverse as the women themselves. Most eventually performed some kind of war work but distinguished what they did, at least in their own minds, from what supporters of the war did. A small minority

STAFFORDSHIRE
UNIVERSITY
LIBRARY

stayed away from all traditional war work, rechanneling their energy into the protection of civil liberties and the preservation of democracy at home. The executive board of the WPP tacitly approved the diverse activities of its branches and members, stating that "the State and Local Branches of the Woman's Peace Party of the United States have entire independence of the National Board of Officers and of each other. . . . This independence has led to great diversity in that work." Some branches performed "service to the Red Cross, to civilian relief, to ameliorative and morally protective work for our soldiers, to food conservation and to general efforts to make our country a reservoir of help to a suffering world." Other branches chose to work for freedom of the press and to protect the civil liberties of conscientious objectors. Still other branches emphasized education in the principles of international justice. And the executive board added admiringly, "Some Branches have been strong enough to engage in all these activities at once."[48]

Persecution and Decline

Those strong branches must have been few and far between, though, because membership in the Woman's Peace Party dropped dramatically during the war years. When the United States entered the war in 1917, the WPP estimated that it had about 25,000 members. By the war's end, when the WPP became the U.S. section of the Women's International League for Peace and Freedom, only 100 members remained.[49]

The kinds of pressure that caused women to flee from the WPP are illustrated by the experiences of some of the most visible and active WPP leaders. Best known, of course, was Jane Addams. Addams came under immense criticism for her opposition to the war and was even placed under surveillance by the Department of Justice.[50] And to make Addams's situation harder, after the United States entered the war, even some of the people with whom Addams had worked to keep the United States out of the war changed their position. Paul Kellogg, a fellow social reformer and the editor of *The Survey*, in which Addams often published, had worked until the last moment to keep the United States neutral, but once the nation abandoned its neutrality, so did he. Addams's good friend John

Dewey also accepted the war and the argument that the restructuring demanded by mobilization for the war could be used to improve society at home. Addams was tempted by this argument, that "militarism might be used as an instrument for advanced social ends," but she resisted that temptation because she suspected that "social advance depends as much upon the process through which it is secured as upon the result itself."[51] Just as Balch did, Addams believed that means and ends had to be consistent, and this belief caused her path to diverge from that taken by old friends such as Paul Kellogg and John Dewey.

As a pacifist in wartime, Addams risked losing friends, power, and influence and forfeiting the enactment of cherished reform goals. She later recalled that she and other pacifists were "constantly told by our friends that to stand aside from the war mood of the country was to surrender all possibility of future influence, that we were committing intellectual suicide, and would never again be trusted as responsible people or judicious advisers." Who were they, friends and critics alike asked Addams and other pacifists, to differ with able and sensitive men, such as President Wilson, "who also absolutely abhorred war, but were convinced that this war for the preservation of democracy would make all future wars impossible, that the priceless values of civilization which were at stake could at this moment be saved only by war?" Addams could only answer: "Was not war in the interest of democracy for the sake of civilization a contradiction of terms, whoever said it or however often it was repeated?" She resented being perceived as purely dogmatic in her opposition to war because she believed that if she had been permitted to explain herself, she "might have cited both historic and scientific tests of our so-called doctrine of Peace." But wartime was not the time for such explanations, and Addams finally admitted that "to hold out against mass suggestion, to honestly differ from the convictions and enthusiasms of one's best friends did in moments of crisis come to depend upon the categorical belief that a man's primary allegiance is to his vision of the truth."[52]

Emily Greene Balch suffered a similar crisis of conscience during the war years. Balch, who had taught at Wellesley College for almost twenty years when the war began, took several leaves of absence from 1915 to 1918 to devote herself to full-time peace activism. She attended the Hague Congress of Women in 1915 and the Neutral

Conference for Continuous Mediation in 1916, and worked with the People's Council of America for Peace and Democracy, the American Union Against Militarism, and the Woman's Peace Party. She spent much of her time with like-minded people, yet she, like Addams, felt the power of wartime propaganda and friends' opinions. It was very difficult, Balch noted, "to stand against the surge of war-feeling, against the endlessly reiterated suggestion of every printed word, of the carefully edited news, of posters, parades, songs, speeches, sermons." She was convinced that she could never support the war, yet at times her conviction weakened. She admitted that she had no satisfactory answer to the question, "What if Germany wins and militarizes the world?" Even more upsetting to her, however, was her belief that if the United States stayed out of the war "it would be largely, perhaps mainly, not for noble reasons, but from greed for profits."[53]

Her uneasiness increased in 1918 when the trustees of Wellesley decided not to rehire Balch, largely because of her peace activism. Had she been wrong to leave her students and her institution for several years? Had she been unfair to expect that Wellesley would rehire her after she had played such a visible and prominent role in opposing the policies of the U.S. government? Balch concluded that she had "overstrained" the "well-known liberality" of the college and refused to make or allow others to make her dismissal a test of academic freedom. She did try to explain her pacifist activities to the trustees, but in 1919, when they affirmed their decision not to rehire her, Balch accepted that decision quietly and devoted the rest of her life to the peace movement.[54]

Another WPP leader who was persecuted during the war was the organization's national secretary, Lucia Ames Mead. Mead had long been involved with the peace movement and had a national reputation as a respectable reformer. That reputation failed to protect her from criticism, however, once the United States entered the war. Unlike Addams, she was not placed under surveillance by the Department of Justice, but she was attacked frequently in the press.[55]

Leader after leader of the WPP came under fire during World War I. Strong women with strong beliefs, they maintained their opposition to the war, buttressed by a deep commitment to the inviolability of human life and to the ideals of nonresistance and nurturing.

Most Americans, and even many (former) WPP members, did not share these beliefs, however, and were quick to condemn Addams, Balch, Mead, and other WPP leaders as traitors. That criticism took its toll, and the WPP sank into inactivity. Its leaders and the philosophy they embodied waited quietly, however, ready to rise from the ashes once the flames of war and patriotic fervor subsided.

The Legacy of the Woman's Peace Party

Although the WPP existed for only four years and was really active for only two, the experiences of its leaders proved formative for their future work in the peace movement. Most notable were the attempts by these women to come to grips with the real differences among women. The internal controversies over the support of women's suffrage, the precise nature of the WPP's pacifism, and the ethics of war relief work demonstrated that although women might share an aversion to war, they did not agree on all tactics and policies. The belief in women's unity, so strong in 1915, was gradually moderated by the reality of women's differences.

Instead of trying to enforce one definition of pacifist action, the WPP leaders allowed members and branches to follow their own consciences. This was a tough balancing act. At the core of the philosophical position assumed by the leaders of the WIL was moral certainty: these women held life sacred and renounced the use of all violence. They also hoped others would share these beliefs, but they refused to require them to do so. Although their worldview had a core of moral certainty, it was surrounded by layers of moral relativism.

Despite their acknowledgment of the differences among women, the WPP leaders maintained their belief that women could and should work together for change. Women, they believed, had been charged with caring for others, and this common responsibility united them across class, racial, and ethnic lines. In the following decades, the leaders of the Women's International League for Peace and Freedom tried to unite first middle-class, activist women and then women from the working class and from other races. These efforts at unification never completely succeeded, but they do testify to the underlying view of women as a social grouping that shared some common, socially constructed characteristics even as they differed in a multiplicity of ways.

Also critical for the work these women would do in the future was the willingness of the majority of WPP members to go on record in support of complete nonresistance. Although many later left the organization, whether they abandoned their belief in nonresistance cannot be determined. It is likely that most continued to believe in nonresistance as an ideal but were convinced by Wilson's rhetoric that it was an ideal that had to be at least temporarily shelved; certainly many of them returned to peace activism after the war's end. About those who stayed in the organization throughout the war, there is no question: they were committed to the ideal of nonresistance and were willing to risk their reputations and even their livelihoods to maintain that commitment.

These leaders and members of the WPP hearkened back to the nonresistants of the nineteenth century, but they also walked in step with other pacifists born during World War I. The Fellowship of Reconciliation (FOR), for example, was organized in the United States in November 1915. Its members were drawn from the Society of Friends, leaders of the Young Men's Christian Association, and clergymen committed to the social application of Christian principles. And like the WPP, the FOR stood for absolute pacifism. The two organizations shared many members, and the FOR and the Women's International League for Peace and Freedom would work together in the decades that followed.

These two organizations also shared a commitment to social justice. Both advocated the essential equality of all people and struggled to establish a more just social, economic, and political system. For the FOR, this position stemmed from its Christian roots; but the WPP's concern for social justice, expressed in rudimentary form in its dilemma over the ethics of war work, came from both the long involvement of its members in social reforms and the strong commitment of its leaders to the importance of nurturing. This commitment to social justice would increase in the following years and eventually become one of the distinguishing characteristics of pacifist activity between the two world wars. The ideal of nonresistance would grow into the practice of nonviolence.

Of these groups, however, only the WPP combined the advocacy of social justice and the ideal of nonresistance with explicit work for the recognition of women's efforts and values. The only peace organization with a similarly broad program had been the Universal Peace Union of the late nineteenth century, but it was tiny and without significant influence. And among organizations that were working for women's rights, both the National American Woman Suffrage Association and the National Woman's Party carefully distanced themselves from opposition to the war.

Women had worked in the peace movement since it first began in the United States, and in the late nineteenth century many women's organizations formed separate committees or departments devoted to peace activity. The WPP continued in this tradition, setting an example that would be replicated again and again throughout the twentieth century. Several women's peace organizations sprang up in the early 1920s and continued throughout the interwar years; one of these, the U.S. section of the Women's International League for Peace and Freedom, was the direct descendant of the WPP. As women continued to organize for peace along gender lines, the tension between unity and diversity grew. How the leaders of the WIL resolved that tension is the subject of the next chapter.

Unity Within Diversity, 1919–1924

WITH THE END OF World War I in November 1918 came the renewal of efforts to prevent future wars. Prominent in these efforts were the women who had led the Woman's Peace Party. Persecuted as they had been during the war, they were nonetheless eager to resume their work for peace as soon as the climate for such work improved. The use of chemical weapons and the specter of trench warfare had helped convince many Americans that war had indeed become too horrible and too costly; efforts to ensure peace became the most popular reform of the 1920s.

This reaction against war that swept the country must have fueled the hopes of the WPP leaders once again. They had failed to stop the first world war; perhaps they could prevent another. Their first step was to attend the second International Congress of Women in May 1919, which had been planned at the first congress in 1915, when women from the United States and Europe had agreed on the necessity of meeting again at the war's conclusion. They had initially hoped to hold their conference in Versailles, where the postwar peace talks were taking place, but because their German members were prevented from traveling there, they chose neutral Zurich instead.

Twenty-three women from the United States attended this meeting: these included national WPP leaders Jane Addams, Emily Greene Balch, and Lucia Ames Mead, as well as physician Alice Hamilton; social reformer Lillian Wald; lecturer, writer, and activist Mary Church Terrell; and former congresswoman Jeannette Rankin, recently defeated in her run for reelection. They were joined by women from 138 other nations. Together for five days, these women renewed and established friendships, commented on the world situation, and most notably issued a strong indictment of the Versailles Treaty, especially its assignment of guilt to Germany, and urged the inclusion of a "women's charter" to ensure equal rights and opportunities for all women.[1]

The congress also agreed to continue the international ties among women by creating a new organization, the Women's International League for Peace and Freedom, open to all women and dedicated to the pursuit of peace, internationalism, and women's rights. Jane Addams was elected president and Emily Greene Balch secretary-treasurer.

Daunting as their new roles must have been, Addams, Balch, and the other delegates returned to the United States committed to forming a U.S. section of the new organization. Because there were so few members of the Woman's Peace Party left, however, they knew they would have to attract members from the ranks of women who had disagreed with their stance during the war years.

Thus they confronted once again the difficulties of uniting women behind a common cause. During the first five years, the leaders of the U.S. section of the Women's International League for Peace and Freedom (WIL) concentrated first on trying to unite women's peace activities. When that did not succeed, the organization then tried to cooperate with other women's organizations. The difficulty of such cooperation, however, gradually persuaded the women leading the WIL to accept that women would express their commitment to peace through a multiplicity of largely independent organizations. It also reinforced their philosophical commitment to pluralism and tolerance.

A Sign of the Future: Divisions Within the New York City Branch

In 1918 the New York City branch of the Woman's Peace Party was one of the strongest remaining branches. The pressures of the war had taken their toll, however, and branch leaders pondered whether changing the name of the organization would help it shake its negative public image. Specifically, they wondered if eliminating "peace" from the title might increase public acceptance. On one side of this issue were those who favored compromise if it increased effectiveness, while on the other side were those who opposed any change that might be perceived as a retraction of their stated position.

The majority of executive board members went on record in favor of changing the organization's name to something they perceived to be less politically charged: the Women's International League. They believed that such a change would "more accurately reflect our goal of internationalism as well as peace" and would "help pro-war people forget that we have differed from them and to see that we all seek permanent peace." Continuing to call themselves the Woman's Peace Party would limit their effectiveness and growth, no longer genuinely reflected their goals, and invited unnecessary misunderstanding from average citizens who equated the WPP with treason. Aware that they would be accused of compromising, these members of the executive board added that they did not consider this name change a "hurling down" of their flag. Rather, it would help them move forward "to a better vantage point from which we can command more practical support for our ideals."[2]

Some members of the New York City executive board, however, believed that changing the name of the New York City WPP would do more harm than good: it would be perceived as an abandonment of principle or perhaps as a calculated move to disguise the organization's true goals. Furthermore, they did not want to try to recruit support from people who found the word "peace" an obstacle. These women preferred the "Women's International League for Permanent Peace" or the "Women's League to Abolish War" as the new name.[3]

The proponents of the change to Women's International League won, and the New York City branch of the WPP moved forward under the leadership of lawyer and labor activist Crystal Eastman. Differences surfaced again the next year, however, and led to a final split in the organization. In September 1919 several members of the executive board resigned because they felt hindered by a "fundamental lack of unity in the membership as a whole and in the executive committee. We all want to prevent war and help establish international relations which will add to the peace and freedom of the world. There our agreement ends." Some of the members sanctioned no violence, while others justified violence in class struggle; some valued organizational and educational work, while others thought only revolution would bring a lasting peace; some accepted the League of Nations, while others condemned that organization and its supporters as reactionary; some desired a strong feminist movement, while others saw feminism as "sex antagonism"; some wanted to work through the political system, while others scorned politics in favor of direct action. This much difference, although understandable in the confusion of the postwar world, made it practically impossible to cooperate effectively, these women believed, and they resigned to work with organizations "with which we can be entirely in sympathy."[4]

This splintering of the New York group was significant for two reasons. First, the variety of opinion among supporters of the peace movement was clearly laid out by the resigning members of the executive committee. Peace was a cause that was hard to oppose, especially as more and more Americans became convinced that U.S. participation in World War I had been futile. But when people tried to work for peace, it became clear that the word meant different things to different people. The peace spectrum encompassed everyone from nonresistants on the left to conservative internationalists on the right; there was common ground, but rather than providing a stable foundation for unity, it more often swirled into an obscuring dust.

Second, the New York branch membership included many who would lead parts of women's peace activity in the following decades. Most notably, Fanny Garrison Villard, Elinor Byrns, and Caroline Babcock organized the Women's Peace Society shortly after they resigned from the New York Women's International League, and then in 1921 Byrns and Babcock began the Women's Peace Union. On the other hand, Emily Greene Balch, Katherine Devereaux Blake, and Madeleine Doty continued to work with the U.S. section of the Women's International League for Peace and Freedom. Although all of these women gave their time, energy, and resources to the peace movement, the differences among them prevented a united effort.

Divisions Among Women Peace Activists

Soon after resigning from the New York City WIL, Fanny Garrison Villard led the organization of a group more in line with her personal philosophy of complete nonresistance, the Women's Peace Society. At its first meeting, Villard was elected permanent chair, at least partly because she gave generously of her considerable wealth. She was assisted by Elinor Byrns, a New York City attorney who also believed unwaveringly in nonresistance. Any woman was eligible to join this new organization if she paid the 25-cent dues and signed a pledge stating that it was wrong to destroy human life under any circumstances.[5]

Approached by Villard about this new organization, Emily Greene Balch expressed the pluralistic view she had developed earlier through her studies of immigrants to the United States. In a city the size of New York, Balch wrote, she would like to see "half a dozen really active peace groups of different types following their own lines freely, not worried by one another's different methods, nor naturally responsible for one another's acts or policies, but cooperating fully on all their common aims and tactics." She maintained her primary allegiance to the WIL but offered to cooperate with Villard in whatever way might be appropriate.[6]

The dissolution of the New York branch of the WPP and the creation of the Women's Peace Society had pushed Balch to evaluate the issues of unity and diversity. Did differences among women mean a proliferation of organizations, or could those differences be encompassed in one organization with a high tolerance for diversity? "In any such movement as ours," she wrote, "there is always the question of how wide to strain the inclusiveness of a group and how to prevent the extreme right and left from breaking apart."[7] One thing that Balch was certain would neither ensure unity nor allow diversity was a membership pledge such as the one required by the Women's Peace Society. A WIL branch in Palo Alto, California, was circulating a pledge stating, "To us the sacredness and inviolability of life is the supreme law" and "we therefore repudiate all organized killing as unworthy of humanity and . . . never again will we render any support to war, including civil war, whether through money, propaganda or work." Balch believed that this kind of pledge, if required by the WIL, would only lead to disagreements.[8]

Not all WIL members or even its leaders agreed with Balch, and the issue of a pledge continued to surface periodically. In 1923, for example, the WIL considered making such a pledge a condition for membership. Both Fanny Garrison Villard and Lola Maverick Lloyd favored such a pledge. Lloyd had become involved in peace work through her association with Rosika Schwimmer, and although she affiliated with the WIL, she consistently criticized it as too conservative. She proffered a pledge she had written, which stated, "In case our country is at war, I will not join nor work for the Red Cross, nor make hospital supplies; I will not urge food conservation; I will not buy Liberty Bonds or any other similar war loans; I will not make munitions nor take a man's place in order to enable him to go to war."[9]

The WIL did not adopt this pledge or any other; this was in part because the many Quakers in the WIL refused to take pledges and in part because of Balch's reservations about the strategic wisdom of such a pledge. More fundamentally, however, the majority of WIL leaders were unwilling to stipulate or require certain beliefs or actions from WIL members. As pacifists, they opposed all support for war; but they also refused to specify how others should act.

The issue of a pledge continued to be a source of disagreement between the Women's Peace Society and the WIL. A few months after she had failed to convince the WIL to adopt Lloyd's pledge, Villard wrote, "Why anyone really desiring to prevent war should be unwilling to say: 'And I declare it to be my intention never to aid in or sanction war' I can't understand."[10] Given Villard's strong support of a pledge, it is ironic that disagreement over the wording of the Women's Peace Society's pledge eventually led to a schism in that organization. Some members of the WPS, especially Elinor Byrns and Caroline Lexow Babcock, felt that the WPS pledge needed to be even more explicit. They wanted a pledge that expressed a total refusal to sanction war or to do war relief work.[11] Villard, however, was reluctant to change the WPS pledge, primarily because she thought the existing, less explicit pledge appealed to more women.

Other issues also separated Villard from Byrns and Babcock and eventually led to the creation of yet another women's peace organization, the Women's Peace Union of the Western Hemisphere (WPU). Created in 1921, the WPU hoped to combine an active political program with a philosophy of total nonresistance. Any woman could join this organization as long as she was willing to sign a pledge stating that she (1) believed "that under no circumstances is it right to take human life"; (2) pledged to work for world peace; and (3) intended never to "aid in or sanction war, offensive or defensive, international or civil, in any way, whether by making or handling munitions, subscribing to war loans, using our labor for the purpose of setting others free for war service, helping by money or work any organization which supports or condones war."[12]

The leaders of the WIL, of course, found this pledge no more agreeable than any other. Indeed, the split in the WPS that led to the formation of the WPU probably confirmed Balch's fear that having a pledge served to divide women more than to unite them. Different opinions about the importance of a peace pledge did not keep these organizations from working together, however, and in the 1920s and 1930s the WIL supported what came to be the single cause of the WPU: a constitutional amendment to outlaw war as an instrument of policy for the U.S. government.[13]

By 1921, then, what had at one time been a central branch of the Woman's Peace Party had split into three separate organizations, all committed to organizing women's work for peace. To some observers, this looked like an unnecessary duplication of effort and expense; but there were crucial differences among the three organizations. Furthermore, the proliferation of diverse women's peace groups could be seen as a source of strength. Emily Greene Balch brought her appreciation of diversity to her leadership of the WILPF. Trying to avoid overlapping efforts and members was a mistake, she wrote. Instead, let there be a variety of organizations working both separately and cooperatively. These different groups, Balch believed, might have broadly similar aims, but if they were placed in one organization, would likely find little on which they could agree. And as far as the WIL was concerned, Balch believed that its program was "so inclusive . . . that there is not only room for but need of groups which emphasize different parts of it."[14]

Perhaps because they accepted Balch's view, the leaders of the WIL began to shift their efforts away from trying to unify women's peace work and toward cooperating with other organizations whose goals were similar to those of the WIL. In 1923 the members of the WIL national board agreed "that it is of first rate importance that the absolutely pacifist character and aims" of their organization always be emphasized; but they also agreed to "be ready to co-operate with all other agencies working toward peace."[15]

Attempts at Cooperation

The WIL leaders' search for allies in the struggle for peace naturally led them first to other women's organizations, with whom many of them already had ties. Early in 1920, Lucia Ames Mead suggested that the WIL cooperate with the League of Women Voters, the General Federation of Women's Clubs, the National Council of Women, and other organizations in getting political candidates to answer a peace-oriented questionnaire. She believed that this effort would force the political candidates "to give satisfactory answers" to women who would be voting for the first time.[16] All of these organizations or their predecessors had helped to organize the Woman's Peace Party in 1915; thus Mead and other WIL leaders most likely knew their leaders and hoped to reestablish the working relationship they had had before the war.

The WIL leaders also hoped to cooperate with the National Woman's Party (NWP), which was committed to achieving legal equality for women. Because the NWP had not supported U.S. participation in World War I, the WIL leaders doubtlessly hoped it would support the postwar cause of peace. The NWP seemed willing to cooperate, for it asked the WIL to send speakers to its annual convention in 1921. Jane Addams attended the convention, as did several other WIL members, and was honored at a ceremony for leaders of the suffrage movement.[17]

When cooperation between the two organizations tried to move beyond the level of ceremony, however, problems arose quickly. Addams and the other WIL members in attendance hoped that members of the National Woman's Party would join the WIL, or that they would at least vote in their own organization to support a disarmament resolution proposed by the WIL. Furthermore, National Woman's Party leader Alice Paul remembered that "there was a very *strong* feeling among most of the delegates, that peace was, after all, the next thing to work for." Paul herself did not share this feeling. She supported women's work in the peace movement but had no intention of taking the focus off the NWP's work for equality. In the end, the National Woman's Party did not decide to devote itself to peace work or even pass the WIL's disarmament resolution.[18] The National Woman's Party members who were most disappointed by this decision withdrew from the NWP; but instead of joining the WIL they formed yet another new organization, the Women's Committee on World Disarmament.[19]

Even when other groups were in sympathy with the WIL program, they often hesitated to cooperate for political reasons. In 1921, for example, the president of the League of Women Voters, Belle Sherwin, told the executive secretary of the WIL that she was very impressed with the WIL's Statement of Policy and that she personally admired the group. As president of a large organization designed to appeal to a variety of women, however, she could not "openly endorse" the WIL.[20]

In spite of this initial rebuff, in 1922 the WIL adopted a resolution that had been previously adopted by the League of Women Voters. This resolution supported the abolition of war through the establishment of equal and just international law. Because this was not a new position for the WIL, it seems likely that WIL leaders adopted it largely to show support for the League of Women Voters. Also, the WIL continued to list the League of Women Voters as one of its primary sources of potential members.[21]

The leaders of the WIL also continued to envision the WIL as the organization that could at least promote and perhaps even coordinate the peace activities of women's organizations. At its annual meeting in March 1923, the WIL resolved to "appeal especially to organizations of women voters, of women in industry, of women in college clubs and church societies, of women in the home and in the school, to recognize the fact that, even unaided by men, we women have the power, if we will exercise it, to abolish war." The WIL even reached out to women assumed to be hostile—members of the Daughters of the American Revolution, the Red Cross, the Army and Navy League, and the Mothers of War Veterans—hoping they could convince these women to work to prevent war rather than to ameliorate its effects. Finally, WIL leaders resolved to try to enlist the help of the press, especially the editors of women's magazines such as *Ladies' Home Journal*, *McCall's*, and *Good Housekeeping*.[22]

Attracting women from one group sometimes meant repelling women from another group. When a previous WIL donor, Laura Williams, decided to switch her support to the League of Women Voters, Williams said that "her chief reason for feeling this way was because of our Woman's Party members." WIL executive secretary Dorothy Detzer believed that Williams was "suspicious of them all and feels that they only blacken and hamper the organization."[23] In such cases, appealing to women from different points on the political spectrum did not further the coordination of peace activities but only cost the WIL needed financial support.

The difficulties caused by attempting to cooperate with other women's organizations and coordinate their peace activities climaxed for the WIL in 1924. The WIL was affiliated with the National Council of Women, an umbrella organization begun in 1888 with which smaller, more specialized women's groups could affiliate. Its main purpose was to serve as the U.S. representative to the International Council of Women. In 1924 the National Council was planning to host the quinquennial meeting for the International Council and wanted to hire the Daughters of the American Revolution mansion as its meeting place. The DAR, which had been especially critical of the peace movement since the end of World War I, wanted to make sure that no pacifist addresses would be made in this hall during the meeting of the International Council; it was particularly worried about the presence of the WIL. The president of the National Council, Eva Perry Moore, responded to the concerns of the DAR by asking the WIL to withdraw, telling the leaders of the WIL that other organizations objected to what they perceived as the WIL's "radical" program.[24]

Charges of radicalism were not new to the leaders of the WIL. Those who had also led the Woman's Peace Party had been accused of treason for opposing U.S. entry into World War I, with Jane Addams coming under particularly strong criticism. The criticism of Addams began again when she dared to criticize the raids on aliens and political radicals organized by Attorney General A. Mitchell Palmer in 1920. These raids were indicative of a general attitude of suspicion, often called the Red Scare, that existed in the United States after the success of the Bolshevik Revolution in 1918. Fearful that this revolution would spread to the United States, some Americans, chief among whom were the leaders of the DAR, applied the label Bolshevik to anyone who criticized the government or its policies. Addams disliked this label but was unable to convince her critics that it was inappropriate. Then, in 1923, Lucia R. Maxwell, librarian of the Chemical Warfare Service of the War Department, prepared the first "spider-web chart" to illustrate the supposed existence of a huge communist conspiracy in the United States, a conspiracy believed to be led by pacifist, progressive, labor, and women's organizations. Organizations listed included the League of Women Voters, the National Consumers' League, the American Civil Liberties Union, the American Federation of Labor, the Fellowship of Reconciliation, and of course, the WIL.[25]

The WIL was suspect not only because of its association with Addams but also because of its policies. Its "sex solidarity" as a women's organization, its links with international organizations, and its support for federal legislation designed to provide public funding for maternal and infant health care all opened it to charges of communism.[26] Although the WIL usually did not dignify accusations of communism with a reply, it could hardly ignore a request for its resignation. Initially, it simply refused. WIL president Hannah Clothier Hull told the president of the National Council, Eva Perry Moore, that the request was "evidently not based on personal incompatibilities, but on some larger question of policies believed to be advocated" by the WIL. To resign under these circumstances, Hull continued, "would be understood as an admission of current calumnies and an encouragement to further attacks upon pacifists all along the line."[27]

Within a few weeks, however, Jane Addams suggested, with an evident tinge of sarcasm, that resignation might be "magnanimous," for otherwise the council would expect the WIL to raise the money the council might have received if it had not been handicapped by the WIL's membership.[28] And a few weeks later, when the executive board of the WIL met with Moore to try to resolve the dispute between the two organizations, Moore told the board members that if the WIL were to remain on the National Council, its members would be expected to support a resolution by Senator William E. Borah, an ardent isolationist and foe of the League of Nations. Hull wrote, "I felt that I could not conscientiously help in seeing Senator Borah to bring an appropriation from Congress." In addition, Hull came to believe that "the whole scheme of the National Council of Women, and of its possibility for usefulness has been outlived." The board members finally agreed to withdraw from the council, but on their own terms. They would "ignore the fact of the Council not wanting us," Hull wrote, and put their resignation "on the ground of our convictions."[29] Hull accordingly wrote Moore that the WIL was committed to eliminating all violence between individuals and nations. Because this program was "not in harmony with the purposes of some of the organizations composing the National Council of Women," the WIL withdrew its membership in the council.[30]

After this incident, it was clear to most of the WIL leaders that it was going to be impossible for the WIL to coordinate women's peace activity and extremely difficult for the organization even to cooperate with other women's organizations. Although most of the women in the organizations with which the WIL tried to cooperate probably knew little about the WIL's actual program and policies, they had heard the charges of radicalism, and those were enough, during the Red Scare years, to cause them to want nothing to do with such women.

The National Conference on the Cause and Cure
of War

If the WIL leaders found it difficult to cooperate with other women's organizations, there was another prominent leader who was ready to try her hand: Carrie Chapman Catt. Catt had left the peace movement in 1917 to lead the National American Woman Suffrage Association in its support of Wilson and U.S. intervention in World War I. She had then presided over the remaining years of the successful suffrage campaign. Once the vote was won, though, Catt became a woman without a cause. The solid block of politically active women who had pushed through the suffrage amendment seemed to melt, then evaporate in disparate droplets. Some women became politically dormant; others returned to work on the social and political problems that had claimed their interest before it had seemed necessary to concentrate almost exclusively on winning the vote; and others returned to the various women's clubs through which they had done volunteer work.

Catt hoped to reunite these women. As she put it, she and other suffragists found themselves longing for "the old days—the struggle, the comradeship, the thrill of working for freedom for the women of all ages." The cause that could provide this sense of unity, Catt believed, was working for world peace. "What hope can there be," she asked, "for women, for democracy, for children, for mankind in a world poisoned, its finest strength running out like water, in war which will become increasingly more hideous?"[31]

It would have been logical for Catt to have tried to work within one of the existing women's peace organizations, but their leaders still resented Catt's decision to support World War I and were skeptical about her renewed commitment to the peace movement. And Catt herself had no interest in working with existing organizations. She believed that she could do what they had been unable to do: attract large numbers of women to the peace movement.[32]

Catt decided to assemble the leaders of nine major women's organizations for a conference she called the National Conference on the Cause and Cure of War (NCCCW). All of the organizations to which she appealed existed for some purpose other than peace: the American Association of University Women, the Council of Women for Home Missions, the Women's Board of Foreign Missions, the General Federation of Women's Clubs, the National Council of Jewish Women, the League of Women Voters, the Women's Christian Temperance Union, the Women's Trade Union League, and the Young Women's Christian Association. Many had also participated in the organizational conference of the Woman's Peace Party nearly ten years earlier; not included this time was the National Association of Colored Women, a group that had been invited to the 1915 conference.

Catt pointedly did not invite any women's peace organizations to this conference, but WIL members who were also affiliated with one of the invited groups did attend. Hannah Clothier Hull found the conference interesting and serious, although the discussion remained simple and basic. She had been heartened by the presence of other WIL members, particularly Anna Garlin Spencer and Lucia Ames Mead, both of whom addressed the assembly.[33] The physician, reformer, and WIL member Alice Hamilton also attended the conference and found it "much more pacifist than I am sure the leaders expected or perhaps realized." She noted that "it was the radically pacifist sentiments which got the most applause and the questions asked were inspired largely by the same spirit."[34] Hamilton's fellow reformer and WIL member Grace Abbott also found the conference useful and, like Hamilton, was especially impressed by "the sound understanding which the missionary ladies and the W.C.T.U. showed of what some of the fundamental difficulties are."[35]

To some extent, attendance at Catt's conference must have encouraged these WIL members. In their eyes, women in whom they had earlier placed their hope for peace—the middle-of-the-road club members and social activists—demonstrated their continued interest in the peace movement. Yet Hamilton and the others also knew that they had been unsuccessful in organizing this group of women. WIL membership had increased—to over 5,000 members in 1924—but it still fell far short of appealing to the majority of women in the United States.

Although the WIL members who attended the National Conference on the Cause and Cure of War may have felt their hope of organizing all women's work for peace through the WIL flicker once more, they did not renew their efforts in this regard. Rather, they revised their conception of the WIL's role. Instead of seeing the organization as one that would unite all women behind the cause of peace, they began to think of themselves as "a fighting peace organization" with a program farther to the left than most women in the United States desired.[36]

The WIL's change of focus suited Catt perfectly, for she believed that the WIL was too idealistic to attract most women. The WIL might "be the power that will blaze the trail," Catt conceded, but "when the trail is blazed a road must be found out of it, and the more conservative groups will have to do that."[37] Catt's role, as the leader of the NCCCW, was to coordinate the actions of those more conservative groups.

Catt was optimistic about the NCCCW's chances for success in 1925, but when she decided to continue the work of the conference in ensuing years she too soon found that organizing women's work for peace was very difficult. Unlike women's suffrage, where there was one clear goal, in the peace movement there were countless goals and strategies for attaining them, all of which varied with an individual's political perspective. After two years, Catt herself admitted doubts about the NCCCW's effectiveness. She expressed those doubts in a meeting with Frederick Libby, the head of the National Council for Prevention of War. This organization, begun in 1923, had essentially the same umbrella structure as the NCCCW, and Libby told Catt that he had begun to doubt its efficacy. Catt then admitted to Libby that, although she had had great hopes for the NCCCW, she had begun to feel "that it was impossible to do anything, that you could not move organizations, that you could only move individuals." The NCCCW, Catt concluded, "had failed in the purpose that she had started out to gain."[38]

A Narrowed Appeal

Catt's experience with the National Conference on the Cause and Cure of War mirrored the experiences of the WIL in trying to attract women's organizations to its cause. That all women would never be combined into one group had to be acknowledged by 1925. Even the language used seemed to reflect the realization of women's diversity; the *Woman's* Peace Party, we have seen, gave way to the *Women's* International League for Peace and Freedom, the *Women's* Peace Society, and the *Women's* Peace Union.[39]

Over the following two decades, all of these groups worked to make their protest against war and injustice heard. The Women's Peace Society was probably the least effective, gradually abandoning activism in favor of educational measures such as letter-writing campaigns. The Women's Peace Union remained small but succeeded in having a constitutional amendment to abolish the government's power to wage war introduced to Congress repeatedly throughout the 1920s and 1930s. The Women's International League grew slowly throughout the 1920s and 1930s, peaking in 1939 with a membership of almost 14,000.

After 1924, the WIL traded its desire to unite women's peace activities for the freedom to became a more committed peace organization with its own distinctive philosophy. Central to this philosophy was a concept that had grown out of the experiences of the women who led the WIL during the first years of its existence: unity within diversity. Many of the women who led the WIL had come together in 1915 to form the Woman's Peace Party, only to see that organization gradually divided by differences over policy and program. When they reorganized as the WIL, they again watched as women committed to the peace movement split into several organizations. And when they tried to cooperate with other women's organizations, they again encountered difficulties.

Ultimately, women joined the organizations with which they were most compatible and still made common cause with other organizations when their goals intersected. This approach had worked within the WIL and the Woman's Peace Party, and gradually WIL leaders realized that they could extend this perspective to the work of other organizations as well.

This perspective had its roots in the commitment to cultural pluralism that had figured prominently in the earlier work of both Jane Addams and Emily Greene Balch. Balch then applied the idea of pluralism to her work in the peace movement and developed the concept of unity within diversity. In 1922 Balch wrote in the WIL's annual report, "With us, there is more than tolerance, there is a vivid pleasure in the element of unlikeness and variety."[40] Conflicts between the WIL and other women's organizations in the following years only confirmed the importance of this perspective.

In 1925 the WIL national board installed Balch in the new position of director of policies. She held the position throughout the 1920s and 1930s and probably did more than any other individual woman to shape the philosophy of the WIL in those years. Under her philosophical leadership, the WIL became a pacifist organization with a strong commitment to justice for all people.

STAFFORDSHIRE
UNIVERSITY
LIBRARY

Nurturing and Nonresistance, 1919–1941

IN THE FALL OF 1941, Dorothy Detzer had served almost twenty years as the executive secretary of the WIL. Spending much of that time as a lobbyist for pacifist causes, she had achieved numerous small victories and at least one major one: convincing Congress to investigate munitions manufacturers. Yet Detzer was not confident that the peace for which she had worked so hard would last much longer. Western Europe was already at war, the United States was providing protection to British convoys, and the conflict between the United States and Japan was escalating. In this climate, Detzer found herself pondering what she called "our WIL failure." She supposed, she said, that "it is somewhat natural that those who have never accepted the pacifist way of life might be prepared to sacrifice ethical values in a period such as this." And certainly the WIL should not feel too bad about not having completely changed the government's attitude toward international relations: "It would be arrogant and ridiculous to imagine that in twenty-five short years a functioning cooperative peace system could have been established." What really nagged at Detzer was her sense that even the WIL membership had not become committed to some of the fundamental concepts of their work. "Our failure," she believed, "lies primarily with our own membership. We have somehow failed to get the mass of our members to understand and to accept certain basic ethical principles."[1]

The ethical principles to which Detzer referred were the commitment to nurturing one's fellows; the feminist belief that women shared some common characteristics and should work with women to advance issues of concern to women; the concept of unity within diversity, both in membership and in policies; and a belief in the ideal of nonresistance. For the organization's pacifism, nurturing and nonresistance were the most important. Because these two principles sometimes conflicted with each other, the organization's commitment to pluralism and tolerance through the concept of unity within diversity was also vital, for it allowed WIL leaders to disagree over policies yet continue working together.

The Link Between Nurturing and Peace

The connection the WIL leaders made between nurturing and peace had its roots in the ideas of Jane Addams. She believed that, if properly cared for by their fellow citizens and their government, the poor residents of the inner city would be transformed into models of cosmopolitanism and might even lead the way to a peaceful world. And, she argued, because women had the most experience in nurturing, the injustice of women's exclusion from the public sphere should be ended and women integrated into all realms of life.

Addams's belief never wavered, and in the books she wrote during and after World War I she tried to make her concept of nurturing more concrete and specific. While working with Herbert Hoover's Department of Food Administration during World War I, for example, Addams made the willingness to provide food fairly to all people a concrete symbol of the commitment to nurturing. She suggested that "the more sophisticated questions of national grouping and territorial control would gradually adjust themselves if the paramount human question of food for the hungry be fearlessly and drastically treated upon an international basis." If President Wilson would ensure that the League of Nations he envisioned was "founded not upon broken bits of international law, but upon ministrations to primitive human needs," then Addams thought such a league would have a chance of being a stable and helpful political institution.[2]

In 1922 Addams developed this idea more fully in her book *Peace and Bread in Time of War*. As she had done years before as a college student, she used bread as a symbol of nurturing and explicitly connected women with its provision. She explained that she had considered her work with the Food Administration so important partly because she saw it as a way to convince women who were not already concerned about the world's affairs that their voices and efforts were needed. Most women traditionally had not been interested in world affairs, Addams implied, because such matters had not seemed relevant to their lives. But anthropological studies showed that women, as farmers and as preparers, had always been involved in the provision of food. If other women could be convinced that an equal distribution of the world's food supply would go a long way toward resolving international conflicts, then Addams thought those women might see their relevance to international affairs. Just as Addams had seen women enter "into politics when clean milk and the premature labor of children became factors in political life," so she thought women might become "concerned with international affairs when at last these were dealing with such human and poignant matters as food for starving peoples who could be fed only through international activities."[3]

Addams wanted women to become involved in international affairs, but she wanted them to do so on their own terms, not those of men.[4] The provision of food, in her mind, was just as important as the negotiation of an international treaty, and women's historic role in the provision of food could provide their entree into the arena of international affairs.

The link Addams drew between women and nurturing seems, to modern readers, to be part of the chain confining women to household and dependent care. Superficially that criticism is valid. Addams believed that women were more committed to nurturing than men were, and that if a woman wanted to spend her life well she would spend it in the service of others. What is often overlooked, however, is that Addams believed that nurturing was important work for all people, not just women. In *Newer Ideals of Peace*, for example, she had offered nurturing others as the "moral substitute for war" for all people. Furthermore, Addams did not envision women nurturing in traditional ways—only their immediate families and within the confines of their own homes—but through active involvement in all realms of society.

In effect, Addams criticized the division of life into public and private spheres. This division had occurred in the middle and upper classes as a result of industrialization, and it had been given intellectual significance by the theorists of the Enlightenment. Those theorists had exalted the importance of rationality while shunting other ways of acquiring knowledge and resolving ethical issues into the private realm. Because most women were not educated in ways that would have allowed them to participate in the public and rational sphere, and because custom gave them primary responsibility for home and family, the theorists relegated most women to the private sphere, where they were supposed to serve primarily as the keepers of the nation's morality.[5]

What Addams envisioned was a reunification of public and private and of rationality and emotionality. She wanted to reintegrate facets of human life and thought that had been separated in the previous century. She did not believe that people moved solely in the private or the public realm, or that they made decisions or responded to situations with pure emotion or pure rationality. Such inaccurate conceptualizations of roles and mental capacities had proved especially limiting to women, Addams believed; the work they did in the home and the emotional support they provided to others had been undervalued. She worked to formulate an understanding of modern life that would allow, even encourage, women to bring their emotional sensitivity and their concern for caretaking into the public realm. She also suggested that men participate in the work of nurturing—work that would cause, even compel, them to heighten their own emotional sensitivity. In this scheme, men and women would begin working together, both at home and outside the home, and would cultivate both their rationality and their emotional sensitivity.

But getting women to take part in public activities, Addams knew, could be difficult because of the ways in which their lives were restricted by their responsibilities at home. Women struggled, she wrote, to make a "synthesis between our ambitions to cure the ills of the world on the one hand, and the need to conform to household requirements on the other." That difficulty had to be overcome, however, for the two realms of private and public, of emotionality and rationality, of women and men, "had become absolutely essential to each other." World peace "could not be achieved without woman's participation founded upon an intelligent understanding and upon the widest sympathy," but neither would a woman be attracted to peace work unless "it were attached to her domestic routine, its very success depending upon a conscious change and modification of her daily habits."[6] The public activity of working for world peace would have to be redefined to include something that related to the realities of most women's lives in the private realm. Addams believed that something was the provision of food.

Addams's belief in the importance of nurturing, and specifically the equitable provision of food to all people, became a central component of WIL policy. In 1927 WIL national board member Katherine Devereaux Blake testified in favor of the so-called Frazier Amendment proposed by the Women's Peace Union. Sponsored by Senator Lynn Frazier, a Republican from North Dakota, this amendment made war illegal and deprived the U.S. government of the power to prepare for or wage war. Blake pointed out that war hurt children the most: "It is they who starve, it is they who die, it is they who grow up with the awful handicap of undernourishment, it is they who bear the burden."[7] Among all the other reasons for opposing war, Blake spotlighted the fact that it interrupted food supplies and caused starvation.

The WIL national board made clear its belief in the importance of providing food in a resolution passed during the darkest months of the Great Depression. President Franklin Roosevelt, struggling to assist ailing farmers, oversaw the passage of the Agricultural Adjustment Act. Under this act, the federal government paid farmers to reduce production by not planting crops and by destroying crops already in the fields. To the WIL, as to many other Americans, this policy was deplorable in the face of starvation in this country as well as in others. The WIL suggested as an alternative that the government purchase the agricultural products and distribute them to Cubans, Puerto Ricans, and others who needed them.[8]

At their 1941 annual meeting the members of the WIL also stated that using food as a weapon was wrong. Blockades that prevented food from getting to the people of a belligerent nation hurt primarily noncombatants. Thus they resolved to appeal to President Roosevelt to do what he could to make sure that food was allowed to pass through such blockades.[9] At this same meeting, a statement by Gertrude Bussey, who had recently become the national president of the WIL, eloquently summarized the centrality of food, of nurturing, and of the impact of the ideas of Addams. Bussey told the assembled WIL members:

One of the fundamental clues which I get from the work of Jane Addams and her fellow-workers is derived from their emphasis on feeding. Food is not only the primary necessity of our life, but for that reason fitly symbolizes all those goods which satisfy the cravings of the human spirit. . . . This emphasis on food must be central in our ideal of building up a constructive

social order in which the vast resources of the earth discovered by the genius of man may be utilized for the feeding of the people and the healing of
the nations.[10]

The WIL also exhibited its commitment to nurturing through its
opposition to what it considered the economic imperialism of the
United States. Since the late nineteenth century, the United States
had been expanding its influence in Latin America and attempting
to do so in Asia. Businessmen were eager to take advantage of plen-
tiful and inexpensive natural resources, including human labor, and
periodically called upon the government of the United States to settle conflicts or negotiate favorable agreements with the host nation.
U.S. foreign policy in the early part of the twentieth century tended
to follow the economic interests of U.S. businesses into places such
as Mexico, Nicaragua, Guatemala, Honduras, Cuba, the Dominican
Republic, and Haiti.

This tendency to put the power of the government of the United
States at the call of private economic interests disturbed the leaders
of the WIL, but they also realized that accusing the United States of
economic imperialism would be unpopular with the American public. As Balch wrote in 1926, "We citizens of the United States are so
innocent of any imperialistic purpose and so complacently unaware
of what is done in our name in inconspicuous but effective ways
that we are aggrieved by any criticism along these lines."[11]

The risk of unpopularity, however, did not deter the WIL leaders from criticizing such imperialistic policies, and Balch and other
WIL leaders began trying to explain to others how the United States
used the natural resources of other nations to its own advantage and
why that policy ran counter to the WIL emphasis on nurturing.
Hannah Clothier Hull, national president of the WIL, understood
this connection well. To attain peace, she wrote, it was not enough
to try to eliminate armaments; one also had to work "to do away
with imperialism and to see justice done to all nations in the matter of free access to food and raw materials for the sustenance of
every race and people." The WIL, she continued, was "convinced
that the prevention of conflict depends upon the solution of such
economic problems."[12] Dorothy Detzer, the executive secretary of
the WIL, agreed with Hull; she even went so far as to compare the
foreign policy of the United States to that of a road hog.[13] Detzer argued that the United States was building a large navy not for pur-

poses of defense, but to protect American economic interests abroad. "Is our money to be sunk in naval vessels and our boys conscripted to fight for rubber interests, fruit interests or oil interests?" she asked. And in answer to her own question, she concluded, "We are building an imperialist navy for the vested interests in war—for those with special privilege in steel and munitions at home and profits in commodities abroad. . . . We are building an imperialist navy, and civilization is threatened as long as the United States and other nations maintain their policies of economic and political imperialism."[14]

When Detzer and Hull expressed these criticisms to President Roosevelt in 1936, their language was more restrained but their message was the same. They took issue with the president's interpretation of the rise of Nazism and fascism. Rather than the products of leaders who were convinced that they were "unique depositories of ultimate truth and right," as Roosevelt had stated, Detzer and Hull suggested that they were "the results of bitter injustices and serious economic ills" and could only be resolved through a "just and rational distribution of the natural riches of the world with a view to satisfying the needs of all men."[15]

Katherine Devereaux Blake agreed with Hull and Detzer. She found herself increasingly upset about the apparent drift to war in the late 1930s. She proposed an international conference for the mediation of national grievances, a campaign to oust militarists from the Congress, and a conference "to consider raw materials, and the possibility of equal accessibility to such materials for all countries" because "it is the desire to control oil and mines that is the basis of most of the danger of war today, and we must face the fact, and try to end the present injustice and imperialism by world control."[16]

Through this critique of economic imperialism, the national leaders of the WIL used and elaborated upon Addams's initial idea of substituting nurture for warfare. Achieving their goal would also require the further integration of women into the public sphere and a heightened appreciation among men of the importance of nurturing.

The Ideal of Nonresistance, the Reality of
International Aggression

The other fundamental principle that shaped WIL policy during the 1920s and 1930s was the ideal of nonresistance. This ideal had also been fundamental to the Woman's Peace Party. Although the WPP's initial platform had positioned it close to the middle of the spectrum of peace organizations, within one year the organization had moved much farther to the left. Responding to the urging of Fanny Garrison Villard, the WPP had passed a resolution condemning the use of violence, even in self-defense. Not all branches of the WPP went so far, but the national group at least had placed itself among those pacifists who considered themselves nonresistants. Furthermore, the controversy within the WPP over whether its members should do war relief work had shown the deep commitment many members had to helping people in need and how that commitment could be perceived as conflicting with their equally strong commitment to peace.

When the WPP was reorganized after the war as the WIL, it again faced the problem of defining its pacifism and of reconciling its pacifism with its belief in helping others. Its earliest and most comprehensive statement, one to which it would reaffirm its commitment periodically throughout the next two decades, was taken from a statement issued by the International Executive Committee of the WILPF:

The League is made up of people who believe that we are not obliged to choose between violence and passive acceptance of unjust conditions for ourselves or others; on the contrary, that courage, determination, moral power, generous indignation, active good-will, can achieve their ends without violence.

We believe that experience condemns force as a self-defeating weapon although men are still so disposed to turn to it in education, in dealing with crime, in effecting or preventing social changes, and above all in carrying out national policies.

WE BELIEVE THAT NEW METHODS, FREE FROM VIOLENCE, MUST BE WORKED OUT FOR ENDING ABUSES AND FOR UNDOING WRONGS, AS WELL AS FOR ACHIEVING POSITIVE ENDS.[17]

In this policy, the WIL condemned the use of violence and called for the use of "new methods" to resolve conflict and to achieve more positive goals such as international cooperation and social justice. Particularly important to this position was the understanding of the WIL leaders that the methods or means used to achieve an end affected the end itself; or to put it more precisely, the achievement of moral ends could *not* justify the use of immoral means. This was not a new insight: Crystal Eastman, Jane Addams, Emily Greene Balch and others had pointed out the importance of method as early as World War I.[18] But it played a major role in shaping the WIL's analysis of how to resolve international conflicts.

Balch argued strongly that the method used affected the end achieved. Balch had written years before, during the war, that in addition to being unethical, the use of coercion was ineffective, and she continued this line of thought in the 1930s. When she heard the news of nonviolent protests in India, for example, Balch was encouraged but not wholly satisfied, for she felt that the Indian resistance leader Mohandas Gandhi was not going far enough in his effort to work with and understand the British. She was particularly critical of Gandhi's decision to issue an ultimatum to the British: "An *ultimatum* is in essence a war method and issues from a war mentality. One never presents an ultimatum to a friend and if Gandhi does not consider the British as friends—however wrong and however wicked—then he has surrendered something more precious than the non-violence principle—the good will principle." For Balch, it was not enough simply to refrain from violence; one's method also had to be governed by good will for one's opponent.[19]

Three years later, Balch again stressed the importance of using proper methods to achieve peace: it was important to try to establish structures, such as international laws, courts, and organizations, and to try to solve the inequities of the present system. But that was not enough. "Fundamental to all else," she wrote, "is the need that men should grow to understand and practice patience and tolerance, and come to substitute for the clumsy, uncertain, cruel tool of violence, the methods of reason and cooperation."[20]

Balch knew that Jane Addams had also realized the importance of the method used to achieve an end. Shortly after Addams's death, Balch recalled that Addams's concern for peace had not been a specific reaction to World War I but a "state of mind, a method of dealing with contentious problems of all sorts." And certainly Addams herself had made evident her belief that using the proper method was necessary by refusing to go along with reformers who eventually supported the war effort.[21]

An identical view was expressed repeatedly by Jeannette Rankin, who worked intermittently with the WIL during the 1920s and 1930s. Looking back on her decision in 1937 to vote against U.S. entry into World War I, she remembered, "Twenty years ago I voted against war because I was convinced that no social problem is ever solved by force and violence. My study of history, of social conditions and all life's experiences had taught me that it is a futile method of adjusting human relationships." And years later, when interviewed about her opposition to both World War I and World War II, Rankin again stated, "War is a method, and you can be either for it or against it and I'm against it because of its futility, its stupidity and its ultimate destruction of humanity—of civilization."[22]

The pacifists of the interwar years, especially the leaders of the Fellowship of Reconciliation, shared the WIL's convictions about the effects of violence. They argued that the value of a result could be judged only in relation to the means used to achieve it. As stated in the pacifist publication *World Tomorrow*, "The pacifist believes that the means and the end are so intimately related that it is impossible to get a coordinated and cooperative world by destructive methods that violate personality and increase antagonism and distrust."[23]

The pacifist belief in the relation between means and ends was related to the philosophy of pragmatism. Particularly as formulated by William James, pragmatism was conceived not as a school of thought but as a possible method. It offered not answers, but theories; and the validity of those theories was determined by their effects in the real world. Jane Addams, for example, opposed World War I and believed that the postwar world would prove that violence was invalid as a means of achieving constructive social change. Pragmatist philosopher John Dewey, on the other hand, decided to support World War I because he believed that under the leadership of Woodrow Wilson the United States would wage war intelligently and for a moral cause: the spread of democracy both domestically and internationally. By the end of the war, however, Dewey had changed his mind; he acknowledged that the war had actually lessened democracy instead of furthering it, and from then on he advocated that means and ends had to be consistent.

This emphasis on method, or the means used to achieve an end,

STAFFORDSHIRE
UNIVERSITY
LIBRARY

was important for two reasons. First, focusing on method allowed the leaders of the WIL, as well as other pacifists, to separate the existence of conflict from the existence of violence. Critics sometimes charged that pacifists naively assumed that perfect harmony could govern human relations; but the leaders of the WIL held no such belief. For them, conflict was a positive good. Dorothy Detzer explained this view in a radio address in 1931: "People so often confuse conflict and war." But, she noted, "Conflict is a part of life. The conflict of ideas, the clash of thought is of the very stuff of progress. When conflict ceases, stagnation begins." But to acknowledge the importance of conflict did not mean that one had to accept war, for Detzer continued, "War is only a method for dealing with conflict."[24]

The second reason that it was important to identify violence as a method can best be understood by envisioning the alternative. If war was not a method for resolving conflict, what was it? One answer was that it sprang from the depths of human nature—it was simply the largest expression of human aggression. If one accepted this view, there was hardly any reason to oppose war. One might be able to make war a bit gentler through the regulation of weapons and laws for treatment of prisoners and civilians, but one could never abolish it altogether. If, however, war was only one method of solving disputes, then other methods could be developed and put in its place. This is what William James and Jane Addams had both suggested at the turn of the century, with their plans for moral equivalents and moral substitutes. It was also what the WIL, and most other pacifist organizations, spent effort and money on in the interwar decades.

What other methods for settling disputes could be developed, and how effective would they be? What exactly was violence? Was it only physical, or could it be mental and emotional as well? If others relied on violence, could they be opposed effectively without violence? Was it moral to use alternative types of coercion if one abstained from violence? If one abstained from the use of all coercion, could injustice be corrected some other way or did it have to be ignored? And if one ignored injustice in order to maintain peace, was it likely that the injustice would breed more conflict? The WIL leaders answered these difficult questions in different ways, but the way in which they dealt with their differences illustrated once again their philosophical commitment to unity within diversity. Their attempts to unify or coordinate women's peace activities had convinced them to tolerate, even appreciate, a multiplicity of views within the organization. Only if they were "acrimonious in differing," Balch believed, would they "be out of accord with the spirit of Jane Addams and of our League and untrue to our peace principles."[25] Gertrude Bussey, who served as the national president of the WIL after 1940, agreed: "As a democratic organization," she explained, the WIL had "always expected differences of opinion among our members. The frank discussion of such differences is an essential part of our program and contributes to the real strength of the League."[26]

Although this tolerance of diversity helped the WIL remain a vital, developing organization, it did not always make for efficient operation. In fact, Dorothy Detzer remembered that prolonged discussions over policy sometimes made the decision-making process painfully slow. Because the WIL leaders tried to encompass differences within a consensus rather than simply accept a majority vote, Detzer recalled that meetings of the national board sometimes lasted days. In those cases, Detzer remembered, it was vital to have women such as Balch who excelled at "finding a third way."[27]

This kind of extended debate helped to ensure a good working relationship among the national leaders, but it would have proved deadly at annual meetings of the entire organization. Thus the structure for formulating policy was designed to allow for differences of opinion, but to do so without sacrificing all effectiveness. The national WIL consisted of a centrally directed national organization with local branches. The local branches had much autonomy, but the national organization hired staff, issued literature, and spoke for the entire organization during emergency situations. Furthermore, the national WIL developed the annual program, which was then distributed to the branches. This program was divided into two sections, one on principles and one on policies. The program could emphasize the general unity of principle among its leaders and members while still allowing for disagreement over specific parts of its plan for action. This strategy worked well, with the national organization and the branches achieving a large degree of consensus during the interwar years.[28]

The WIL's core commitment to nonresistance still allowed for a

STAFFORDSHIRE
UNIVERSITY
LIBRARY

great deal of disagreement over specific policies. The organization struggled most with disarmament, national and international outlawry of war, the use of boycotts and sanctions, and national neutrality legislation. Disarmament and outlawry were designed to diminish or at best abolish the means of waging war; boycotts and sanctions were attempts to solve conflicts without resorting to violence; and neutrality legislation was designed to prevent the shipment of weapons to belligerent nations and to keep the United States out of war if war began despite all efforts to prevent it.

The leaders of the WIL consistently advocated disarmament, and in doing so they built on the tradition begun by the Woman's Peace Party. Early on, the WPP had emphasized its opposition to a standing peacetime military or "preparedness." Preparedness did not ensure safety, WPP members had stated, but only increased the chance that conflict would escalate into war. As Crystal Eastman told the WPP in 1916, "The road to war is paved with preparedness." As an alternative, and in order to have genuine security, Eastman proposed that the United States spend its money and energy on building internationalism, not more weapons.[29] In its statement of policies in 1929, for example, the WIL advocated "international agreements not merely for reduction of armaments all around, but for the fundamental transformation of the whole type and purpose of armed forces, giving them a purely police character and abandoning everything—staff studies, manoeuvres or weapons—directed to the making of war."[30] And in a hearing on the constitutional amendment to outlaw war proposed by the Women's Peace Union, WIL leader Katherine Devereaux Blake said unequivocally, "The real way to end war is to end preparedness. Without an army and navy there can be no war."[31]

To gain support for the World Disarmament Conference, convened by the League of Nations in February 1932, the WIL used a strategy that women had found effective in earlier reform movements: the circulation of petitions. It organized a "peace caravan," a motorcade that traveled from Hollywood to Washington, D.C., stopping at 125 cities along the way. By the time the caravan arrived in Washington, WIL members had collected 150,000 signatures to present to President Hoover.[32]

Disappointingly, the World Disarmament Conference to which the WIL devoted so much energy accomplished little. Hannah Clothier Hull observed the conference and gradually grew more and more discouraged. In May 1932 she wrote to Jane Addams that the support of the people for disarmament, expressed through the petition campaign and early enthusiastic speeches, had all been forgotten and that the military experts had begun dominating the discussions. Nevertheless, Hull maintained her faith that disarmament was the only solution to war.[33]

Jane Addams was also convinced that disarmament was necessary to peace. In fact, not long after receiving Hull's report on the World Disarmament Conference, Addams told an interviewer that she had "come to regard with horror the results of the unrestricted trade in armaments and of the profit derived from their manufacture and sale" because she believed that "private profits accruing from the great armament factories are a powerful hindrance to the abolition of war." She suggested as a first step toward the solution of this problem the nationalization of armaments manufacturing. She believed that nationalization would help "reduce war scares," which were "from time to time deliberately fomented" by armament manufacturers. Addams apparently referred to the revelations in 1930 and 1931 that shipbuilders had hired a representative to disrupt the Geneva Disarmament Conference of 1927.[34]

These revelations combined with Addams's suspicion of armament manufacturers to prompt the WIL in 1933 to ask President Roosevelt to propose a Senate investigation of the private manufacturers of armaments.[35] Soon thereafter, Dorothy Detzer began to work with other pacifist leaders to organize a congressional investigation, led by Gerald P. Nye of North Dakota. After a thorough investigation, Nye and the other committee members eventually charged that "private armament interests circumvented national policies as defined in arms embargoes and treaties, sold weapons to both sides in time of war, bribed government officials, lobbied for military appropriations and against embargoes, stimulated arms races between friendly nations, and thrived on excess profits and favoritism from the government."[36]

Exposing the ways in which private interests profited from governmental policies and distorted foreign affairs for private gain was a major victory for the WIL; but it was a short-lived one. Over the long term, the WIL leaders continued to support the general goal of disarmament, but they began to disagree over whether they should work for total and complete disarmament or simply for arms reductions and limitations. This general issue had been addressed as early as 1923, when the national board had decided always to emphasize "the absolutely pacifist character and aims" of the organization but also to support partial measures that showed promise of achieving the WIL's goals. The WIL also decided at that time to cooperate with other peace groups as long as the specific project on which they cooperated did not conflict with the basic principles and goals of the WIL.[37]

The reconsideration of this policy was led by Hannah Clothier Hull. Having witnessed the deliberations of the World Disarmament Conference, Hull had become convinced of the futility of "the attempts to regulate in the discussions and deliberations on the tonnage of battleships, the size and weight of tanks, the length of guns and all the rest of such measures."[38] Hull acknowledged that the WIL supported partial measures, but she also emphasized that only complete disarmament would be significant.

Other WIL leaders agreed with Hull in principle but differed in regard to strategy. Although the WIL wanted total disarmament, Balch believed it was only realistic for the WIL to support partial measures such as arms reductions, prohibitions of particular types of weapons, and the limitation of expenditures on armaments.[39] And WIL executive secretary Dorothy Detzer felt that standing for total disarmament as war loomed relegated the WIL to ineffectiveness at best and ridicule at worst. "I certainly claim to be as eager for total disarmament, or disarmament alone, as you," she told Hull, "but I want to be able to talk to the men on Capitol Hill without having them become irritated immediately by an idea which has no relationship to political reality today."[40]

Detzer's argument eventually won Hull's reluctant support. As Hull explained to Lola Maverick Lloyd, who was critical of Detzer's position, she did not agree with Detzer, "but I do not work in Washington and I find that people like Jeannette Rankin who gave up her political career in order to vote against war, and who is certainly as good a pacifist as either you or I, agree with Miss Detzer on this strategy." Hull concluded that the WIL had to choose: "We can either work alone, or we can try to do the thing which is in demand all over the country, as you know—to have a minimum united program." Although still unsure, she was willing to experiment "to see whether in situations like conventions, it may not be better strategy to unite on a minimum program, even though we do not agree 100% on it, than to stand up for our own; all the time, however, working vigorously for our own position when we are working as a separate organization."[41]

The organization had taken the same position in 1923 when it had decided to cooperate with other organizations while still emphasizing its absolute pacifism. It made the WIL vulnerable to charges of compromise from the left and radicalism from the right, but it allowed the WIL to work in the real world while also reaffirming its conviction, as it stated during the last months of peace before the United States entered World War II, "that the goal of total world disarmament is the only basis for a lasting and permanent peace."[42]

Another strategy for achieving a peaceful world was to abolish war through law. The "outlawry movement," as it was sometimes called, reached its peak in the interwar years and was embodied in two proposals: the Frazier Amendment sponsored by the Women's Peace Union and the Kellogg-Briand Pact. Also related, although not truly calling for the outlawry of war, was the Ludlow Amendment, which required a public referendum on any declaration of war.

The constitutional amendment sponsored by the Women's Peace Union was written by two of its most devoted leaders, Elinor Byrns and Caroline Lexow Babcock, in 1923. They then searched for the right person to introduce the amendment in Congress, finally settling on Lynn Joseph Frazier, a Republican senator from North Dakota. Frazier introduced the amendment for the first time in 1926 and then again in every session through 1939. The amendment itself was straightforward: "War for any purpose shall be illegal, and neither the United States nor any State, territory, association, or person subject to its jurisdiction shall prepare for, declare, engage in or carry on war or other armed conflict, expedition, invasion, or undertaking within or without the United States, nor shall any funds be raised, appropriated, or expended for such purpose." The amendment also provided that any provisions of the Constitution in conflict with the amendment would become void upon its passage.[43]

The leaders of the WIL divided over the wisdom of this amendment. In 1925, at a meeting of the Academy of Political and Social Sciences attended by Dorothy Detzer, several speakers favored outlawing war, but someone also used the WPU amendment as an example of how ridiculous outlawing war was. Detzer reported that this man read the amendment with ridicule, "expecting that by so doing he would amuse the audience," but when he finished and dropped the amendment on the table with a smile, the audience "burst into a storm of applause." Detzer then commented that in her opinion the amendment was "the most complete and waterproof amendment on absolute American disarmament immediately. There are simply no loopholes in it." She also added that she knew "of nothing which is such a radical peace measure" and that it was "a most interesting sign of the times to have it receive such spontaneous applause."[44]

The following year, a majority of the WIL voted to endorse the Frazier Amendment at its annual meeting. Lucia Ames Mead, who was no longer on the WIL national board but who was still active in the Massachusetts branch of the WIL, wrote to Addams that the younger members had pushed the endorsement through and that she resented the fact that the vote had taken place after many of the older, more experienced members had already left the meeting. She also believed that it committed the WIL to "a fourth step" before "a first step had been taken." This, she noted, was a hindrance not only to the work of the WIL but also to the work of the National Council for Prevention of War, the organization to which she devoted most of her time.[45] Mead maintained this position into the 1930s, but apparently her view was in the minority. The WIL sent representatives to the congressional hearings on the amendment in both 1930 and 1934, and those representatives spoke in favor of the amendment. On the other hand, the WIL never made working for the amendment a top priority; the WIL leaders seemed to be content to let the WPU lead the struggle in this area. Support was also being provided by the Fellowship of Reconciliation, the American Friends Service Committee, the War Resisters League, the Women's Peace Society, and the Pennsylvania Committee for Total Disarmament.[46]

The WIL also had lots of company in its support of the Kellogg-Briand Pact. An international treaty that outlawed offensive war, the Kellogg-Briand Pact did on the international level what the Frazier Amendment hoped to accomplish nationally. The leaders of the WIL believed they had to support the pact, for its symbolic value if for no other reason. They had been asking that war be renounced as the means of settling differences; when the U.S. government did so in cooperation with many other countries, they could hardly refuse their support. They believed that this pact and the role of the United States in its creation demonstrated the leadership and commitment of the United States in the peace movement and were eager to see it ratified by the U.S. Senate.[47]

The WIL leaders were not, however, totally naive about the possibilities for peace provided by this treaty. Balch probably summarized the feelings of most WIL leaders when she wrote, "I am a great believer in the possibilities of the Pact, but rather in spite of the politicians than through them. It is going to mean what the people of the world choose to make it mean, no more and no less."[48] Perhaps even more indicative of WIL skepticism about the effectiveness of the treaty is the absence of any strong endorsement of it in the organization's Statement of Policies issued in April 1929, only three months before the president proclaimed the treaty in force.[49]

The leaders of the WIL were similarly skeptical about the Ludlow Amendment, a constitutional amendment that said a declaration of extraterritorial war and the taking of property for public use had to be validated by a national referendum. The members of the WIL national board decided to support the amendment nonetheless because they believed that such measures served to educate the general public about peace issues. Any objections were outweighed, they suggested, by the obligation the WIL had to "make its attitude clear to the world."[50]

Their support of outlawry and disarmament was essentially an attempt to conform national and international policy to their ideals; but if they were to be taken seriously and to be at all effective, they also had to conform their policies to national and international realities. This proved to be challenging and divisive work, especially during the 1930s, when the post–World War I determination to end war gave way to desperate attempts to squelch aggression without resorting to war once again. What should be done, WIL leaders had to ask themselves, when blatant aggression occurred? It certainly helped to be able to understand the historical causes of such aggression, and it doubtless provided some grim satisfaction to believe that if the policies you had recommended had been followed, the aggression would never have occurred. But such understanding and self-satisfaction did nothing to stop the aggression from escalating or to

STAFFORDSHIRE
UNIVERSITY
LIBRARY

help the victims of aggression. For these purposes the WIL leaders relied on sanctions and embargoes and on neutrality legislation. This policy decision was controversial, however, for it modified the WIL's commitment to the ideal of nonresistance and made it appear that the WIL was advocating isolation, not international cooperation.

Sanctions are measures designed to ensure compliance with international law; they can demand the use of military force but most often call for economic boycotts or diplomatic and moral condemnation. The first extended discussion of the WIL policy on sanctions occurred over the desirability of U.S. membership in the League of Nations. Although most WIL leaders found the internationalism of the league attractive, many objected to its ability to use military force against aggressor nations. In order to prevent a dangerous split in the WIL, Hull urged that the WIL avoid the issue of U.S. membership and "work for a reformed League of Nations whether we are within or without."[51]

The same issue resurfaced in 1927. In an open letter to WIL members, Balch encouraged them to support a resolution urging the United States to join the league, but only if the resolution specified that "the United States is exempt from any obligation to supply military forces, or to join in exerting military pressure in any case." She also wanted the United States to register its disapproval of the league's use of military sanctions, noting that, in its admittedly short history, the League of Nations had relied on moral condemnations even though it could have applied military or economic sanctions. In 1929 Balch's proposal became the official policy of the WIL.[52]

The WIL's position began to change once again as conflicts escalated around the world in the 1930s. When Japan marched into Manchuria in the fall of 1931, for example, the WIL groped for an adequate response to this act of aggression and the breaking of international law. Moral sanctions would have little effect, Balch realized, so as director of policies she suggested first that the WIL work to stop arms shipments to Japan. Second, she wanted the United States to appeal to the Japanese ambassador, "begging him to present to his government an appeal to desist from further slaughter on humanitarian grounds." Balch acknowledged that this suggestion was probably futile, but she hoped that "it might conceivably serve as a face-saving ground for a change of policy, a change for which there are also more hard-boiled reasons, especially economic ones." Finally, Balch admitted that she had "with many qualms given my name as one of those who without any thought of hostility to Japan do not propose to buy any known Japanese goods while the present situation continues." She stopped short, however, of supporting an organized, mass boycott because she feared that such a movement "would probably involve the working up of a mass movement of hatred and war spirit."[53]

Balch's response was mirrored by the national WIL. At its annual meeting in 1932 it modified its opposition to economic sanctions. Noting that both the international WILPF and the Indian pacifist leader Mohandas Gandhi considered economic sanctions proper in extreme cases, the WIL now hesitatingly approved their use against Japan with the hope that they would move the dispute "out of the hands of militarists and put it in the hands of economists."[54] And the following year, the WIL national board completely reevaluated its policy on sanctions, concluding that "all action must be based on friendliness to all, yet we must judge concrete cases and not hesitate to disapprove recognized aggression." Methods of expressing disapproval supported by the national board included support for legislation blocking arms sales to belligerent nations and opposition to the extension of credit or loans for military purposes and to aggressor countries. It also acknowledged that supposedly neutral policies often hurt one country more than another. If this happened to a country that had been victimized by an aggressor, the injured country should be given nonmilitary aid to help correct the imbalance and deter the aggressor. Finally, the national board acknowledged that it had supported economic sanctions against Japan and might be forced to do so in other cases; it would never, however, approve of a food blockade.[55]

With these changes, the WIL adjusted its commitment to the ideal of nonresistance to the reality of international aggression. Had it not done so and continued to countenance only moral pressure, it would have done nothing to ensure the peace and freedom of the victims of aggression. And that was an impossible position for women who were committed not only to peace, but also to justice and freedom. Much like the majority of members of the WPP, who had performed humanitarian work during World War I even though some pacifists believed that to do so was to cooperate with the war effort, the leaders of the WIL tried to find some way to help the victims of aggression even while they worked to keep the United States free from war.

As usual, not all WIL leaders agreed with the policy supporting the use of economic sanctions. One of the strongest dissenters was the Quaker Hannah Clothier Hull. Hull remained strongly opposed to all but moral sanctions. As she told her daughter in 1936, "Compromises, sanctions, and all the rest amount to nothing. Good will is the only oil that will make the wheels go round even where a Hitler is concerned."[56] Hull understood the feeling of other WIL leaders that they needed to help the victims of aggression; she even admitted that if she were to follow her feelings, she would support boycotts. She did not do so, however, because she saw the struggle against war as a long one. Success in that struggle might "not be in my life time," Hull wrote, "but I cannot conscientiously work for any other end. Were all of us now to go into condemnation of the aggressor, boycott, and all the other coercive measures the world would have the same problems before it in the future and even more and more suffering."[57]

In frequent disagreement with Hull was Mildred Scott Olmsted, the national organization secretary of the WIL. "Not since the Japanese first invaded Manchuria have I been able to agree with Mrs. Hull," Olmsted wrote to Balch; "It has seemed to me that the successive international developments of the last five years have indicated very clearly that [her] alternative to international action both in determining an aggressor state and in combining against it in some way was international anarchy." Olmsted hastened to add, however, that she did not favor military sanctions, only "economic, financial, social etc."[58]

During the early 1930s, the WIL's position on sanctions evolved from one that approved only moral sanctions to one that approved virtually any sanction except military. Committed to nonresistance, the WIL nonetheless tried to adjust to the reality of acts of aggression by supporting sanctions short of violent force. By 1935, though, the hope of WIL leaders that such sanctions would preserve world peace had begun to fade. Acts of aggression in the Far East and in Ethiopia, the rise of Adolf Hitler in Germany, civil war in Spain— all of these events combined with the failure of the Geneva Disarmament Conference and the revelations of the Nye committee to make the leaders of the WIL, as well as other pacifists, increasingly pessimistic about maintaining world peace and increasingly concerned about keeping the United States out of the looming war. The United States had, of course, tried to remain neutral during World War I, maintaining that a neutral nation had the right to trade freely on the open seas, but it had been drawn into the war by this position. As war brewed once again, many Americans worked to avoid repeating the nation's earlier mistakes by establishing a neutrality policy that would compel the United States to remain neutral in a European war.

Opinion on neutrality legislation divided into two general positions. Many leaders advocated strict or impartial neutrality: a truly neutral nation would forgo its chance to profit from trade with the belligerents and maintain strict noninvolvement. Other leaders favored having the United States constructively engage with conflict; the United States would decide which belligerent nation was the aggressor and then cooperate with other nations to place economic and diplomatic sanctions against that aggressor. Opinion was further complicated by disagreement over the degree to which foreign policy should be prescribed by legislation or left to the discretion of the administration in power.[59]

The opinion among WIL leaders was divided also. Dorothy Detzer supported neutrality legislation because she saw little hope "for an internationally organized world." She also wanted the legislation to be mandatory and strict: "After the revelations of the Munitions Committee," she wrote to Balch in 1936, "I want to leave as little to the discretion of the President as possible."[60] Balch was less certain. "I want us to keep out of war. . . . I think now we ought to take (and especially that earlier on other occasions we ought to have taken) not a neutral attitude any more than a belligerent one but that we ought to cooperate, if necessary assuming leadership, to restrain aggression by non-military pressure of various sorts."[61]

A year later Balch was still torn between two unsatisfactory choices. She wrote her longtime WILPF colleague Gertrude Baer, "I try not to make myself sick over the situation which grows more menacing all the time. My judgement twists and turns. I feel so strongly the danger of Czech armed resistance or the threat of it setting off the powder pile like another Sarajevo and on the other hand we have accumulating evidence of the effect on Hitler and Mussolini of yielding and conceding." The only option she could envision was one of widespread nonviolent resistance such as that practiced by Gandhi and his followers in India; but she did not believe that the people of Europe were ready for this form of resistance.[62]

Unlike Balch, WIL president Hull was certain of her position. Hull supported mandatory and strict neutrality. Only such neutrality would secure the United States "from the impending dangers of possible 'incidents' which might easily drag us into war" as well as make it possible for the United States to "go ahead enthusiastically and energetically to invoke peaceful and constructive methods of helping to stop the present war through conference with other nations, and of helping to negotiate and to make concessions needed on the part of all nations in order that peace may be permanently maintained." Hull did want it understood, however, that she was not advocating isolationism; the advocates of neutrality legislation, she wrote, "are not isolationists, as frequently charged, except in the sense of isolation from participation in war."[63]

Even these serious differences of opinion among the leaders of the WIL, however, did not lead to hostility or an organizational breakdown. Hull set the tone of compromise and tolerance: Although she told Balch that she worried about a breach in the WIL, she hoped that "our unity, so whole heartedly in most of our policies and aims, is going to make it possible for us still to do very responsible work together." She also noted that this difference of opinion characterized the entire peace movement, not just the WIL. For her part, she believed that she understood "perfectly the opposite point of view from my own and with such people as you, Mildred and others I could name, I go along very happily agreeing to disagree."[64]

Although the leaders could disagree, the organization did have to agree on a policy, and a decision was finally made in 1939 by polling WIL members. Nearly a thousand women from 45 chapters voted; of these, 75 percent supported the mandatory neutrality position. Furthermore, a substantial majority of the delegates to the annual meeting then voted to confirm the results of the poll. But like Hull, these WIL members also wanted it to be clear that although they wanted the United States to stay out of war, they were not advocating isolationism. A report on the poll published in the WILPF journal, *Pax International*, made clear that the WIL still supported international action; and in the printed program for 1939, for the first time in many years, international measures such as support for world government and a world conference headed the list of measures supported by the WIL.[65]

Although WIL leadership was divided, the membership voted decisively in favor of strict neutrality. As one European nation after another fell before Hitler's advance, the members of the WIL were forced to assume a defensive position. They believed that the world was too poisoned by the mistakes made after World War I for nonviolent methods to succeed and that Europe would have to suffer through another war. They fervently hoped, though, that this time the United States would stay truly neutral, and that when the craziness ended the United States would serve as the impartial advocate of peace and justice for all.

There was one important leader for whom this position was unsatisfactory: Emily Greene Balch. In a poignant illustration of her struggle for honesty and authenticity, Balch eventually admitted her private support for the Allies. She told her longtime associate in the peace movement, Anna Melissa Graves, that Graves's argument that war was like "driving Beelzebub out through Beelzebub" struck her "poignantly and cogently," yet she could not agree. "I grieve to say that I cannot believe as you do," Balch wrote, then added sadly, "I think I never did believe individuals and nations may not be driven by a series of crimes and blunders into a position where only evil is open to one, where every possible alternative is evil." She told Graves that although she had believed "that war was the worst of public evils," she had become "most unwillingly convinced that it is *more* evil to (in effect) connive at what Hitler is doing to plastic minds to say nothing of the policy toward Jews and the effort to exterminate political dissenters from his doctrine." Balch still did not believe "that war will solve any problem or do any constructive good at all equal to its harm" but she also did not believe that anything constructive could be accomplished "till the barrier of the power of the Hitler regime is swept aside and the door opened so the forces of reason and good can function in Germany."

For Balch, this position was the least evil of only evil alternatives, but she was never happy in it. "I do not pretend that my position is consistent or logical," she told Graves. "I play as much as possible with pacifists. I am less unhappy when with them—usually.

I do not try to win people to my own unsatisfactory position." The only satisfaction she had was that she was at least being honest with herself: "Of this I am sure, that one must not pretend to oneself or others to believe what one does not believe and one cannot believe a thing because one wants to. Be sure that just as soon as I can honestly repudiate my repudiation . . . I will do so with joy."[66]

The Choice Between Nurturing
and Nonresistance

During the 1920s and 1930s, the WIL's position on disarmament, outlawry, sanctions, collective security, and neutrality changed as the world situation changed. The underlying criterion for deciding where to draw the WIL policy line was whether physical violence was involved and if so, for how many people. The WIL leaders understood and generally agreed with the argument made by Balch during World War I and advanced during the 1930s by Hannah Clothier Hull: that any type of coercion was wrongful. By the mid-1930s, however, that position seemed a luxury of a more peaceful age. Furthermore, the WIL leaders were committed to nurturing others and strongly believed that a peaceful world could exist only if justice and freedom also existed; to allow aggression to continue would only increase injustice and deprive more people of freedom.

But when every method short of violence had been tried and failed, the leaders of the WIL were faced with a hard choice: they had to either condone the use of violence or abandon their emphasis on justice and freedom. Early in the 1930s, their agreement to support the collective use of sanctions against aggressors was an attempt to avoid this choice, to work for freedom and justice with nonviolent methods. But by the mid-1930s, when nonviolent methods had failed to deter or redress aggression, the WIL finally acknowledged that its balancing act had also failed. The choice it made then, to support the strict neutrality of the United States, showed that no matter how valid the cause, the WIL would never support the use of violent force. WIL leaders abhorred injustice and believed that it bred violence; but their belief that the means determined the end was even more fundamental. Someone had to stop the merry-go-round; perhaps the United States could do so.

On one level, the WIL had been forced to contradict its basic statement of principles. But the entire time that it was struggling to conform international policy to the ideal of nonresistance it was also working to create social justice through peaceful methods at home. In that smaller arena, one the WIL saw as less corrupted by past errors, the WIL was able to avoid choosing between its ideals of nonresistance and nurturing others.

Nonviolence and Social Justice, 1919–1941

EVEN WHILE MANY Americans worked to prevent another war during the 1920s and 1930s, many others wanted only to relax and enjoy life. This became increasingly possible as steady economic growth during the 1920s raised the average family's standard of living. The sale of consumer goods soared, and electricity reached all but the poorest and most sparsely populated areas. There was more time for recreation, too, and people increasingly spent some of their growing income on movies, spectator sports, and hobbies. There were, of course, those who did not enjoy this prosperity, but they were easily overlooked.

Then the economy crashed, and it became impossible to overlook the poor and the unemployed. As it had before World War I, reform again dominated the minds of many Americans: how should the economic and political structure be changed to get things working again? Offering an approach untried in the United States, the Communist and Socialist Parties gained members, and many Americans feared that their nation would soon be embroiled in a revolution. It was a grim time, and few people felt generous enough or had the financial resources to enable them to work for the welfare of others. Especially hurt were those who had historically occupied the lowest rungs of the socioeconomic ladder: African Americans, Native Americans, small farmers, sharecroppers, and migrant laborers. Racially based violence increased, and thousands of agricultural workers were displaced.

For very different reasons, most Americans did not want to focus on helping others: the self-indulgence of the 1920s became the self-survival of the 1930s. Some, however, took a less restricted view of self-survival, believing that their own well-being was intimately connected to the well-being of others. For the leaders of the WIL, this position was made possible both by solidly middle- to upper-class economic standing and by their personal principles. Throughout the 1920s and 1930s, these women guided the WIL in its work for "the establishment of social, political and economic justice for all, without distinction of sex, race, class or creed."[1] They concentrated their efforts in four areas: work for women's advancement, the defense of civil liberties, the elimination of racial discrimination, and the establishment of economic equality.

Undergirding the WIL's work were its commitment to nurturing others and its feminist belief that women shared some socially constructed characteristics and should work together on behalf of women. Also apparent in the WIL's work for social justice was the vision of a unified society of diverse components—unity within diversity. WIL leaders worked during these years to further the integration of women into areas previously dominated by men, to promote the integration of African Americans and other traditionally disadvantaged ethnic groups, and to lessen differences among economic classes by redistributing the nation's wealth. Yet the leaders of the WIL simultaneously appreciated the importance of separatist institutions for women and African Americans and of cultural traditions different from those of the dominant culture. Somewhat paradoxically, WIL leaders worked for integration through separatist action and highlighted people's differences while also championing their equality.

Working with Women for Women

Fundamental to the women leading the WIL was their work to improve the condition of women. Most of their working lives had been spent in the company of other women, and almost all of them had actively supported women's suffrage. Through this work, they had developed a sense of collective identity: women, they believed, were more sensitive to the value of human life than men and could work for peace most effectively separate from men. This belief had figured largely in their decision to organize the Woman's Peace Party during World War I as well as in their efforts to unite women behind the cause of peace during the first half of the 1920s. By 1925, when those efforts had failed, the leaders of the WIL had stopped trying to unite all women.

In the 1920s and 1930s, the WIL emphasized instead women's inclusion and more equal representation in international organizations and conferences. As early as 1920, for example, the WIL suggested that the League of Nations charter include an explicit provision "for the admission of women to all positions, thus making them eligible for the Assembly, Executive Council and the Commissions."[2] And in 1923, when the WIL urged calling a conference to revise the 1919 Peace of Paris, it emphasized that the selection of representatives was one of the points needing change. It stated its belief that "since the women of the world are equally concerned with the men of the world in the settlement of these problems, every nation should have women as well as men as its official representatives, and that all delegates from every nation, both men and women, should have equal powers and responsibilities, and stand upon identical terms in this conference."[3]

The WIL's demand for female representation at international conferences was finally met in 1932. Perhaps because women had been actively campaigning for disarmament throughout his administration, President Herbert Hoover consented to appoint a woman to the U.S. delegation to the disarmament conference. He selected Mary Woolley, president of Mt. Holyoke College and longtime peace activist. Dorothy Detzer greeted the announcement of Woolley's selection by expressing her gratitude that women, who "are half of the population and pay taxes also which are taken for war purposes," finally had a representative with a woman's point of view who was a peace advocate. But at the disarmament conference she criticized Woolley for being too timid to make her influence felt. Detzer did admit, however, that Woolley had a daunting task; when Detzer arrived at the conference, all of the other women delegates had left and, as Detzer described the scene, "the delegations were all black with men and the galleries almost solidly women." Hannah Clothier Hull was less critical of Woolley, writing to Addams that Woolley was doing a fine job in spite of "the suspicion and intrigue which is abroad among all nations."[4]

The WIL defended its requests for the inclusion of women with its usual arguments about equality, but running under the surface was the sense that women were also different from men. This emphasis on women's differences from men was also implicit in the belief of WIL leaders that "fundamental to the welfare and progress of humanity" was the establishment of political rights for women.[5] As the leaders of the Woman's Peace Party had said during World War I, so the WIL leaders stated during the interwar years: "The political rights of women are very closely allied to the subject of Peace and Freedom."[6]

This argument—that women and men should be treated equally because it was fair but also because women were different from men—was essentially the same position these women had expressed in organizing the Woman's Peace Party years earlier and in justifying women's participation in many other realms of activity. For decades they and many others had used it to argue that women deserved political rights; furthermore, they had long argued that one of the differences between men and women was women's greater desire for and commitment to peace. Women's attainment of full political power would advance the cause of peace, they argued, and a peaceful world would be one in which women's characteristics would be more greatly appreciated.

The continuing belief in women's differences from men also underlay one of the most controversial positions taken by the WIL: its opposition to the Equal Rights Amendment. Although its position may seem to the modern reader to conflict with the WIL's support for the integration of women into areas previously dominated by men, the women of the WIL saw it as a consistent acknowledgment of reality.

Proposed by the National Woman's Party in the early 1920s, the Equal Rights Amendment stated simply that "men and women shall have equal rights throughout the United States and every place subject to its jurisdiction." This amendment, far more complicated than its wording suggested, became the main source of discord among activist women in the following decades. Its supporters tended to be white professional women for whom gender-specific, "protective" legislation was the major barrier to success and advancement in the public realm. These were women who, as historian Nancy Cott stated, had the privilege of perceiving themselves "first and foremost as 'woman,'" who could "gloss over their class, racial, and other status identifications because those are culturally dominant and therefore relatively invisible." The opponents of the Equal Rights

Amendment, in contrast, were usually poorer women and reformers who had worked to secure laws regulating the hours and conditions of women's work.[7]

Most of the leaders of the WIL fell into this second camp. Throughout the 1920s and 1930s, the WIL repeatedly refused to endorse the Equal Rights Amendment. In 1924, for example, the annual meeting of the WIL rejected a resolution that stated, "Whereas the WIL has as one of its fundamental principles equality between men and women; and Whereas the Equal Rights Amendment now pending in Congress is the only measure before the country that would bring absolute equality, with the least possible delay; Resolved: that we endorse this amendment and work for it." Similar resolutions were defeated in 1936 and 1937 and tabled in 1941.[8]

Not all WIL leaders agreed with this position. Katherine Devereaux Blake supported the amendment, as did Lola Maverick Lloyd and Madeline Doty.[9] Of these women, however, only Blake served more or less constantly on the national board of the WIL. Lloyd worked primarily with Rosika Schwimmer on developing a plan for world government; her involvement with the WIL consisted largely of attending international conferences. Doty also spent much of her time in Europe, serving as the editor of the WILPF journal, *Pax International*, from 1926 until 1932. Even had Doty and Lloyd been more active in the United States, however, it is doubtful that they would have changed the WIL's position. The majority of leaders and members opposed the ERA.[10]

This opposition makes sense for two reasons. First, as social reformers many WIL leaders had campaigned for the protective legislation that they now feared would be abolished by the ERA. And second, as they argued repeatedly, these women believed that women were different from men and different from each other as well. In their minds, legislation that was blind to these differences would, in a world in which men still held most of the power and in which there were clear class differences among women, not assist all women but make the lives of poorer women even harder. Equality in the abstract would ensure inequality in reality; as Jane Addams put it, the ERA was " 'legalistic'—opposed to life and opposed to history."[11]

For the leaders of the WIL, to oppose the ERA was to inhabit the real world where women were not and would not soon be equal to men or to each other. This did not, however, stop these women from working for equality. Just as they had worked for universal disarmament while simultaneously sanctioning agreements that only limited arms, they worked for women's equality while simultaneously supporting laws that only limited the ways in which women could be harmed. It was never "all or nothing" for the leaders of the WIL; they lived their lives and made their policies in the ambiguous territory between the two alternatives.

This appreciation of ambiguity extended even to a consideration of the WIL's basic identity. With its roots in the Woman's Peace Party, the WIL began as a separatist women's organization. But throughout the interwar years, that identity was challenged periodically. Should the WIL remain an organization for women only? Why not admit men? A peaceful world would see women and men cooperating; should not an organization dedicated to world peace see the same? How would allowing men into the organization change it?

One of the leaders who struggled with these questions was Dorothy Detzer, the executive secretary of the WIL.[12] As she told Addams, Hull, and Balch in 1927, "I do wish that we were not exclusively a women's organization yet I suppose in that very fact lies a great deal of strength too."[13] Later in her life, however, Detzer acknowledged that she had become firmly convinced of the importance of working through a separatist organization. She recalled that during the interwar years the only organizations that had women as executives were women's organizations. "If I had been in the National Council for Prevention of War, I would have been an assistant of Fred Libby's or in the Fellowship of Reconciliation . . . an assistant of Nevin Sayre's. Or the Emergency Peace Committee . . . an assistant probably of Norman Thomas. The only way to really have the officers and executives women . . . was to have a women's organization."[14]

Not all members of the WIL, of course, shared Detzer's belief in the importance of separatism, and consequently there were occasionally moves to get the organization to admit men as members. Initially, men served on the WIL Advisory Council but were not admitted into national membership.[15] This policy was reconsidered by the national board again in 1929 and 1932 but was not changed.[16] Finally in 1934, the WIL changed its rules and allowed men to join; it even gave local branches the option of changing the name of the lo-

STAFFORDSHIRE
UNIVERSITY
LIBRARY

cal organization. This change of policy evidently reflected the difficulties the WIL was having recruiting members as well as the increasing success of organizations such as the National Council for
Prevention of War, which recruited both women and men.[17]

But this change in the requirements for membership did not result in a flood of male members, and the men who did join the WIL
served more as figureheads than as equal and active participants. In
response to an inquiry about starting a new branch of the WIL in
1935, for example, the WIL organization secretary Mildred Scott
Olmsted noted that if a new branch was started, it could admit men
as "full-fledged members." She added that there were three new
branches in West Virginia that were "headed by men." This had
been done, she believed, because "the local committees seem to feel
that if they can get some prominent man to be the nominal head
their work will be easier." Olmsted then added, "I must say it seems
to be the women, vice-chairmen and secretaries, who are doing the
most of the work."[18]

The issue of the WIL's identity as a women's organization arose
again during 1939 and 1940. As war in Europe spread and the likeli-
hood of U.S. participation increased, peace activists in the United
States tried to join forces whenever possible. One coalition of so-
cialist-pacifist organizations, the Keep America Out of War Congress, wanted the WIL to join its effort, but only if it dropped
"Women's" from its title and worked to organize both women and
men. Emily Greene Balch warned that such a change might make
women virtually invisible again, yet even she decided it was an idea
at least worth considering, especially if it would make the WIL more
attractive to younger members. The WIL appointed a committee to
study this issue and to present its findings at the annual meeting in
1940.[19]

The committee's chair, Ruth Gage-Colby, asked the presidents of
all the WIL state branches to poll their members on including men
as equal members and dropping "Women" from the organization's
name. The poll asked members to select one of the following options: (1) eliminating "Women's" from the title, (2) changing the
name more drastically—for example, by dropping "and Freedom," or
(3) keeping the existing name. In the final count of an admittedly
small sample, 251 members voted to eliminate "Women's," 132
voted for more drastic change, and 1,042 voted to keep the existing

name. And when put to a vote at the annual meeting in April 1940, the motion to drop "Women's" failed overwhelmingly.[20]

The majority of WIL members wanted to maintain the organization's identity as a women's organization even though they would also admit men as members. They realized that it was "probably true that peace will never come as a result of the efforts of women alone." Even so, they valued the history and traditions of the WIL, especially the experience of "women working with women for peace the world over." Adelaide Nichols Baker expressed her fear that making the WIL "less of a women's organization might generalize its attack and make it more like the National Peace Conference in which men do make their contribution to peace already." And both Lois Eliot and Faye L. Mitchell worried that men might come to dominate the league. Mitchell noted that she had "tried the experiment of having men belong, University Professors . . . and others. There was the attitude on the part of some of the women that they must stand back: 'What does Mr. —— think?' These men did not try to run the League . . . but some of the women felt they should!" All in all, Eliot concluded, "It is better for women to struggle along by themselves."[21]

The WIL's reaffirmation of its identity as a separatist women's organization and its belief in differences among men and women were unusual in the postsuffrage era; it was much more common then to emphasize that women were human beings and as such deserved opportunities equal to those of men. To most people, the emphasis on "sex solidarity" that had been common in the previous decades seemed old-fashioned at best and threatening at worst. A few women scattered around the country argued the importance of acknowledging differences between men and women—Emily Newell Blair, a leader of the Democratic Party, and the historian Mary Beard, for example—but most did not, emphasizing instead the possibilities of individual achievement in a society that claimed to provide equal opportunity for all.[22]

Against this background, the strong desire of both WIL leaders and members to remain a separatist women's organization commands consideration. Their willingness to admit men shows that they were willing to work with men and that they were comfortable with the ambiguous identity of a women's organization that had male members. Furthermore, their willingness to consider trans-

forming the WIL into an organization that recruited both women
and men shows that they were aware of the trend, especially among
younger women, to deemphasize the differences between women
and men. Yet in the final analysis, their decision to remain a
women's organization is more significant. These were women who
had struggled for social reform for decades. They had worked in
women's organizations and in male-dominated ones; they were experienced, talented, and wise. And all of those qualities combined
to make them wary. One can almost see them, cocking their aging
heads toward the proffered promise of equal opportunity and saying
politely but forcefully, Thank you, but no. We know better. And so
they remained, "women working with women for peace the world
over," out of touch with the times but a model for those who would
follow.

The Defense of Civil Liberties

Like most WIL policies, the commitment to defend civil liberties began when the WIL was the Woman's Peace Party. The WPP had
protested the increasing militarism of the United States, especially
compulsory military training for boys, forced conscription and military service, and governmental repression of the freedoms of speech
and of the press. It had also enthusiastically supported the right to
conscientiously object to military service.[23]

The WIL continued down this path, never making the defense of
civil liberties a primary cause but always endorsing the general principle of freedom from government coercion and surveillance. Following the so-called Palmer raids in 1920, for example, the executive board of the WIL sent Jeannette Rankin and Florence Kelley to
Washington, D.C., to "protest against the spirit and methods of the
'raids' and sudden seizures for deportation and exile of those desig-
nated as 'reds'" and "to appeal for the immediate release from prison
of political offenders whose only offense is opposition to war." The
WIL reiterated this position two years later, still trying to rectify the
injustices committed during World War I.[24]

Because the WIL leaders believed that such injustices would re-
cur if the United States became involved in another war, when a second world war became increasingly probable, the WIL again empha-

sized the importance of civil liberties. In 1934 its national president, Hannah Clothier Hull, made explicit the connection between those liberties and peace. Watching as Hitler gradually restricted individual freedom in Germany, Hull noted that "lack of freedom the world over is indeed evil." Moreover, even the United States was in danger. "No longer can we claim to be the free country our fathers won for us," Hull wrote, "while such things exist as compulsory military training in schools, the drafting of men and the regimentation of industry for war, and the terrorization of laborers and resident aliens in peace."[25] After war started in Europe, the WIL became even more concerned about protecting civil liberties. In 1939 its national board observed that "only in a condition of peace is it possible to retain for all people their Constitutional rights." For this reason, among many others, it urged the United States to remain neutral.[26] And in January 1941, the WIL again acknowledged that fascism threatened liberty, yet it held firmly to its conviction that liberty was best defended not by war but by maintaining democracy and working to bring it to others who had never known it. Accordingly, it urged its branches and members to work diligently to ensure civil liberties.[27]

The WIL also became involved with the specific cause of defending the right to conscientious objection. Because other organizations, such as the American Civil Liberties Union and the historic peace churches, made the defense of this right one of their primary causes, the WIL did not generally expend a great deal of energy in this area. But during the 1920s and 1930s there were two cases in which women who had been affiliated with the WPP or the WIL in some way claimed the right to conscientious objection and were denied citizenship for doing so. One such case involved Rosika Schwimmer, the Hungarian pacifist and advocate for women who had traveled to the United States in 1914 to arouse opposition to the war then beginning in Europe. In 1921 Schwimmer immigrated to the United States after the Hungarian government in which she had served fell from power. But in 1927 she was denied citizenship because she refused to swear that she would bear arms in the defense of the country. The district court's decision was overturned by the U.S. Court of Appeals but upheld by a 6 to 3 vote of the Supreme Court.[28]

The WIL saw the ruling in this case, in the words of the WIL executive secretary Dorothy Detzer, as a "challenge to all pacifists." Because Schwimmer's military service was purely hypothetical—she was disqualified from service by both sex and age—Detzer believed that the decision was based less on Schwimmer's conscientious objection than on the belief that she would be a bad influence on other citizens. The WIL interpreted the decision as an attack "not only on the principle of free thought but possibly as well [on the] freedom to talk peace whenever and wherever individuals wish to." It urged its members to "take a more rigid position on the right of a government to dictate the right of free thought and private conscience."[29] As an organization, it expressed its belief that citizenship should not be denied on the basis of conscientious objection to war and that citizenship should be granted to those to whom it had been denied.[30]

Two years after the Schwimmer decision, Rebecca Shelley began her fight for citizenship as a conscientious objector. Shelley, born in 1887, had attended the 1915 Hague Congress of Women and been very active in the World War I peace movement. She had not continued her activism, however, after suffering a nervous breakdown in 1919 and retreating to her home in Michigan. In 1922 she married Felix Rathmer, a German national living in the United States. Under the Expatriation Act of 1907, this marriage caused Shelley to lose her citizenship; but only one month after the marriage, the Cable Act, which abolished expatriation on marriage to a noncitizen, went into effect. Given the new law, regaining her citizenship would have been simple—if Shelley had not objected to military service. She refused, however, to take the oath of allegiance without specifying that she would not bear arms in the service of her country; likewise, the officials she encountered refused to administer the oath under that condition.[31]

In her ensuing thirteen-year struggle, Shelley attempted to enlist both women's and peace organizations in support of her case. She looked particularly to the friends she had made during World War I, especially through her work in the People's Council of America for Peace and Democracy: Roger Baldwin, who had become head of the American Civil Liberties Union; Frances Witherspoon and Tracy Mygatt of the Women's Peace Union and the War Resisters League; and Emily Greene Balch. Because Shelley had been active in the National Woman's Party, she also expected support from the friends she had made through it.

Shelley's expectations, however, were not met. Male friends such as Roger Baldwin apparently thought that since women could not be drafted, Shelley's argument that women had an equal right to conscientious objection was silly. And some of Shelley's friends in the National Woman's Party took an equally narrow point of view: to them, her case was a pacifist, not a feminist, issue.[32] She received support from Witherspoon, Mygatt, and Balch, but they were able to make only small financial contributions to help defray her legal costs. Even the WIL, for reasons that are not clear, did not make a strong statement in her support, as it had for Schwimmer.

It seems likely, however, that both Shelley's and Schwimmer's cases caused the WIL to pay more attention to the issue of conscientious objection, especially women's, than it had before. In 1934, just as Shelley's struggle was heating up, Hannah Clothier Hull noted that the WIL had become aware that "especially endangered are the rights of women which have been so laboriously and slowly acquired throughout the ages." And in 1938 Hull wrote that the WIL "has had conscientious objectors to war very much on its mind and heart this past year" and that it planned to consider the subject at its next annual meeting.[33]

Although the defense of conscientious objectors was usually left to other organizations, the WIL did stand solidly behind the principle of conscientious objection. As they put it at their annual meeting in May 1941: "Liberty of the human spirit is a basic value," and individuals "must have the right to contribute to decisions and express definite opinions through free democratic processes. Contrary to this freedom are all forms of dictatorship, all imperialisms, all suppressions of civil liberty, all discriminations based on race, class, or creed."[34] This statement highlighted the importance of defending civil liberties, but it also identified the abolition of racial and class discrimination as essential to genuine freedom. And indeed, these were also areas of crucial concern to the WIL during the interwar years.

"What Had Race to Do with the Issues of Peace and Freedom?"

Dorothy Detzer recalled that she and other WIL leaders were frequently asked, "Why did we have to jeopardize the appeal of that [WIL] program by cluttering it up with the irrelevant issues of race?"

To people who defined peace narrowly as the prevention or absence of war, efforts to establish racial justice seemed irrelevant; but to the leaders of the WIL, these efforts were just as essential as work for disarmament or international organizations. As Detzer pointed out, just on practical grounds the WIL had to deal with issues of race: "An organization whose membership included Hindus, Chinese, Japanese, and Negroes could neither be unaware of the dangers inherent in racial tensions nor indifferent to the values of interracial solidarity."[35]

But equally important to the WIL was that its policies reflect its strong moral principles: nonresistance, nurturing, a feminist consciousness of the importance of women working with and for other women, and unity within diversity. Detzer elaborated on this last principle, pointing out that "self-interest . . . could only be realized when merged with the interests of all." This principle, as well as the others mentioned, Detzer believed, were considered by WIL leaders as "mysterious but inflexible moral laws . . . to be applied in every realm of life. Race was no exception." In fact, Detzer noted, concern with racial issues and working with people from races other than one's own brought unexpected rewards. Echoing Balch's earlier praise for the increasing heterogeneity of women's peace activity, Detzer proclaimed: "Difference always seemed to bring enrichment to life; it was not to be avoided."[36]

This appreciation of cultural pluralism and commitment to racial justice had deep roots. As early as 1901 Jane Addams had written an article thoroughly condemning the practice of lynching and the racial prejudice that generated it, and in 1909 she had helped organize the National Association for the Advancement of Colored People (NAACP).[37] Furthermore, during World War I the Pennsylvania branch of the Woman's Peace Party had discussed ways of integrating African-American women into its organization and recorded its opposition to the racist film *The Birth of a Nation*.[38]

The WIL first demonstrated its commitment to racial justice even before the organization was officially founded. As Addams and other leaders prepared to travel to Zurich in 1919 for what would become the organizational conference of the WILPF, there was considerable discussion about who should attend the conference. Alice Thacher Post, who had been a founding member of the WPP and earlier a member of the Anti-Imperialist League, suggested that they invite Mary Church Terrell. Terrell was a prominent leader of African-American women, having served as the first president of the National Association of Colored Women and as its honorary president for life after 1901; she was also a charter member of the NAACP and a lecturer, writer, and activist. Addams agreed that inviting Terrell was an excellent idea, and when Terrell agreed to go Post said that she would "be happy to share a stateroom" with her on the voyage over.[39]

It would have been easier for Addams and Post to have invited only the women they had worked closely with in the WPP, but instead they actively sought Terrell's participation. Aware that she had not previously been active in peace work, Post sent her some materials to help familiarize her with their efforts.[40] Thirty-five women had agreed to attend the conference, but the State Department would give passports to only twelve. "It would have been very easy in reducing the number from thirty-five to twelve to leave the colored delegate out," Terrell recalled, but Addams "insisted that I should be one of the twelve and did everything in her power to have me go."[41]

Terrell did go, and she found her participation in the conference to be both stimulating and frustrating. On the passage across the Atlantic, she and the other delegates read about the peace movement and drafted resolutions that they planned to propose at the conference. Terrell found these discussions fascinating and later recalled that after the other delegates had offered their resolutions, "I then offered one protesting against the discriminations, humiliations and injustices perpetrated, not only upon the colored people of the United States, but upon the dark races all over the world." This resolution was questioned by some who "thought they could improve upon it," but the changes they suggested in wording were not acceptable to Terrell. Finally they agreed to allow Terrell to offer her resolution as she had written it: "We believe no human being should be deprived of an education, prevented from earning a living, debarred from any legitimate pursuit in which he wishes to engage or be subjected to humiliations of various kinds on account of race, color or creed."[42]

At the conference itself, Terrell was asked to represent the U.S. delegation by speaking at a large public gathering. She addressed the audience, in German, on the topic of "the race problem." She emphasized the "progress we have made as a race along all lines of human endeavor in spite of almost insurmountable obstacles" and appealed "for justice and fair play to all the dark races of the earth." She also emphasized strongly her belief that "white people might talk about permanent peace till doomsday, but they could never have it, till the dark races were treated fair and square."[43] Terrell felt that her talk was well received, but she was surprised when Emily Balch notified her of a last-minute decision to alter the text of her resolution against racism. Although irritated that she had not been consulted about the changes, Terrell discovered that the translators of the resolution had apparently misunderstood Balch's directions and translated her original resolution instead of the altered one.[44] Terrell was victorious in this struggle over the resolution, but only by accident; furthermore, the action taken by Balch surely infuriated Terrell and made it difficult for her to trust Balch in the future. Terrell was also bothered by the lack of representation of women of color. In her report on the conference, she noted that "women from all over the white world were present, for there was not a single solitary delegate from Japan, or China or India or from any other country whose inhabitants were not white. . . . In fact, I was the only delegate who gave any color to the occasion at all."[45]

When the delegates returned to the United States to begin the hard work of building an organization, Terrell remained on the national board for several years. But these years did not pass without further conflict. In 1921 the other members of the national board asked Terrell to sign a petition requesting the removal of African-American troops from occupied German territory because they were reputed to have assaulted German women. Although as a woman Terrell sympathized "deeply with the German women if they are really the victims of the passions of black men," as an African American, she believed that this charge was "simply another violent and plausible appeal to race prejudice." Terrell decided that her only choice was to offer to resign from the executive board, telling Addams she was "certain that the black troops are committing no more assaults upon the German women than the German men committed upon the French women or than any race of soldiers would probably commit upon women in occupied territory." She also offered evidence that the charges against the troops were not true.[46]

In response, Addams told Terrell that she had come "to exactly the same conclusion which you have reached—that we should protest against the occupation of enemy territory—not against any special troops," and she expressed her hope that Terrell would attend the annual meeting the following month. For her part, Terrell was relieved by Addams's response. "I was glad not to be forced to resign," she wrote; "I enjoyed working for peace, and the contacts with the fine women who were members were an education to me."[47]

This episode may have convinced the WIL to pass its first thorough condemnation of racism. In 1922, the WIL resolved that because "race prejudice is based on ignorance, and is without reason or justice," and because it "creates distrust, suspicion, antagonism, and hatred towards the people of other nations thus helping to breed and encourage the war spirit," the WIL would "condemn race prejudice as unamerican and unworthy of civilized human beings" and do all it could "to uproot and eradicate it from the minds of the people."[48]

After this action, the WIL did little in the area of race relations for several years and even failed to reelect Terrell to the national board.[49] Nonetheless, it is likely that the sensitivity of WIL leaders to racial issues was gradually increasing. The number of African Americans in the North and East had grown rapidly during World War I, when 500,000 African Americans had left the South. After the war ended, and economic opportunities began to decline, many lost their wartime jobs but stayed in the North, building communities such as Harlem, supporting a "renaissance" of African-American culture, and in some cases participating in nationalist movements such as the one founded by Marcus Garvey. Garvey, an activist from Jamaica, rallied working-class African Americans around the country by calling for separatism and economic independence. In 1914 he founded the Universal Negro Improvement Association, which by 1925 claimed a million followers.[50]

Against this background of increasing African-American visibility and activity in the North, the leaders of the WIL began to make racial issues more central to their programs and policies. In 1928 they decided to form an Interracial Committee. The leaders of the organization did not realize the difficulty of the task they undertook. The meaning of the word "interracial," specifically whether such a committee would be composed of women of all races or be one on

STAFFORDSHIRE
UNIVERSITY
LIBRARY

which only African-American women worked, would become a periodic point of controversy throughout the following years.[51]

The initial manifestation of this controversy occurred as the Interracial Committee was being organized. The head of the committee was Addie Waites Hunton, an African-American woman from New York who had helped organize the National Association of Colored Women in 1896, served as the YWCA secretary for work among African-American women, and volunteered with the YWCA in France from 1918 to 1920. While organizing the Interracial Committee, Hunton talked to her old friend, Mary Church Terrell. Hunton had been enthusiastic about working with the Interracial Committee, but Terrell evidently dampened that enthusiasm by telling Hunton that she had left the WIL years earlier because it segregated African-American members. Hunton then began to worry that the "interracial" committee would actually be a segregated committee for African-American women only. She told Mildred Scott Olmsted that this incident had convinced her that it would be better to proceed cautiously, "as all colored women are more suspicious of the ordinary interpretation of interracial."[52]

Hunton's comments disturbed Olmsted, and she wrote immediately to Emily Greene Balch asking for clarifying information. Olmsted recalled that Terrell had not been reelected because she had not been an active contributor but wanted to resolve the matter in a way that cleared up any misunderstandings and retained the support of the African-American women.[53] Balch responded quickly but offered little in the way of clarification. "I cannot conceive of anything giving a shadow of an excuse" for the idea that the WIL advocated segregation, Balch wrote Olmsted. She also remembered that Terrell "never, as far as I can recall, came to Board meetings or did the least thing"; she softened this comment, however, by adding "but I may not remember things correctly."[54]

Balch also wrote immediately to Addie Waites Hunton. Again Balch maintained that the charge of segregation was untrue, but she also asked Hunton to try to get more information from Terrell. "It seems to me rather important," Balch wrote; "Perhaps this misunderstanding on her part may be the reason that while she was nominally on the Board, she was, so far as I can recall, entirely inactive."[55]

Hunton then wrote to Terrell, asking for the clarification Balch sought. Hunton told Terrell that since becoming active in the WIL and the Interracial Committee, she "had seen no evidence of segregation and not much of that patronizing spirit which we so frequently experience in our contacts." Fearing that she had missed something, however, she asked Terrell to "indicate a little more clearly the ground for your criticism."[56]

Shortly after this letter, Terrell and Balch met in person at a dinner party. Balch evidently took this opportunity to ask Terrell directly about the reputed charge of segregation. Balch then reported to Hunton that Terrell had said "that of course the WIL has never stood for segregation or anything like it." One of the WIL board members had, however, apparently asked Terrell whether she could help secure some additional African-American members. Balch felt that this was "a natural thing to ask" and that the request in no way connoted a policy of segregation: "Nobody had any idea of colored members being in any way separated from all the rest of them."[57]

Balch apparently felt somewhat reassured by this exchange, but Terrell did not. In fact, she felt so humiliated that she wrote Balch a scathing letter in which she listed numerous occasions on which she felt Balch had slighted her. "I realize that I have always rubbed you the wrong way, so to speak," Terrell wrote; "From the day we first met many years ago you have given me indisputable evidence of the fact that there are many things which I do and say which you do not like." The first incident had occurred while Balch was still teaching at Wellesley and others had occurred while Terrell served on the national board.[58] The most recent incident had been Balch's query at the dinner party; Terrell was appalled that Balch had quizzed her in front of the other guests. Still, she assured Balch that she had always admired her and the WIL. Furthermore, she now told Balch that Hunton had misunderstood her comment; she had not told her that the WIL had pursued a policy of segregation, but that she "hoped the W.I.L. would never segregate our group," a comment she often made when discussing "an organization which has never adopted segregation as a policy." She then closed her letter by assuring Balch that she bore her no ill will: "I can forget disagreeable things very easily," she cryptically wrote; "I can retain them also if it is necessary."[59]

Terrell was also angry at Hunton and wrote her a letter only slightly less hostile than the one sent to Balch. She was particularly upset that when she and Hunton had initially talked, Hunton had not identified herself as the head of the Interracial Committee or challenged what she had perceived to be Terrell's belief that the WIL practiced segregation. Terrell thought that Hunton's failure to be forthcoming did not help the cause of racial understanding or peace. Furthermore, Terrell essentially accused Hunton of disloyalty to her race: "It seems to me that a colored woman who was earnestly trying to tie colored women up to work white women are doing would not go to a white woman to report to her what a colored woman had said . . . unless she had tried to show the colored woman she had made a mistake and convince her that she was wrong." At the end of her letter, however, Terrell expressed her admiration for the WIL, as she had done in the letter to Balch. "Finally," she told Hunton, "I feel like emphasizing my gratitude toward and love for the women who stand at the head of the W.I.L. I owe a great deal to Miss Jane Addams and her co-workers which I shall never be able to repay. I would not say . . . anything which would injure the organization, if I could."[60]

Clearly the WIL's Interracial Committee began in a flurry of misunderstanding and hurt feelings. It is indicative of the difficulties of interracial cooperation that these women, who shared a belief in racial equality and cooperation as well as a commitment to the peace movement, could find themselves so at odds. Balch and Olmsted explained the conflict by suggesting that Terrell had overreacted, but they also admitted that her reaction was understandable. As Olmsted put it, "It certainly is distressing to have Mrs. Terrell so super-sensitive, even though it is entirely understandable, in the light of the many slights she must have received in her life." For her part, Balch simply made a note to herself: "Isn't it pitiful what this segregation business does to people? Can we be patient enough or careful enough when we have hurt them and twisted them so? *Think* what it has meant to Mrs. Terrell."[61] Both Balch and Olmsted portrayed Terrell as a victim of segregation, but neither considered how their own perspectives may have been limited by segregation. If they had offended Terrell in some way, they remained ignorant of their offense, instead chalking this misunderstanding up to Terrell's heightened sensitivity to racial slights.

Terrell's reaction went unrecorded, but it seems clear that she would not have judged her actions as inappropriate. She doubtlessly felt slights by European Americans, such as the condescension evident in these comments by Balch and Olmsted, which were probably unintentional. Furthermore, the issue of how to recruit African Americans to the WIL—whether through a separate committee for that purpose and if so, who should serve on that committee—was a genuinely difficult issue and one that continued to plague the WIL in the following years.

The attention Terrell's perceived charge of segregation brought to the issue of race relations was most likely responsible for the strong statement the WIL made that year in opposition to racism. In its annual statement of policies, the WIL wrote that "the Negro problem is one that everyone can help in singlehanded for it arises mainly because of the stupidities and cruelty of race prejudice." The WIL also anticipated the "day when there will be no more inconvenience or self consciousness connected with race than with the possession of blue eyes or brown eyes."[62]

Perhaps this statement helped ease the tensions among Terrell, Hunton, Olmsted, and Balch, for Hunton remained the head of the Interracial Committee and Terrell soon offered to resume work for the WIL. She wrote to Olmsted in 1930 to say that she regarded the previous year's misunderstanding as unfortunate. She also volunteered to travel to "the negro institutions all over the country, so as to tell young people that they would never gain anything by war and ought to support the peace movements." Olmsted was a bit hesitant but suggested that the WIL accept her offer. "Mrs. Terrell seems to carry such weight with her own people," Olmsted wrote to Balch, "that I think it would be highly desireable for us to use her in this way."[63]

Had Terrell read Olmsted's comment, she might have taken offense at the suggestion of exploitation; she did not, however, and apparently began working more closely with the WIL. By 1932 she had written a pamphlet for the WIL entitled "Colored Women and World Peace," which explained the principles and goals of the WIL and argued that African Americans should support the peace movement, especially the WIL. "No group of citizens in the United States should desire peace more than colored people, and none should strive harder to put an end to war than they should," Terrell wrote. She argued that "any group whose population and wealth are small and whose advantages are few, when compared with others, will suffer more from war than the more highly favored." She went on to

explain that African Americans had suffered from World War I and
that prominent African-American leaders such as W.E.B. Du Bois
supported the peace movement. She concluded by suggesting that
"it is the duty of colored people who want to smooth out some of
the rough places over which they have to travel every day, and who
wish to enjoy the privileges to which they are entitled as citizens,
to support an organization" such as the WIL, an organization that
Terrell characterized as "trying to end war and to remove friction
between the races at one and the same time."[64]

Hunton, in her role as chair of the Interracial Committee, also
stressed that the WIL understood the connection between racial justice and peace. In a solicitation for contributions, Hunton wrote that
the WIL "has realized that good will is absolutely necessary among
all races and people before universal peace can come, and has its
whole program built on that basis."[65]

In spite of the conviction of Terrell, Hunton, and other WIL leaders that working for peace and racial justice went hand in hand,
there was confusion about exactly how to focus the two efforts. This
confusion was most apparent in the repeated debates over the exact
meaning of interracial work and the role of interracial committees.
Did "interracial" mean cooperation between African Americans and
European Americans or among all kinds of racial and ethnic groups?
Was "interracial" in fact a code word for "segregated"? Were interracial committees supposed to work on racial problems directly, or
were they a sort of social experiment in which people from different
races cooperated to further the peace movement?

Different branches of the WIL took different positions on these
issues. In the annual report of the Interracial Committee in 1932,
Hunton noted that there were interracial committees flourishing in
seven local branches of the WIL: Boston, Cleveland, Detroit,
Newark, New York, Philadelphia, and Washington, D.C. These committees had pursued interracial work in various ways. The branches
in Boston and Cleveland seemed to have interpreted interracial to
mean cooperation among all races and ethnicities focused on furthering the peace movement. For example, Boston had sponsored an
evening study meeting on the Chinese-Japanese situation and had
held the meeting in an African-American facility, the center of the
Urban League. The Cleveland branch boasted that its group included
"five nationalities," but did not make clear whether that phrase in-

corporated groups from different continents or only different European national origins. This branch met the charge for interracial work by having African-American speakers and performers. On one occasion, Dean William Pickens, the field secretary for the NAACP, attended a branch meeting that was held at a Chinese restaurant and followed by a tour of the Tong temple; the purpose of Pickens's visit was not stated.

Branches in Detroit and Newark dealt more directly with race relations. The Detroit branch found it "somewhat difficult for us to hold ourselves to our aim of being strictly a peace committee with inter-racial members, because inevitably race relations has come [up] for a short time at each meeting." Newark's experience was similar. Although this branch believed in "the broader interpretation of the word inter-racial," it was frequently asked to help other organizations promote better race relations. It had divided its work between arranging for speakers on peace and holding meetings with the primary purpose of discussing and improving race relations.[66]

This confusion over the nature and purpose of interracial work continued to hamper the WIL's efforts to recruit African-American women. Hunton herself wrote in 1933 that "the claim cannot be made as yet that any great number of colored people have come to a recognition of the deeper implications of the Peace movement, and so it has not yet won their first and deepest loyalties." Hunton believed African Americans were too busy struggling just to survive to give the peace movement much devotion, but she continued to hope that "when they are able to visualize their own relations to this new world of peace and realize how their strivings and yearnings are bound up in it, they will seek to be a part of it." Hunton concluded that it was up to the WIL to continue working to explain the connections between peace and racial justice. "To me," she wrote, "it seems that the [WIL] is challenged by its basic principles to meet this need of this particular group for larger knowledge and participation in the movement."[67]

In the following years, the WIL continued its efforts to meet Hunton's challenge but also continued to struggle with the meaning and nature of interracial work. In 1934 the Interracial Committee reported that although the WIL had originally wanted the interracial committees to be composed of a variety of racial and ethnic groups, the committees had remained largely biracial, with only African

Americans and European Americans represented. Furthermore, there was the continued sense that, in some cases, the African-American women who served on the interracial committees were not fully integrated into the larger organization. The national Interracial Committee condemned this practice: "There should be no separate organization of these [African-American] women, nor should they be restricted to the work of the Interracial Committee, but should serve on any or all of the committees of the branch."[68]

Some WIL branches evidently decided that the best way to ensure integration was to disband their interracial committees. The Massachusetts branch took this step in 1936, replacing this committee with the commitment to "take up more seriously the study and understanding of the Interracial problem, and have one meeting during each season truly integrated with a free discussion of interrelated subjects." When notified of this change, Hunton, who was serving her last term as chair of the Interracial Committee, expressed her approval. Writing to her successor, Bertha McNeill of Washington, D.C., Hunton said, "It is a fine move and I hope our group will join."[69]

When McNeill took over as the chair of the Interracial Committee in 1937, she stepped into the middle of this debate. McNeill apparently wanted to follow the traditional WIL policy of allowing state and local branches a great deal of autonomy in making decisions of this sort. She did express her disapproval, however, of the fact that in some branches women were members of the Interracial Committee without being members of the WIL. This would not promote integration, and McNeill reminded branches that individuals needed to be members of the larger organization in order to serve on a committee.[70]

It also became clear that dissolving interracial committees could have an effect just the opposite of the one desired. Instead of integrating African-American women and concern with racial justice into the larger WIL, disbanding interracial committees could instead effectively exclude those women and limit the discussion of racial issues. In Massachusetts, for example, the secretary of the state branch, Doris McElwain, felt that disbanding the Interracial Committee had been a mistake. "Not very many of that group joined the League, as had been hoped," she noted. Furthermore, the only activity on racial issues held by the branch since disbanding the committee had been a meeting on anti-Semitism.[71]

These debates over racial issues and the participation of African Americans in the WIL were remarkably similar to the discussion about whether the WIL should remain a separatist women's organization. Each discussion grew from a central question: Was it better to work separately from the dominant culture and risk marginalization, or to work within the dominant culture and risk having one's special perspective and causes become less visible, perhaps even excluded? The WIL had overwhelmingly decided in favor of separatism when faced with the issue of becoming a mixed-gender organization, but its position on integrating African Americans and on racial issues in general was less clear. The general commitment to racial justice was evident, but opinion on how to achieve that justice, even within the WIL, was genuinely divided. The crucial issue was how to deal with perceived difference. Should the WIL try to appeal to the different historical experiences of African Americans by providing a committee that was charged with exploring racial issues, or should it simply treat African Americans as it did European Americans? If it followed the second course, it could be charged with ignoring racial injustice; if it followed the first, it opened itself to charges of segregation.

This dilemma came into focus sharply when the WIL national board considered employing an African American to recruit African-American women as members. This policy had been recommended by the Interracial Committee, but the national board decided "to proceed thoughtfully and carefully before making a decision on this complex issue."[72] If the board approved this recommendation, it could be condemned for fostering segregation; but if it voted against the recommendation, it could be criticized for not trying hard enough to recruit African Americans, for denying this position of leadership to an African American, or for thinking that a European American could effectively recruit African Americans.

The WIL never successfully resolved this dilemma, but the intense and sustained examination of this issue serves to demonstrate its commitment to integration. At a time when African Americans were still segregated in most realms of public life, they were welcomed into the WIL. Furthermore, the WIL did not automatically assume that differences in historical experiences should simply be overlooked; rather, its leaders tried to balance respect for cultural differences with the desire to bridge those differences in the name of a common humanity. It is likely that the history of the WIL as a separatist women's organization influenced this position. The leaders of the organization knew the virtues of separatism and the risks of working in mixed-gender organizations. They doubtlessly suspected that working in a mixed-race organization would be equally risky for African-American women and that at least a separate committee, where racial issues were given priority, could provide a comfortable and supportive niche for African-American women who had decided to join the WIL.

Other aspects of the WIL's work for racial justice caused less debate within the organization. For example, the WIL consistently opposed the segregation of African Americans in public facilities; it was particularly critical of other peace organizations that ignored the issue of segregation when selecting a conference site. In June 1930, WIL executive secretary Dorothy Detzer protested the choice of a segregated hotel by the National Council for Prevention of War.[73] The WIL's protest was supported by the Fellowship of Reconciliation and the Pacifist Action Committee, and eventually the NCPW moved its convention to the Friends' Meeting House. The hotel, economically affected and evidently impressed by the power of the WIL, requested a copy of the WIL policy on interracial matters.[74]

The WIL also consistently supported legislation to make lynching a federal offense. African Americans had protested openly against lynchings since the late nineteenth century. In 1910 the National Association for the Advancement of Colored People joined the protest, responding to lynchings by quickly gathering and publicizing the facts of the incidents. It also worked for the passage of state and federal antilynching legislation. In 1922 the NAACP founded a women's group called the Anti-Lynching Crusaders to generate support for the antilynching legislation that had been introduced into Congress in 1921 by Representative L. C. Dyer. The Crusaders were unable to reach their goal of raising a million dollars and recruiting a million supporters, but they did generate wide publicity for the movement, particularly in leading women's publications.[75]

This publicity probably combined with the WIL's concern for racial justice to cause the WIL to support antilynching legislation.

The WIL supported the Dyer bill for years, and in the 1930s lobbied forcefully on behalf of other such bills.[76] In 1933 Dorothy Detzer suggested to Walter White, the secretary of the NAACP, that their two organizations coordinate their efforts, and White agreed to do so. This work continued in the following years; in 1940, for example, the WIL asked President Roosevelt to use his influence to get antilynching legislation passed.[77]

The WIL's support for antilynching legislation stemmed from its commitment to racial justice, but it was also obviously influenced by the organization's condemnation of the use of violence. Furthermore, Dorothy Detzer tied the WIL's condemnation of lynching to its commitment to economic justice. In a meeting with the assistant attorney general in August 1933, Detzer suggested that the federal government took quick action in kidnapping cases "because this crime affected the lives, liberty, and money of the rich." She said that the federal government should act as decisively against lynchings, "a crime which had for years menaced underprivileged and helpless people in the south." This suggestion angered the assistant attorney general so much, Detzer gleefully noted, "that he would hardly let me finish and interrupted me constantly. We literally had a verbal battle while he insisted on making a denial that 'wealth' affected the actions of the Dept. of Justice or the federal government."[78]

The WIL's commitment to racial and economic justice as well as its commitment to nonviolence also led it to work on behalf of other disadvantaged groups. In particular, the WIL favored less discriminatory treatment of Native Americans and Asian Americans. In 1929, for example, the comptroller general of the United States declared that Native American landless tribes were ineligible for federal aid. For those Native Americans living on infertile land and in harsh weather conditions, this ruling meant increased malnutrition and illness. The WIL responded by condemning the treatment of Native Americans by the United States and calling upon the secretary of the interior and the Congress to increase appropriations for Native Americans instead of for the military.[79]

The WIL also stated its opposition to racial discrimination in immigration and in granting citizenship and urged that "qualifications for citizenship should be personal, not racial, and that so long as our immigration is regulated by the quota system, the quota should be extended to Asiatic peoples."[80] WIL national president Hannah Clothier Hull saw the restriction on Asian immigration as particularly dangerous when relations with Japan deteriorated steadily during the 1930s. This restriction, she believed, had "caused friction and ill will toward the United States" and needed to be abolished.[81]

The WIL also protested against anti-Semitism, particularly as Hitler escalated his persecution of German Jews during the 1930s. In March 1933 the WIL issued a protest directly to Adolf Hitler expressing shock and dismay over the reports from Germany of violence and torture and asking him to provide "justice and civic protection to all, without regard to religion, class, race, or political opinions." Similar protests were repeated throughout the remainder of the year as the reports from Germany worsened.[82] About reports of concentration camps in Germany, Emily Greene Balch wrote to Jane Addams for advice: "Do you see how anything can be done to get the Red Cross or some other neutral body to investigate [the] German concentration camps? No one knows what goes on there and they alarm me almost more than the incredible performances as regards the Jews."[83]

The WIL found no way to change Hitler's policies, however, so it began trying to ameliorate their effects. By 1938 it had organized the Committee on Refugees to help WILPF members and others in Europe to immigrate to the United States. And in 1941 the WIL urged the United States to become more active in the rescue of refugees. "We demand," the WIL stated in its principles and policies for that year, "that the United States government secure ships for the immediate rescue of thousands of refugees now caught at Lisbon and elsewhere whose papers are in order, or who are only awaiting passage to the United States. If it is possible for the United States to police the Atlantic, we are convinced that ways can be found to secure ships of mercy."[84] Finally, shortly before the United States entered World War II, the WIL national board acknowledged the existence of anti-Semitism within the United States as well as in Europe. It cautioned its members to watch for and denounce anti-Semitism and also to guard against its spread in their own communities.[85]

The final area in which the WIL identified and condemned racism was the extension of American business interests and the military into some African, Asian, and Latin American nations. The WIL had condemned U.S. economic imperialism, arguing that it ran counter to the general WIL philosophy of nurturing others. This exploitation of the natural resources of other nations caused hostility and set the stage for military conflict.

The first situation to attract WIL attention was in Haiti. This small Caribbean nation had been occupied by U.S. Marines in 1915. Soon thereafter, Emily Greene Balch suggested that a commission be appointed to investigate the situation there. Such a suggestion was made again in 1920 by the executive board of the WIL, and the board stipulated that such a commission should have "both women and blacks" as members.[86] Finally, in 1926, Balch, Addie Waites Hunton, and four others were appointed to an unofficial investigatory commission. After visiting Haiti, Balch was struck most strongly, she wrote, by "the complete hiatus between the sense of what is important in life in the eyes of members of the American occupation and in the eyes of the Haitians themselves." The Americans emphasized the good they had done by overseeing the building of roads, bridges, and health care facilities; the Haitians emphasized that American occupation "had broken down self-government and left a whole generation to grow up without any sense of political responsibility or experience of it." Even worse, in the view of the Haitians, was that the American occupation had created "a situation between the races powerfully influenced by that which has developed in the former slave states of the U.S." and produced within the Haitians a sense of "racial self-consciousness" from which they had before been free.[87]

Balch later clarified these remarks with examples of racism and condescension she had witnessed. "Among American officials in Haiti, even those who pass for the most friendly" she noted, "there is a good deal of joking about Haitians having just stopped living in trees, and that sort of thing." Balch believed that it was impossible for Americans to hide their contempt for the Haitians, and this failure doomed any attempts at mutual cooperation: "If black men, however cultivated, strike our men in Haiti as a sort of nigger minstrels masquerading in Paris clothes and aping real men like ourselves, there can never be effective cooperation."[88]

The commission with which Balch worked concluded that there was little justification for the continued occupation of Haiti and that self-government should be restored. When the commission returned to the United States, Balch presented the group's conclusions during an interview with President Calvin Coolidge. Then, when President Herbert Hoover formed an official committee to investigate the situation in Haiti, Balch submitted a memorandum outlining the WIL commission's findings to it. The report eventually issued by the Hoover commission echoed many of the recommendations made earlier by the WIL commission, recommendations that were implemented in 1934 when U.S. troops were finally withdrawn from Haiti.[89]

The WIL also urged that the United States grant independence to the Philippines and Samoa, end its military occupation and financial supervision of Nicaragua, and loan money to Latin American countries only for "constructive projects that will contribute to the prosperity and well-being of the people."[90] The WIL also condemned United States policy in Liberia, particularly because it seemed designed to benefit the American-based Firestone Corporation at the expense of the Liberian people.[91]

Underlying U.S. policy in Liberia as well as in the nations of Latin America and the Pacific, WIL leaders believed, was a racist disregard for different cultural traditions, a disregard in direct conflict with the WIL's commitment to cultural pluralism. Detzer argued, for example, that "the darker world has long been convinced that it is being used and exploited by Europe and America for the benefit and power and luxury of white folk and at the expense of poverty, and slavery for yellow, brown and black." Detzer thought that African Americans were particularly sensitive in this regard: "They are especially astounded and embittered when they think they see in the whole white world and in its attitude toward self-determination and opportunities for development among colored peoples and particularly among Negroes a disposition to shut the gates of opportunity in their faces and to reduce every colored country where possible to complete vassalage to white countries."[92] Balch also thought the United States erred by denying the validity of other people's cultural traditions and demanding that they mimic American ones. "I loathe and repudiate," she wrote her friend Anna Melissa Graves, "the exploitation of peoples outside the line of development of White European civilization who have their own culture, their own art and full human rights as much as anyone."[93]

To counter the detrimental effects of the racist and exploitative policies of the United States, the WIL protested government actions, but it also tried to organize branches of the WILPF throughout Latin America. This effort was headed by Heloise Brainerd, a graduate of Smith College who devoted her life to fostering educational, artistic, literary, and scientific exchanges among the nations of the Americas. In 1935 Brainerd became the head of the WIL Inter-American Committee, which changed its name to the Committee of the Americas in 1938. In this capacity Brainerd toured Latin America, contacting women who might be interested in the WILPF and trying to organize them into WILPF branches. She also tried to "eradicate the imperialist phases of U.S. policy."[94] She was largely unsuccessful on both counts, but the support of her efforts by the WIL shows that the organization's leaders realized the importance of trying to cooperate with women from elsewhere in the western hemisphere, of practicing what they were preaching to the U.S. government. That the WIL failed to achieve lasting results in this area, however, may also indicate that it was trying to graft an organizational structure and commitment onto others with little regard for how it meshed with their own cultural traditions.

Efforts to interest Latin American women in the work of the WILPF; opposition to the racist assumptions underlying much of United States foreign policy; condemnation of discrimination based on race or ethnicity; commitment to the equality of all peoples: all of these characterized the policies and principles of the WIL during the interwar years. To the leaders of the WIL, then, the answer to the question, "What had race to do with issues of peace and freedom?" was simple.[95] Only when all people were treated fairly would peace exist, the WIL leaders believed; work to eradicate injustices committed because of racial and ethnic discrimination was just as essential as work for disarmament or international organization. But even working for racial justice and peace was not enough. Dangerous distinctions among people were also made on the basis of economic class.

The Covert Violence of Economic Inequality

Central to the WIL's work for peace was the belief that economic injustice—the deprivation of vital necessities from many and the provision of excessive luxuries to a few—would eventually lead to vio-

STAFFORDSHIRE
UNIVERSITY
LIBRARY

lent conflict between the haves and the have nots. This belief had been expressed as early as the organizational conference of the Woman's Peace Party, and a commitment to economic justice had always been a component of WIL policy.[96] During the severe economic dislocation caused by the Great Depression, however, this commitment demanded action as it had not before.

The WIL's commitment to economic justice grew partially from the insights and leadership of Jane Addams. Addams, as we saw earlier, had long argued that the working class had an important role to play in the development of a peaceful world; workers understood the importance of producing instead of destroying, and they were accustomed to mixing with other workers of different nationalities. She maintained this position into the 1930s and urged leaders of the peace movement to cooperate with workers. At the very least, she noted, such cooperation was necessary because workers could deter war by refusing to manufacture or transport war-related goods.[97]

Dorothy Detzer shared Addams's assessment of the importance of cooperating with laborers. She too wanted to ensure that workers would "be prepared to strike against war, to do their part in refusing to cooperate in carrying on a war if conflict should come."[98] This was difficult to do, however, for in the short run, workers benefited from war and its preparations: military expenditures brought increased employment. But, Detzer argued, to look only at the short run was deceptive. Would proponents of increased armaments be willing to argue that "for the sake of employment, men should be hired to increase the output of soul-destroying, body-destroying narcotics?" Probably not, but Detzer believed that argument was no more ridiculous than the argument of the militarists. Rather than providing constructive, beneficial employment, Detzer concluded, "Employment in armaments and munitions means that labor prepares the instruments of death to be used on other laborers in other lands for the profits of the few."[99]

The increased employment accompanying war preparations and war was not the only barrier to cooperation between labor and the women's peace movement. The other major problem was the common use of violence by and against labor during strikes. The WIL realized that it would have to convince labor that peaceful techniques could be used as effectively as violent ones; and it would have to convince employers not to resort to violence to settle strikes.[100]

In order to carry this work forward effectively, the WIL organized the Labor Committee in 1937. This committee was chaired by Elisabeth Christman, who was also secretary of the Women's Trade Union League, and its secretary was Eleanor Fowler, who had earned a doctorate in international law from Columbia University. Fowler noted that although working with organized labor was relatively new to the WIL, the importance of such work had long been implicit in its principles. The annual statements of "Program and Policies" had often stated that "the basis of peace and freedom is a just economic and social order," had condemned "the inequalities of the present economic system," and had acknowledged the "close connection between peace and a decent standard of living for the people of the world."[101]

This was a solid foundation on which to build, but the principles that would govern WIL work with labor henceforth still needed to be clearly articulated. Fowler believed that the WIL needed to commit itself to work that would benefit organized labor as well as the peace movement. She suggested that previous attempts at cooperation between peace activists and labor had failed largely because the peace activists had gone to labor "for the most part as outsiders with no interest in or understanding of labor's problems." For example, Fowler asked, did peace activists really think that the pamphlets they directed at organized labor would receive a sympathetic response when the workers noted that the pamphlets had been printed by a nonunionized printer? This sort of thoughtlessness and insensitivity had caused labor to resent the overtures from the peace movement.[102]

Fowler suggested a new approach—one that would emphasize the common interests and principles of labor and the peace movement rather than see labor only as a source of support for the peace movement. "Our first undertaking in the labor field," she wrote, "must be to educate ourselves in the trade union movement and in the problems of the workers generally." WIL members who wanted to work with labor "must join some workers groups, serve on committees, learn labor's viewpoint, help in its struggles." Furthermore, the WIL should not conceive of its work with labor as simply winning friends whom it could later rouse for peace action. Instead, the WIL needed to realize that "helping workers to organize is in itself work for peace because a strong trade union movement is a bulwark of peace." Like Addams and Detzer, Fowler believed that labor had "the power to stop war by stopping shipment of certain materials without which wars cannot be fought." To exercise that power, though, labor had to be solidly organized. Fowler reasoned that when the WIL helped organize workers, it simultaneously strengthened the forces of peace.[103]

The vision of a mutually beneficial relationship between labor and peace activists was compelling, but equally important to Fowler were the common principles and goals of the two groups. The WIL, she pointed out, believed "that the present economic and social order is a danger to peace and that it is our duty to work for a 'better economic and social order' by every pacific means." Organized labor also directed "its whole energy to building up a more just economic and social order." By helping labor to organize for better working and living conditions, the WIL was also "working for that more just society which we all recognize to be essential to permanent peace."[104]

A first step in this work was for the national office of the WIL to unionize its staff; this was done in 1937.[105] The following year, Fowler and the Labor Committee suggested additional ways in which the WIL could fulfill its moral responsibility to organized labor. The committee encouraged the WIL to do what it could to secure unemployment insurance, to support the minimum wage and maximum hours legislation, and to uphold labor's right to organize and bargain collectively. This emphasis on the freedom portion of the WIL's "peace and freedom" program, the committee believed, would help counteract the growing national as well as international reaction against such social reforms.[106]

The WIL did support such reforms in the following years, especially labor's right to collective bargaining. This method of peacefully settling disputes between workers and employers was a domestic version of what the WIL and other peace organizations wanted to happen between nations. Hannah Clothier Hull, for example, wrote that she believed "thoroughly in the method of conference between employer and employed—in collective bargaining which many of our business corporations are successfully recognizing and practicing and which others are not willingly recognizing causing thereby much of the trouble throughout the industrial world." Then, in a comment that she could just as easily have made about the mediation of international disputes, Hull stated, "When the method of conference is tried, it works." It might not work immediately, she admitted, but it still worked "more quickly than does force which must lead to conference after all in the end." The WIL as a whole echoed Hull's commitment to collective bargaining.[107]

The WIL's work with organized labor enacted basic principles of the WIL: the use of peaceful methods to resolve disputes and the importance of nurturing all people in pursuit of a more just distribution of economic resources. It also gave new life to the charge that the WIL was a communist organization. Such charges had plagued the WIL since the early 1920s but gained new intensity when the WIL began to work with labor organizations, which often contained socialists and communists, and to advocate economic justice, attainable only through a redistribution of resources. Particularly problematic was the WIL's association with the American League Against War and Fascism. The twin threats of war and fascism had led to a European movement to unite leftist forces against fascism; and in the United States this movement had led to the formation of the American League Against War and Fascism. Drawing members from both the American Federation of Labor Trade Union Committee for Unemployment Relief and the Fellowship of Reconciliation, the American League included both communists and pacifists.[108]

Whether and to what extent the WIL should join efforts with the American League was a difficult issue for WIL leaders. When the issue first arose, soon after the founding of the American League in 1933, the WIL made clear that although it wanted to cooperate with all forces opposing war and the economic injustices leading to war, it refused to sanction the use of violent force to end such injustices. "While we sympathize with all generous indignation against economic injustices and stupidities, and understand the view that adequate change can be brought about only by violence, we deplore this and all acceptance of violence as a tolerable method. We believe they are short-sighted and mistaken." The WIL would, then, "cooperate in all expressions of antipathy to war just so far as they do not imply that class war and revolutionary violence are legitimate."[109]

The WIL followed this policy from 1934 until 1938, during which time most of the cooperation between the two organizations was organized by Dorothy Detzer. Yet even the WIL's carefully delineated basis and limited nature of cooperation with the American League did not stop critics from using the connection between the organizations as evidence for the charge of communism. WIL leaders found themselves having to respond to such charges and to defend their position even to WIL members. The standard WIL response was that the WIL could not be a communist organization because it opposed all use of violence, even for a supposedly just cause.[110]

The WIL's affiliation with the American League ended in 1938, partially because the American League had begun to abandon pacifism in favor of collective security and partially because the WIL believed the American League did not sufficiently respect individual civil liberties.[111] But charges that the WIL was a communist organization did not stop, because they had more to do with the public perception of its general goals than with its precise principles or actions. The leaders of the WIL believed in and worked for the advancement of all repressed people, whether they were distinguished from the dominant culture by race, ethnicity, sex, religion, economic class, or political philosophy. But working for these goals threatened the distribution of power in the United States. The WIL could defend itself with careful explanations of its policies and principles; it could justify its work through an appeal to the American ideals of liberty and justice for all; but it could not deny that if its program were successful, power and wealth would be redistributed. Although the WIL was not a communist organization, it sought exactly the changes that many Americans associated with communism. What the leaders of the WIL called "democracy" the dominant culture had redefined as "communism."

But the WIL did not give up. Even as the United States moved ever closer to entering World War II, the WIL continued its work both against the war and for greater economic justice within the United States. In May 1941 the WIL expressed it conviction that "there can be no real domestic security or true democracy until the mass of the people can be released from poverty." To live in poverty, deprived of the "right to decent living and health through inadequate wages," was "a covert form of violence and the soil out of which fascism grows."[112] War and economic injustice were opposite sides of the same coin; they had to be opposed simultaneously.

Peace and Social Justice

To the women leading the WIL, economic injustice, racism, the repression of civil liberties, and the oppression of women were forms of violence, different only in magnitude from international war. Their work for solutions to these problems was essential to their work for world peace: the causes of violence had to be eradicated, they believed, to give international organizations or laws a chance to work. The WIL leaders' early commitment to nonresistance—the rejection of the use of violence—had blossomed into a commitment to nonviolence—using peaceful methods to eradicate the causes of violence.

In part, this change reflected the changing times. During World War I it had seemed most important to protest against the war that was raging; by the 1930s it seemed most important to address the deep-seated social and economic problems manifested by the Great Depression. There were major problems on the international level, to be sure, but as the solutions proffered by the WIL and other pacifists failed to lessen hostilities, the WIL gradually redirected its energy to domestic problems. The world seemed to be marching straight to another war; all the WIL could do was to try to keep the United States out of such a war, and failing that, to minimize the effects of the war at home.

But the advocacy of nonviolence and social justice also illustrated the philosophical basis of the WIL's work. By the 1930s the WIL's program represented the "substitution of nurture for warfare" that had been envisioned by Jane Addams so many years before. In its work for the equality of women as well as racial and ethnic minorities, in its protection of civil liberties, and in its work for the economic equality of all people, the WIL struggled to nurture people in ways that would allow them to achieve their fullest potential. Reflecting on her career in 1930, Addams said: "I came to believe that 'the ancient kindliness which sat beside the cradle of the race,' cannot assert itself in our generation against the waste of life in warfare, so long as we remain indifferent to the shocking destruction of life in other areas. To protect life in industry may be a natural beginning, a response to the brother we have seen."[113]

Throughout the interwar years, the women who led the WIL

maintained a vision: that a few basic moral principles could guide people into a world where difference was tolerated, even valued; where arbitrary divisions based on color or sex faded before the realization of a common humanity; where honest labor was valued honestly; where all people could live at peace and free from want. Their vision, as well as the organization they created, still stands today, a challenge to us all.

Jane Addams, founder of Hull House and leader of the Woman's Peace Party and the Women's International League for Peace and Freedom, 1913. Jane Addams Papers, Swarthmore College Peace Collection.

Leaders of the WILPF. Left to right: Madame Ramondt-Hirschman, Holland; Chrystal Macmillan, Great Britain; Dr. S. Jawein, Petrograd; Baroness Ellen Palonstierna, Sweden; Emily Greene Balch, United States. Taken in Dr. Jawein's office in Petrograd, 1915. Records of the Women's International League for Peace and Freedom, U.S. Section, Swarthmore College Peace Collection.

U.S. members at the WILPF conference in Zurich, Switzerland, 1919. Bottom row: far right, Emily Greene Balch; third from right, Jane Addams. Back row: fifth from right, Lucy Biddle Lewis; seventh from right, Mary Church Terrell (?). Records of the Women's International League for Peace and Freedom, U.S. Section, Swarthmore College Peace Collection.

Official delegates of WIL to Disarmament Conference of League of Nations, February 1932. Left to right: Meta Berger, Hannah Clothier Hull, Katherine Devereaux Blake. Flowers sent by Eleanor Roosevelt. Records of the Women's International League for Peace and Freedom, U.S. Section, Swarthmore College Peace Collection.

Katherine Devereaux Blake. Records of the Women's International League for Peace and Freedom, U.S. Section, Swarthmore College Peace Collection.

Hannah Clothier Hull. Photo by Bain News Service. Records of the Women's International League for Peace and Freedom, U.S. Section, Swarthmore College Peace Collection.

Dorothy Detzer, circa 1924. Photo by Underwood and Underwood, Washington, D.C. Records of the Women's International League for Peace and Freedom, U.S. Section, Swarthmore College Peace Collection.

Mildred Scott Olmsted, circa 1930. Copyright Bachrach. Mildred Scott Olmsted Papers, Swarthmore College Peace Collection.

Gertrude Bussey. Records
of the Women's Interna-
tional League for Peace and
Freedom, Swarthmore Col-
lege Peace Collection.

Mary Church Terrell.
Prints and Photographs
Collection, Moorland-
Spingarn Research Center,
Howard University.

Bertha McNeill. Prints and Photographs Collection, Moorland-Spingarn Research Center, Howard University.

Emily Greene Balch reading telegram notifying her that she had been awarded the Nobel Prize for Peace, 1946. Courtesy of *Boston Globe*. Records of the Women's International League for Peace and Freedom, U.S. Section, Swarthmore College Peace Collection.

The Implications of Reconstructing
Women's Thoughts

DESPITE THE SUSTAINED efforts of the leaders of the WIL, the United States declared war once again on December 8, 1941. Two days later, the WIL national board convened for an emergency meeting. "The war in which we find ourselves today," the board members wrote, "is the inevitable result of a world organized for war and not for peace." They would not oppose the decision of their nation's elected representatives; they believed too strongly in democratic processes to do so. But neither would they support a war they had seen coming for many years. Instead, the WIL leaders decided to redirect their energies: to cooperate with the British section of the WILPF "in directing our joint energies toward the problems of the post-war world and by striving to create the attitudes and the will which will eliminate both a narrow isolationism on the one hand and an Anglo-American imperialism on the other." Changing attitudes and the creation of a will for peace were vital: "Neither the United States nor the rest of the world can ever be truly free until the conditions of peace have been established for all nations and all peoples. Mankind must some day be released from the violence and waste and suffering of this recurring tragedy. For us, war remains the final infamy."[1]

With this rhetorical flourish, the WIL leaders began the long war years. Their exhaustion and disappointment were great and doubtlessly made greater by their increasing age. Emily Greene Balch was 71; Katherine Devereaux Blake, 83; and Hannah Clothier Hull, 69 (Jane Addams had died in 1935 at the age of 74). Even the younger leaders were well into middle age: Dorothy Detzer was 48, and Mildred Scott Olmsted was 51. With the advantage of relative youth, Detzer and Olmsted remained active leaders throughout the war. Detzer finally left her position as executive secretary in 1946, partially because of conflicts with Olmsted; Olmsted remained an active leader until 1966. Balch, Blake, and Hull had gradually reduced their participation, and all had assumed honorary offices by the beginning of the war.

The World War II years stand as a period of clear transition in the life of the WIL. The organization would emerge at the end of the war with new leaders and with a slight shift of emphasis: working for social justice remained important, but opposition to nuclear weapons and testing also took considerable energy and time. The war years form a vantage point from which to review and evaluate the ideas of the women who led the WIL before World War II.

Emotional Attachment and the Ideology of the WIL

As we have seen, the leaders of the WIL based their work on their conviction that although they lived in a world where little was certain they could be sure of two things: put simply, that violence was bad and nurturing was good. These basic convictions underlay their advocacy of nonviolence and their opposition to a patriarchal system that they believed minimized the importance of women's traditional work of nurturing.

First, their understanding of human history and human relationships led them to believe that violence was never an effective tool for change: violence of all sorts—the overt violence of physical conflict as well as the more subtle violence of all forms of inequality—only bred more violence. These women believed strongly that a wrongful means could not be used to secure a just end: means and ends had to be both consistent and just. If the world were to exist in peace, nations had to renounce violence as a method of solving conflicts and defuse the causes of conflict by working to ensure for all people a satisfactory standard of living. The leaders of the WIL combined nonresistance and a commitment to social justice into the philosophical position of nonviolence. They stood with other groups such as the Fellowship of Reconciliation and the American Friends Service Committee on the left end of the spectrum of peace activism.

Simultaneously, the leaders of the WIL stood apart from these other groups in their insistence on resisting sex hierarchy.[2] This resistance grew at least partially from their particular socialization as women growing up in the Victorian era of the late nineteenth and early twentieth centuries. This socialization had caused them to value the nurturing work traditionally done by women. Because men had not been taught to nurture others, the WIL leaders believed, men had devalued the importance of such work. In the view of the WIL leaders, the political, social, and economic system that men had established in the United States was fundamentally flawed. During the nineteenth century, the developing industrial and urban nation had posited a strict division between public and private and assigned the work of nurturing to the private realm. Women had assumed this work willingly, performing tremendous amounts of charitable and voluntary work; but they had also gradually realized that such a populous nation could never meet all of its "nurturing" needs in this way. The government would have to assume responsibility for nurturing its citizens. And the easiest way to make government do so, the leaders of the WIL believed, was to allow women to serve and be fairly represented in government and in the public realm in general.

But the leaders of the WIL did not argue only that women should be integrated into the public realm because they brought distinctive and much-needed characteristics with them. They combined that argument first with the argument that women were equal to men and later with the acknowledgment that women were a diverse group. The positions taken by the leaders of the WIL show that a dichotomous model of these women's consciousness—that they either argued that women were the same as men or that they were different from men, that they were either "hard-core" or "social" feminists— does not adequately characterize their stance.[3] Rather, the worldview developed by the leaders of the WIL shows a more complex understanding of gender, race, and class differences.

They emphasized their belief in the differences between women and men most strongly during the years of the Woman's Peace Party but maintained this position throughout the 1920s and 1930s. At the same time, they also came to see that women differed from each other. After a last attempt at uniting women behind the cause of peace in the early 1920s, they increasingly acknowledged that political, racial, and class differences could overshadow the similarities associated with gender. They then urged that such differences be respected and carefully balanced with some degree of gender solidarity. That it was difficult to maintain this balance is clear: conflicts with other women's organizations, the intermittent controversies involving the WIL's Interracial Committee, and the difficulty of working with organized labor all stand witness in this regard.

The WIL succeeded, though, because its worldview included a profound appreciation of pluralism, both cultural and political. The women who led the WIL understood that women varied in many ways—ethnically, racially, religiously, politically—but they also believed that women shared some common socially constructed characteristics. Likewise, they acknowledged and appreciated the diversity among cultures but never lost sight of the common humanity shared by all.

This same attitude, a careful balancing of similarities and differences, also governed the conduct of the WIL itself. The WIL leaders identified a few basic principles that were essential, but they allowed members to enact those principles in whatever ways suited them best. In fact, during the 1920s and 1930s the policies of the WIL encompassed such a spectrum of beliefs that more narrowly focused activists occasionally accused the WIL of trying to be all things to all people, of lacking the courage to be a truly pacifist organization. The WIL leaders understood this criticism, but in their minds they could not change without compromising their commitment to diversity and pluralism.

The balancing of similarities and differences led the organization to develop the concept of "unity within diversity." The choice of prepositions in this phrase was crucial. Unity *through* diversity would have connoted the faith that even though each individual might pursue her or his own ends, the ends would eventually constitute some common good (as in capitalism). Unity *from* diversity would have connoted the sense that people would move from their diverse positions to shared ones or that they would forsake their cultural differences to create a new, unified culture (as the motto of the United States, e pluribus unum, suggests). Unity *within* diversity, however, signified the belief that some basic elements are common to all people and all cultures, regardless of how different they might appear. To practice unity within diversity, then, meant to recognize and build upon those basic common elements while simultaneously tolerating, and even enjoying, the differences among people and cultures.[4]

Perhaps most important, the concept of unity within diversity dissolved the us-them, insider-outsider dichotomy. Committing violence or injustice was much easier when the victim was characterized as fundamentally different from the perpetrator. In wartime, national propaganda often dehumanizes the enemy; instead of people, the enemy becomes Huns or rats or Nazis or madmen. But to keep constantly in mind the commonalities of humanity makes this dehumanization much more difficult and emphasizes instead the connectedness among people.

Connectedness and the dissolution of dichotomies were vital to the worldview of the WIL in other ways as well. Its leaders wanted to end the harmful aspects of separation of women from men, blacks from whites, and ethnic group from ethnic group. From the organization of the Woman's Peace Party in 1915 through the interwar years, they called for women's integration into the public sphere. In the late 1920s and the 1930s, they devoted increasing amounts of energy to integrating racial and ethnic groups and minimizing class differences. Finally, the WIL worked to reduce conflict between nations by eliminating the use of violence and forging an understanding of what the nations had in common.

Implicit in the WIL's work to heal divisions based on race, ethnicity, economic class, or gender was a realization of the need to reunite public and private interests. Women could never achieve the reforms they believed necessary if they were relegated to the private sphere, and the nation could never genuinely provide for the welfare of its citizens as long as nurturing was also relegated to the private sphere. When some women challenged this division of responsibilities and resources by asking for the vote or calling for reforms or serving in prominent professional positions, they were essentially challenging the relegation of some people and some topics to the private sphere. And simply enlarging the purview of the public sphere was not enough; for women such as Jane Addams, the boundaries between the two realms needed to be completely revised, perhaps even abolished.

This revision of the public-private split was also implicit in calls for integration on the grounds of race, ethnicity, and economic class.

It was not just women who had been defined out of the public realm; it was also people of color and the poor. The financial problems of a large corporation, the wealthy argued, were obviously of concern to the government; but the poverty of individuals was simply a personal failure resulting from lack of effort or intelligence. Certainly the government should provide subsidies for railroads, for example; but caring for the welfare of Asian railroad workers was an entirely different matter. Thus a structure was established that defined concerns of the wealthy as public while concerns of the poor remained private; and because in the United States wealth was correlated with skin color, what was defined as public was usually of most importance to whites, and what was defined as private was of most importance to people of color.

This division of public and private was fundamentally shaken by at least some of the political and social reforms at the turn of the century. During this so-called Progressive Era, the government began accepting responsibility for the welfare of more and more of its citizens, spurred on by reformers such as the future leaders of the WIL. With the advent of Franklin Roosevelt's New Deal, again the leaders of the WIL, as well as many other activist women and men, were there, carrying the torch for themselves and other women, the poor, and people of color. Not the least of the contributions of the WIL leaders was their work to erase the strict division between public and private by enlarging the understanding of governmental responsibility for all its citizens.

At first glance, the work of the WIL leaders to heal divisions seems at odds with their leadership of a separate women's organization. However, the WIL leaders believed that integration could best be achieved, at least in the short run, through separatist action. They struggled, as society does today, with the issue of providing equal access without losing distinctive characteristics or perspectives.[5] They eventually puzzled out a modus operandi that was workable and that was entirely consistent with their philosophy of unity within diversity: a separatist, female-dominated organization that admitted men as members and worked in cooperation with male-dominated organizations. Likewise, in their effort to bring more African-American women into the WIL, they acknowledged that separatist organizing and a committee that focused solely on racial issues might be the appropriate means to their eventual goal of an integrated organization.

The principles that were at the heart of the WIL's philosophy—unity within diversity, nonviolence, nurturing, and the importance of women working with and for women—were shaped by, and then in turn deepened, the emotional attachment to others that had been a hallmark of the nineteenth-century "women's sphere." We have seen how the nineteenth-century ideology of separate spheres and the theory of complementarianism shaped the early experiences of the leaders of the WIL; these women then remained convinced of the importance of "feminine" values even after they moved well beyond the limits prescribed by the original ideology.

Although intellectual historians have sometimes given the impression that human ideas are developed only in response to the ideas of others, it seems clear that, at least in part, humans develop ideas based upon their life experiences. And if people are deprived of education and knowledge of others' ideas, they are even more likely to develop their ideas based upon personal experience.[6] The leaders of the WIL were educated, but they were also deeply influenced by their socialization as caretakers. It should not be surprising, then, that they developed a worldview in which emotional attachment to others was central.

Victorianism, Modernism, and Men's Ideas

The leaders of the WIL developed a distinctive worldview that shaped the contours of their work for peace and social justice throughout the early twentieth century. To appreciate its distinctiveness, however, it is necessary to compare it to the worldviews that historians have identified as dominant during this same time period. Historians have labeled the dominant intellectual currents of the late nineteenth century as "Victorian" and those of the early twentieth century as "modernist." And as I said in the introduction to this book, their generalizations about Victorianism and modernism have been based almost exclusively on the writings of men. Are they, then, helpful in understanding the ideas of the women who led the WIL? How do the principles that underlay the work of the WIL mesh with what are understood to be the central tenets of Victorianism and modernism?

First, the concepts of nurturing and nonviolence that were central to the philosophy of the WIL leaders echo some characteristics of Victorianism. The belief that women were more nurturing, caring, and sensitive than men certainly would have sounded familiar to many Victorian women. Indeed, historians have argued repeatedly that middle- and upper-class women in the late nineteenth century preached their moral superiority to men and used this view to expand their own participation in the public realm.[7]

In the rhetoric of the Woman's Peace Party, and occasionally in that of the WIL, the equation of women and certain moral values is clear; but it is also clear that the leaders of the WIL did not advocate the moral superiority of women. They believed that women had distinctive—but neither superior nor inferior—moral values that needed to be appreciated by men and also integrated into the public realm. They sought "moral authority," but they did not seek or claim superiority.[8]

The insistence by the leaders of the WIL that separatist action by women was desirable also echoes the Victorian era. By the twentieth century, and certainly after the passage of the Nineteenth Amendment, women began to downplay women's solidarity and separate organization in favor of cooperation and friendship in gender-neutral (though still male-dominated) groups. In this regard, the leaders of the WIL seem to have been out of step with their times, remnants from the Victorian era.

Finally, the conviction held by the leaders of the WIL that nonviolence and nurturing were good and violence was bad bespeaks a degree of moral certainty usually associated with Victorianism. It was the Victorians who saw clear distinctions between right and wrong and made judgments based on those distinctions. By the early twentieth century, such certainty was fading as tolerance of others' values and a willingness to reserve judgment of others' actions began to shine more brightly. In this regard too, then, the ideas of the WIL leaders seem Victorian.

But if on one level the rhetoric and actions of the WIL leaders echoed Victorianism, on another they sounded themes that we now associate with modernism. On the issue of moral certainty, for example, WIL policy shows that surrounding their core moral principles of nurturing and nonviolence was a profound appreciation of diversity, uncertainty, and ambiguity. Although during World War I and early in the 1920s the leaders of the WPP and WIL assumed that most women shared their moral principles, by the late 1920s and the 1930s they acknowledged that their members held a wide range of beliefs. Their sustained discussions of neutrality legislation and the use of sanctions during the 1930s, for example, showed how carefully they listened to each other and how hard they worked to accommodate opinions that differed from their own.

Furthermore, WIL leaders believed that diversity among its members was as desirable as diversity in its policies. The organization struggled to recruit African-American women; it also struggled to reconcile its historic identity as a women's separatist organization with the growing sense, especially among the younger generation, that women and men should work together, not separately. The position on which WIL leaders finally agreed was an ambiguous one: a women's organization that nevertheless had male members. The appreciation of pluralism, diversity, and uncertainty guided its work as surely as the appreciation of separatism and a belief in the importance of nurturing and nonviolence.

Finally, despite their strenuous efforts on behalf of integration and peaceful coexistence, the leaders of the WIL realized the inadequacy of that work. Like modernists in general, they sought integration and harmony but lived with the understanding that what they sought would never be completely realized.[9] The leaders of the WIL realized that life had to be lived, and policies made, in the breach between the ideal and the real, the desired and the actual.

It is clear that the leaders of the WIL built upon some ideas that are consistent with a modernist sensibility. Yet in their work these ideas took on new forms. For example, one of the frustrations of many modernists was the difficulty of living a life with no certainties. They applauded the existence of "tension," but they found that complete uncertainty and lack of resolution created a degree of tension that was ultimately unlivable. The leaders of the WIL, however, wrapped their appreciation of conflict, tension, diversity, uncertainty, and ambiguity around a core of moral certainty—the commitment to nonviolence and nurturing—thereby sculpting a philosophical position that served them, and others, well throughout their lives. While many of their modernist contemporaries immersed themselves in theoretical, scholarly, or artistic work, the leaders of the WIL actively engaged with the world.

The ideas held by the WIL leaders fit only uncomfortably and partially into the categories that have been used by intellectual historians to characterize the late nineteenth and early twentieth centuries. Although Victorianism and modernism are supposed to have oppositional characteristics, the worldview of the leaders of the WIL encompasses some ideas from both as well as some that are not associated with either. They did not hold unthinkingly to the Victorian beliefs in moral certainty and separate spheres for men and women. Neither did they unthinkingly embrace the modernist call for moral relativism and the argument that women and men were equal and thus should work together. Rather, they held these beliefs up to the light of their own experiences and objectives, kept what was useful, and discarded the rest.

Reintegrating Reason and Emotion

The concepts of Victorianism and modernism help us understand some things about the philosophy of the women who led the WIL, but they do not fully explain that philosophy. How can we explain their ideas, and how does such an explanation change our understanding of our intellectual heritage?

Historian Gerda Lerner suggests why accepted notions of intellectual trends and changes do not adequately explain the ideas of women. Lerner argues that "the hegemony of patriarchal thought in Western civilization is not due to its superiority in content, form and achievement over all other thought; it is built upon the systematic silencing of other voices." She details the heartrending stories of women trying to become educated, to create and think and write, to assert that their minds were as good as men's. Although many of them preserved a record of their accomplishments, most were only narrowly distributed and sometimes lost for centuries.[10] Women who were denied knowledge of women's history could not build upon the ideas of women who worked before them, and they worked through the same issues over and over instead of moving on to new ones. Also, when men were denied knowledge of women's history they could not include women's ideas in their own work, even if they had been inclined to do so. For these reasons, Lerner concludes, "The female questions, the woman's point of view, the paradigm which would include the female experience has, until very recently, never entered the common discourse."[11]

It is this new paradigm that reconstructing the ideas of the WIL leaders allows us to bring to our understanding of intellectual life in the first half of the twentieth century. Like all women before them, the leaders of the WIL lived in the world both as human beings and as women. That is, they had been socialized as women and brought to their work a perspective considered by them to be distinctively female; but they were also simply people, affected as were all other people by the momentous changes in society and culture that occurred around the turn of the century. Their ideas were shaped by the same forces that shaped the ideas of the men who were usually considered the outstanding examples of Victorianism and modernism, but their ideas were also shaped by their distinctive experiences as women.

Perhaps most influential was their early training that nurturing others was something done by women, not men. This emphasis on nurturing was undergirded by an emphasis on emotional attachment to others. And understanding the importance of emotional attachment in the underlying philosophy of the WIL leaders allows us to formulate at last an intellectual paradigm that includes the experiences of some women.

For centuries, beginning at least with Plato, Western thought associated reason with men, emotion with women. The Enlightenment strengthened this association, as did the economic and social developments of the nineteenth century. The ideology of separate but complementary spheres for men and women portrayed men and women as having different characteristics and thus being suited to the public and private realms, respectively. The increasing distance between work and home brought about by industrialization and urbanization, the willingness to relegate matters of morality to the private sphere of women while men did the business of the nation, and the declining involvement of men with religion and the family all furthered the division between private and public and served to link emotion firmly with women, reason firmly with men. Most important, the rational, public, male realm was privileged over the emotional, private, female realm. In spite of protestations of equality, the rationality associated with the public realm and with men became the preferred method of determining proper action; to betray emotion was to betray feminine weakness and to corrupt the operation of reason.

A reaction against this separation of reason and emotion arose during the early part of the twentieth century. Just as modernists called for the reintegration of other divisions, so they called for a reintegration of reason and emotion. No less visible a modernist than T. S. Eliot believed that the problem with modern life was that "thought and emotion ceased to be coordinated activities, and human utterances became dried up or sentimental, in any case dissevered from the full complexity of experience." Southerners Allen Tate and John Crow Ransom agreed that the "dissociation of sensibility" was a fundamental problem of modern civilization. And the preeminent philosopher of the 1920s and 1930s, John Dewey, spent those years struggling to coordinate intelligence (rationality) with emotion, eventually positing what he called "passionate intelligence."[12] But when these men identified the split between reason and emotion as an artificial division that needed to be dissolved, they had little in their past to guide them. Even worse, they had to fight their own tendency to link emotion with women and the private sphere, which they sometimes claimed to be inferior.

In spite of the historical privileging of reason, the leaders of the WIL had been convinced early of the importance of emotional attachment. Simultaneously, however, these women had also been taught the virtues of rationality. Their educations had demanded rationality, as had their careers in the public realm. To some critics, their assumption of rationality had even "unsexed" them, made them "manly women." In a nation that valued the male over the female, however, it was easier to be a manly woman than it was to be a womanly man. It was one thing for a woman to aspire to the superiority assigned to men, quite another for a man willingly to embrace the inferiority assigned to women.

Paradoxically, the sexism of the United States at the turn of the century favored the women who led the WIL in this one regard: trained early in the importance of emotional attachment, they had also acquired the habits of mind associated with rationality as they battled their way into higher education and careers. Men, on the other hand, had been trained early to restrain emotionality; their educations had only reinforced that training. For men to reclaim emotion, to reintegrate it into their understanding of the world, they would have had to reclaim what they had previously dismissed as feminine. Although it was male modernists who called most loudly for the reintegration of reason and emotion, it was the women of the WIL who accomplished it, both philosophically and through their work for peace and social justice.

The philosophy of the WIL leaders has been largely invisible in traditional constructions of the Western intellectual heritage. One could suppose that this is because the philosophy was fundamentally flawed or held by only a handful of women. But what if instead this philosophy better represents the realities of many people's lives and reflects the ideas of as many people as the central philosophies of the so-called Western intellectual tradition? Gerda Lerner has suggested that "throughout the millennia of their subordination the kind of knowledge women acquired was more nearly correct and adequate than was the knowledge of men. It was knowledge not based on theoretical propositions and on works collected in books, but practical knowledge derived from essential social interaction with their families, their children, their neighbors." Lerner notes that this "thorough knowledge of how the world works and how people work within it and with each other" was often shared by "men of subordinate castes, classes and races." For the oppressed, such knowledge could ensure their survival. This knowledge was not made available to society as whole, however, "because of patriarchal hegemony and instead found expression in what we now call women's culture."[13]

If Lerner is correct, and I believe she is, then the philosophy formulated by the women who led the WIL may have much in common with the ideas of other women and oppressed groups.[14] The ideas of other historically disadvantaged groups and individuals will need to be intensively studied before any firm conclusions can be drawn, and when those studies are done, it is certain that the ideas of other groups will differ in some ways from those of the WIL leaders. But it is also likely that some ideas will be similar. Nonviolence and unity within diversity are ideas that would be beneficial to many oppressed groups; and nurturing has been central to the lives of practically all women. The feminist consciousness of the need for women to work with other women may be less common, especially

STAFFORDSHIRE
UNIVERSITY
LIBRARY

among men, but because it is consistent with the ideas of nurturing, nonviolence, and unity within diversity, it will likely appear occasionally at least.

Reconstructing the thoughts of the women who led the WIL suggests that intellectual historians have overlooked the existence of an important alternative philosophical tradition. This tradition posits the importance of nurturing and nonviolence; views humanity as united by common elements but also appreciates differences among individuals and cultures; and values the work of women, especially on behalf of other women. If this tradition is reinstated as a central component of the Western intellectual heritage, it will validate the work of those who strove for peace and social justice through the ages, encourage those who are doing this work today, and provide hope for a peaceful and harmonious future as we move together into the twenty-first century.

Reference Matter

≺ ≻

Appendix

Biographical Information on Leaders of the U.S. Section,
Women's International League for Peace and Freedom

STAFFORDSHIRE
UNIVERSITY
LIBRARY

Leader	Ethnicity	Education (with terminal date and degree if known)	Career	Religion	Leadership period
Addams (1860–1935)	European American	Rockford Female Seminary, 1882	Social reformer; writer; peace activist	Presbyterian at 25; then no open affiliation	1915–35
Balch (1867–1961)	European American	Bryn Mawr, 1889; postgrad., Harvard Annex, Univ. of Chicago, Univ. of Berlin	Professor, Wellesley; peace activist	Unitarian; Society of Friends	1915–41
Blake (1858–1950)	European American	Hunter College, 1876	Teacher; principal	Unknown	1924–41
Brainerd (1881–1969)	European American	Smith College, 1904	Latin American specialist	Unknown	1935–41
Bussey (1888–1961)	European American	Wellesley College, 1908; M.A., 1910; Northwestern Univ., Ph.D., 1915	Professor, Goucher College	Episcopalian— League for Social Action and Pacifist Fellowship	1924–41
Detzer (1893–1981)	European American	Chicago School of Civics and Philanthropy, no degree	Social reformer; peace activist, lobbyist	Unknown	1924–41
Fowler (1908–87)	European American	Bryn Mawr College, 1927; Columbia University, Ph.D.	Social reformer; labor activist	Unknown	1937–?
Gage-Colby (1899–1984)	European American	University of Minnesota; Radcliffe, A.B., n.d.	Journalist; speaker; child welfare worker	Methodist— Federation for Social Action	1932–41
Hommel (Unknown)	European American	Syracuse University, B.A., n.d.	Social reformer	Unknown	1934–41
Hull (1872–1958)	European American	Swarthmore College, B.L., 1891; Bryn Mawr, 1896–97	Peace activist	Society of Friends	1919–41

Name	Race/ethnicity	Education	Occupation	Religion	Years active
Hunton (1875–1943)	African American	Spencerian College of Commerce, 1889	Social activist for women's and African-American rights	Reared African Methodist Episcopal	c1925–37
Lewis (1861–1941)	European American	No college	Volunteer worker for humanitarian causes	Society of Friends	1915–41
Libby (1902–84)	European American	Smith College, B.A., 1925; Harvard summer study, 1928	Teacher; peace activist	Society of Friends	1935–41
Lloyd (1875–1944)	European American	Smith College, B.A., 1897	Peace activist	Unknown	1920–41
McNeill (1887–1979)	African American	Howard Univ., 1908; Catholic Univ., M.A., 1945	Teacher; professor	Church of Christ	1933–41
Martin (1875–1951)	European American	Univ. of Nevada, A.B., 1894; Stanford Univ., A.B., 1896; A.M., 1897	Professor; politician; peace activist	Unknown	1926–36
Olmsted (1890–1988)	European American	Smith College, 1912; Univ. of Pennsylvania, 1913	Social worker; peace activist	Society of Friends	1922–41
Rankin (1880–1973)	European American	Univ. of Montana, 1902; New York School of Philanthropy; University of Washington	Politician; peace activist	Unknown	1920–25
Terrell (1863–1954)	African American	Oberlin, 1894	Teacher; writer; social activist	Lincoln Temple; Congregational Church	1919–c1935
Vernon (1883–1975)	European American	Swarthmore College, 1906; Columbia Univ., A.M., 1924	Teacher; activist for women's rights, peace	Unknown	1930–35
Woods (Unknown)	European American	Boston University	Teacher; social worker	Unknown	1922–36

SOURCE: Biographical Sketches, WIL Records, SCPC Series A,1, boxes 4.1 and 4.2; and Anne Marie Pois, "The Politics of Organizing for Change: The United States Section of the Women's International League for Peace and Freedom, 1919–1939" [Ph.D. diss., University of Colorado, 1988].

≺ ≻

Notes

Depositories

LOC   Library of Congress, Manuscripts Division, Washington, D.C.
NYPL New York Public Library, Manuscripts and Archives Division, New York, N.Y.
SCPC Swarthmore College Peace Collection, Swarthmore, Penn.
SL   Schlesinger Library, Radcliffe College, Cambridge, Mass.

Introduction

1. Once political history was reconceptualized to include activity that influenced the political process, it became clear that women have been extremely active in this area. Through voluntary associations, petition campaigns, and lobbying, women have worked for causes such as temperance, abolition of slavery, extension (and sometimes limitation) of the franchise, campaign reform, municipal cleanliness and beautification, historic preservation, the rights of labor, and civil rights. Many of these endeavors are cited later in this book; for an overview of women's political activity, see Sara Evans, *Born for Liberty: A History of Women in America* (New York: Basic Books, 1989). On expanding the understanding of political activity, see Paula Baker, "The Domestication of Politics: Women and American Political Society, 1780–1920," *American Historical Review* 89 (June 1984): 620–47. On women in international politics, see Cynthia Enloe, *Bananas, Beaches, and Bases: Making Feminist Sense of International Politics* (Berkeley: University of California Press, 1990), and Edward P. Crapol, *Women and American Foreign Policy: Lobbyists, Critics, and Insiders* (New York: Greenwood Press, 1987).

2. On the history of feminism and the women's rights movement, see Nancy Cott, *The Grounding of Modern Feminism* (New Haven, Conn.: Yale University Press, 1987); Rosalind Rosenberg, *Beyond Separate Spheres: Intellectual Roots of Modern Feminism* (New Haven, Conn.: Yale University Press, 1982); William L. O'Neill, *Everyone Was Brave: The Rise and Fall of Feminism in America* (Chicago: Quadrangle, 1969); and Eleanor Flexner, *Century of Struggle: The Woman's Rights Movement in the United States* (Cambridge, Mass.: Harvard University Press, Belknap Press, 1975). On suf-

frage, see Aileen Kraditor, *The Ideas of the Woman Suffrage Movement,
1890–1920* (New York: Columbia University Press, 1965). See also Paula
Blanchard, *Margaret Fuller: From Transcendentalism to Revolution* (New
York: Delacorte Press, 1978); Bell Gale Chevigny, *The Woman and the
Myth: Margaret Fuller's Life and Writings* (Old Westbury, N.Y.: Feminist
Press, 1976); David Watson, *Margaret Fuller: An American Romantic* (New
York: St. Martin's Press, 1988); Mary A. Hill, *Charlotte Perkins Gilman: The
Making of a Radical Feminist, 1860–1896* (Philadelphia: Temple University
Press, 1980); Patricia Ann Palmieri, *In Adamless Eden: The Community of
Women Faculty at Wellesley* (New Haven, Conn.: Yale University Press,
1995); and Ann J. Lane, *To Herland and Beyond: The Life and Work of Char-
lotte Perkins Gilman* (New York: Pantheon Books, 1990). On the engender-
ing of philosophy, see Lorraine Code, *What Can She Know? Feminist Theory and the Construction of Knowledge* (Ithaca, N.Y.: Cornell University
Press, 1991); Jean Grimshaw, *Philosophy and Feminist Thinking* (Minneapolis: University of Minnesota Press, 1986); Sandra Harding and Merrill
B. Hintikka, eds., *Discovering Reality: Feminist Perspectives on Epistemol-
ogy, Metaphysics, Methodology, and Philosophy of Science* (Boston: D. Rei-
del, 1983); and Sandra Harding, *Whose Science? Whose Knowledge? Thinking from Women's Lives* (Ithaca, N.Y.: Cornell University Press, 1991).

3. Of the nine articles about women or mentioning women in the title,
two examined Mary Wollstonecraft, one looked at Christine de Pisan and
one at Simone De Beauvoir, one analyzed the treatment of women in Nietz-
sche's writings, and three discussed feminist themes or attitudes toward
women. Any analysis of women in the United States was glaringly absent.

4. David Hollinger, "American Intellectual History: Some Issues for the
1980s," in *In the American Province: Studies in the History and Historiography of Ideas* (Bloomington: Indiana University Press, 1985), p. 180.
Hollinger suggests that these assumptions have governed the choice of subjects by intellectual historians and have brought charges of elitism against
intellectual historians.

5. Jane Arscott, "Opening Up the Canon," *Journal of History and Politics* 6 (1988/89): 47–48.

6. Feminist scholars have begun to analyze women in regard to central
concepts such as republicanism, individualism, and the public; see Linda
Kerber, *Women of the Republic: Intellect and Ideology in Revolutionary
America* (Chapel Hill: University of North Carolina Press, 1980); Gillian
Brown, *Domestic Individualism: Imagining Self in Nineteenth-Century
America* (Berkeley: University of California Press, 1990); and Mary P. Ryan,
Women in Public: Between Banners and Ballots, 1825–1880 (Baltimore,
Md.: The Johns Hopkins University Press, 1990).

7. Historian Gerda Lerner recently noted the difficulty of restoring
women's ideas to the historical record: "Oppression brings with it the hegemony of the thought and ideas of the dominant; thus women's oppression
has meant that much of their mental product and creation has been lost for-

ever." See Gerda Lerner, *The Creation of Feminist Consciousness* (New York: Oxford University Press, 1993), pp. 16–17.

8. Ibid., p. 11.

9. Elizabeth Karmarck Minnich, *Transforming Knowledge* (Philadelphia: Temple University Press, 1990), p. xiii.

10. As Gerda Lerner explains, "The absence of heroines and of Women's History crippled even the most talented women or deflected their talents into less ambitious or shorter forms: poems rather than drama cycles; letters and journals rather than works of philosophy." See Lerner, *The Creation of Feminist Consciousness*, p. 179.

11. To distinguish between the U.S. section and the international organization, hereafter I use WIL for the former and WILPF for the latter. WIL leaders themselves commonly used this abbreviation throughout the interwar years. To avoid confusion, it should be noted that the New York branch of the Woman's Peace Party reorganized itself under the name the Women's International League in 1918 and used the acronym WIL briefly; it later became the New York branch of the U.S. section of the WILPF.

12. See Harriet Alonso, *Peace as a Women's Issue: A History of the U.S. Movement for World Peace and Women's Rights* (Syracuse, N.Y.: Syracuse University Press, 1993); Anne Marie Pois, "The Politics of Organizing for Change: The United States Section of the Women's International League for Peace and Freedom, 1919–1939" (Ph.D. diss., University of Colorado, 1988); and Carrie Foster, *The Women and the Warriors: The U.S. Section of the Women's International League for Peace and Freedom, 1915–1946* (Syracuse, N.Y.: Syracuse University Press, 1995).

13. The names of many other women appeared on WIL stationery as members of the National Board, especially after the board was enlarged in 1938. The ones listed here contributed regularly to annual meetings or corresponded frequently with the central core of leaders.

14. Around the time of the hundredth anniversary of Jane Addams's birth (1960), and before the rise of women's history, for example, noted historian Merle Curti explored Addams's ideas in "Jane Addams on Human Nature," *Journal of the History of Ideas* 22 (Apr.–June 1961): 240–53; and Christopher Lasch edited a volume of her works, *The Social Thought of Jane Addams* (Indianapolis, Ind.: Bobbs Merrill, 1965).

15. James to Addams, Sept. 17, 1902, in Frederick J. Down Scott, ed., *William James: Unpublished Correspondence, 1885–1910* (Columbus: Ohio State University Press, 1986), pp. 293–94.

16. James to Addams, Feb. 12, 1907, in ibid., pp. 433–34.

17. See John Nevin Sayre to Balch, Oct. 27, 1928, Emily Greene Balch Papers, SCPC, microfilm, reel 129.8, frames 76–77; Boas to Balch, May 13, 1940, Balch Papers, reel 129.11, frame 69; and John Dewey, "Emily Greene Balch—An Appraisal" [n.d.], McNeill Papers, SCPC, box 2.

18. See Pois, "The Politics of Organizing for Change," p. 229. Some of my biographical information relies on Pois's composite profile of WIL leaders,

pp. 228–33. Additional information comes from published biographical dictionaries and files on individual leaders found in WIL records; see Biographical Sketches, WIL Records, SCPC, Series A,1, boxes 4.1 and 4.2.

19. For an example of the importance of these friendships and networks, see Blanche Wiesen Cook, "Female Support Networks and Political Activism: Lillian Wald, Crystal Eastman, Emma Goldman," *Chrysalis* (Autumn 1977): 43–61.

20. See Pois, "The Politics of Organizing for Change," pp. 241, 441–42.

21. The following summary is drawn from Charles DeBenedetti, *The Peace Reform in American History* (Bloomington: Indiana University Press, 1980).

22. See Alonso, *Peace as a Women's Issue*, chap. 2.

23. See Cott, *The Grounding of Modern Feminism*, pp. 4–5; and Lerner, *The Creation of Feminist Consciousness*, p. 14.

24. This ideology has been well explicated by historians; for a recent overview of the ideology and reality of "separate spheres" for different economic classes and ethnic groups, see Evans, *Born for Liberty*, especially chaps. 4–6. See also Linda Kerber's excellent essay, "Separate Spheres, Female Worlds, Woman's Place: The Rhetoric of Women's History," *Journal of American History* 75 (June 1988): 9–39. On complementarianism, see Londa Schiebinger, *The Mind Has No Sex? Women in the Origins of Modern Science* (Cambridge, Mass.: Harvard University Press, 1989).

25. Women's activity in nineteenth-century benevolent, moral, and social reform has received ample attention from scholars. For a sample of this literature, see Ruth Bordin, *Women and Temperance: The Quest for Power and Liberty, 1873–1900* (Philadelphia: Temple University Press, 1981); Barbara Epstein, *The Politics of Domesticity: Women, Evangelism, and Temperance in Nineteenth-Century America* (Middletown, Conn.: Wesleyan University Press, 1981); Estelle B. Freedman, *Their Sisters' Keepers: Women's Prison Reform in America, 1830–1930* (Ann Arbor: University of Michigan Press, 1981); Nancy Hewitt, *Women's Activism and Social Change: Rochester, New York, 1822–1871* (Ithaca, N.Y.: Cornell University Press, 1984); Lori Ginzberg, *Women and the Work of Benevolence: Morality, Politics, and Class in the 19th-Century United States* (New Haven, Conn.: Yale University Press, 1990); Peggy Pascoe, *Relations of Rescue: The Search for Female Moral Authority in the American West, 1874–1939* (New York: Oxford University Press, 1990); and Anne Firor Scott, *Natural Allies: Women's Associations in American History* (Urbana: University of Illinois Press, 1991).

26. Daniel Joseph Singal, "Towards a Definition of Modernism," in *Modernist Culture in America*, ed. Daniel Joseph Singal (Belmont, Calif.: Wadsworth, 1991), pp. 4–5. Singal has done the best job of summarizing philosophical and cultural modernism in the United States, and the following overview relies heavily on his insights. See also his entry on modernism in Richard Wightman Fox and James T. Kloppenberg, eds., *A Companion to American Thought* (Cambridge, Mass.: Blackwell, 1995), and Singal, *The*

War Within: From Victorian to Modernist Thought in the South, 1919–1945 (Chapel Hill: University of North Carolina Press, 1982); Henry May, *The End of American Innocence: A Study of the First Years of Our Own Time, 1912–1917* (New York: Oxford University Press, 1959); Stanley Coben, *Rebellion Against Victorianism: The Impetus for Cultural Change in 1920s America* (New York: Oxford University Press, 1991); and George Cotkin, *Reluctant Modernism: American Thought and Culture, 1880–1900* (New York: Twayne, 1992). For insight into modernism by looking at its opponents, see T. J. Jackson Lears, *No Place of Grace: Antimodernism and the Transformation of American Culture, 1880–1920* (New York: Pantheon Books, 1981).

27. Singal, *The War Within*; Cotkin, *Reluctant Modernism*.

28. For interpretations of these women as advocates of women's moral superiority, see Jill Conway, "The Woman's Peace Party and the First World War," in *War and Society in North America*, ed. J. L. Granatstein and Robert D. Cuff (Toronto: Thomas Nelson, 1971); Conway, "Women Reformers and American Culture, 1870–1930," *Journal of Social History* 5 (Winter 1971–72): 164–77; William Chafe, *Women and Equality: Changing Patterns in American Culture* (New York: Oxford University Press, 1977); Barbara J. Steinson, "The Mother Half of Humanity: American Women in the Peace and Preparedness Movements in World War I," in *Women, War, and Revolution*, ed. Carol R. Berkin and Clara M. Lovett (New York: Holmes and Meier, 1980); and Steinson, *American Women's Activism in World War I* (New York: Garland, 1982).

CHAPTER I

1. This biographical sketch is drawn from Allen Davis, *American Heroine: The Life and Legend of Jane Addams* (New York: Oxford University Press, 1973).

2. Jane Addams, *Newer Ideals of Peace* (New York: Macmillan, 1916), p. viii.

3. Ibid., p. 8. Throughout this book, Addams refers to the difficulty of finding words to express her ideas.

4. Ibid., p. 25.

5. T. J. Jackson Lears identified this strain of antimodernism in *No Place of Grace: Antimodernism and the Transformation of American Culture, 1880–1920* (New York: Pantheon Books, 1981), chap. 3.

6. Addams, *Newer Ideals*, pp. 27, 210–14.

7. William James, "The Moral Equivalent of War," in *William James: The Essential Writings*, ed. Bruce W. Wilshire (New York: Harper and Row, 1971), p. 359.

8. Addams, *Newer Ideals*, pp. 25, 212.

9. Addams, *Rockford Register*, Apr. 2, 1880, quoted in Davis, *American Heroine*, pp. 19–20.

10. Addams, *Newer Ideals*, p. 183.

11. Ibid., pp. 182–86.

12. Ibid., p. 207. Addams wanted women to have the vote, but she did not believe that the vote was as important as the founders of this country had believed: "We ignore the fact that world-wide problems can no longer be solved by a political constitution assuring us against opposition, but that we must frankly face the proposition that the whole situation is more industrial than political" (p. 42).

13. Jane Addams, address to the Workingmen's Public Meeting, Oct. 5, 1904, *Official Report of the Thirteenth Universal Peace Congress* (Boston: Peace Congress Committee, 1904), p. 146.

14. Addams, *Newer Ideals*, pp. 16–17.

15. Ibid., pp. 18–19.

16. Ibid., p. 15.

17. For an overview of the pre–World War I peace movements, see Charles DeBenedetti, *The Peace Reform in American History* (Bloomington: Indiana University Press, 1980); C. Roland Marchand, *The American Peace Movement and Social Reform, 1898–1918* (Princeton, N.J.: Princeton University Press, 1972); and David S. Patterson, *Toward a Warless World: The Travail of the American Peace Movement, 1887–1914* (Bloomington: Indiana University Press, 1976).

18. James, "The Moral Equivalent of War," p. 359. For an extended comparison of the alternatives to war posed by James and Addams, see Linda Schott, "Jane Addams and William James on Alternatives to War," *Journal of the History of Ideas* (Apr. 1993): 241–54. George Cotkin pointed out the elitism of James's plan in *William James: Public Philosopher* (Baltimore, Md.: Johns Hopkins University Press, 1990), pp. 149–50.

19. Addams, *Newer Ideals*, p. 150.

20. Addams, address to the Public Meeting of Women, *Official Report of the Thirteenth Universal Peace Congress* (Boston: Peace Congress Committee, 1904), pp. 121–22.

21. Addams, *Newer Ideals*, pp. 221–22.

22. This biographical information is summarized from Mercedes M. Randall, *Improper Bostonian: Emily Greene Balch, Nobel Peace Laureate 1946* (New York: Twayne, 1964).

23. Ibid., p. 51.

24. Ibid., p. 66.

25. Ibid., p. 70.

26. Ibid., p. 73.

27. Balch to "Dear M," Jan. 2, 1893, Emily Greene Balch Papers, SCPC, microfilm, reel 129.4.

28. Addams to Balch, May 11, 1893, and Balch to Father, n.d. [c1893], Balch Papers, reel 129.4.

29. Randall, *Improper Bostonian*, pp. 86–87.

30. Balch to Father, Apr. 6, 1896, Balch Papers, reel 129.5.

31. Balch to Father, n.d. [c1896], Balch Papers, reel 129.5.

32. Balch to Father, Jan. 5, 1896, and Jan. 19, 1896, Balch Papers, reel 129.5.

33. Father to Balch, Mar. 8, 1896, Balch Papers, reel 129.5. For an intriguing analysis of how Balch's father influenced her life, see Patricia Ann Palmieri, *In Adamless Eden: The Community of Women Faculty at Wellesley* (New Haven, Conn.: Yale University Press, 1995), pp. 63–66.

34. Carl Degler, *In Search of Human Nature: The Decline and Revival of Darwinism in American Social Thought* (New York: Oxford University Press, 1991), pp. 48–49. See also George Cotkin, *Reluctant Modernism: American Thought and Culture, 1880–1900* (New York: Twayne, 1992), chap. 3.

35. Emily Greene Balch, *Our Slavic Fellow Citizens* (New York: New York Charities Publication Committee, 1910), pp. 410–12.

36. Ibid., pp. 417–18. See also Randall, *Improper Bostonian*, pp. 118–22.

37. Balch, *Our Slavic Fellow Citizens*, pp. 424–25.

38. Degler, *In Search of Human Nature*, p. 104.

39. Balch to George Sylvester Viereck, Nov. 9, 1914, Balch Papers, reel 129.5.

40. Quoted in Randall, *Improper Bostonian*, p. 127.

CHAPTER 2

1. Balch to Maidee, Aug. 8, 1914, Emily Greene Balch Papers, SCPC, microfilm, reel 129.5.

2. Catt to Addams, Dec. 14, 1914, Addams correspondence, Carrie Chapman Catt Papers, LOC, box 4.

3. For a complete analysis of Mead's life and work for peace, see John Craig, *Lucia Ames Mead (1856–1936) and the American Peace Movement* (Lewiston, N.Y.: Mellen Press, 1990).

4. Catt to Addams, Dec. 14, 1914, Addams correspondence, Catt Papers, box 4.

5. Addams to Catt, Dec. 21, 1914, Woman's Peace Party Records, SCPC, microfilm, reel 12.17 (hereafter cited as WPP Records).

6. Catt to Addams, Dec. 14, 1914, Addams correspondence, Catt Papers, box 4.

7. Harriet Alonso, *Peace as a Women's Issue: A History of the U.S. Movement for World Peace and Women's Rights* (Syracuse, N.Y.: Syracuse University Press, 1993), pp. 62–63.

8. Compiled from "Roll of Charter Members" and a list of the Co-operating Council at the Organizational Conference, Jan. 10–11, 1915, WPP Records, reel 12.17.

9. Lori Ginzberg, *Women and the Work of Benevolence: Morality, Politics, and Class in the Nineteenth-Century United States* (New Haven, Conn.: Yale University Press, 1990), chap. 6.

10. Minutes of Organizational Conference, WPP Records, box 1, folder 2, reel 12.17, p. 2.

11. Ibid., pp. 4–5.

12. Ibid., pp. 17, 19–20.

STAFFORDSHIRE
UNIVERSITY
LIBRARY

13. Ibid., p. 17.

14. Ibid., pp. 17–19.

15. Ibid., pp. 26–29.

16. Because Shaw and Addams differed on the importance of biological motherhood, I hesitate to apply the label "maternalist" to them and other founders of the Woman's Peace Party. Some of the rhetoric at the organizational conference sounds clearly maternalist while some does not. Furthermore, this rhetoric recedes in the following years. A good overview of the current historiography of maternalism can be found in a series of essays entitled "Maternalism as a Paradigm" in the *Journal of Women's History* 5 (Fall 1993): 95–131. Gerda Lerner argues that women used the concept of motherhood to advance their claims for equality much earlier than they used the concept of sisterhood. Lerner writes: "Motherhood, as fate and experience, was something women could share with other women. The rituals of motherhood involved women with one another and were dominated by female support networks, whether made up of female kin or neighbors. . . . Motherhood was then the only basis on which sisterhood could even be conceptualized." See Gerda Lerner, *The Creation of Feminist Consciousness: From the Middle Ages to Eighteen-seventy* (New York: Oxford University Press, 1993), p. 122.

17. Other historians have argued that the leaders of the Woman's Peace Party based their activities on a traditional concept of femininity that held that women were "naturally" more peaceful than men—a concept closely related to the argument for women's moral superiority used by some suffragists and women reformers. They have then criticized these women for not understanding that basing their activity on a gender-linked view of social problems undermined any possibility of true sexual equality. For this interpretation, see Jill Conway, "The Woman's Peace Party and the First World War" in *War and Society in North America*, ed. J. L. Granatstein and Robert D. Cuff (Toronto: Thomas Nelson, 1971), and "Women Reformers and American Culture, 1870–1930," *Journal of Social History* 5 (Winter 1971–72): 164–77; William Chafe, *Women and Equality: Changing Patterns in American Culture* (New York: Oxford University Press, 1977); Barbara J. Steinson, "The Mother Half of Humanity: American Women in the Peace and Preparedness Movements in World War I," in *Women, War, and Revolution*, ed. Carol R. Berkin and Clara M. Lovett (New York: Holmes and Meier, 1980). See also Steinson, *American Women's Activism in World War I* (New York: Garland, 1982). One speaker at the WPP organizational conference, Janet E. Richards, stated that "woman is naturally constructive, not destructive." Richards later decided to support U.S. involvement in World War I; she did not remain active in the Woman's Peace Party. For her comments, see the Minutes of Organizational Conference, WPP Records, box 1, folder 2, reel 12.17, p. 23.

18. Minutes of Organizational Conference, WPP Records, pp. 29, 27.

19. Ibid., pp. 13–14. Many people would not have agreed with Schwimmer. Antisuffragists often argued that if women voted disruptive minorities

would know that half the electorate could not enforce its vote; chaos and upheaval would result. See Aileen Kraditor, *The Ideas of the Woman Suffrage Movement, 1890–1920* (New York: Columbia University Press, 1965), pp. 28–29.

20. Preamble, reprinted in Marie L. Degen, *The History of the Woman's Peace Party* (Baltimore, Md.: Johns Hopkins Press, 1939), pp. 40–41.

21. Ibid.

22. Historian Molly Ladd-Taylor characterizes "maternalists" as believing that "women were united across class, race, and nation by their common capacity for motherhood and therefore shared a responsibility for all the world's children." The statements made by the founders of the Woman's Peace Party are similar to this position, but they are not the same. The founders of the WPP emphasized not women's common capacity for motherhood but the ways in which society made women responsible for the care of children. See Ladd-Taylor's essay, "Toward Defining Maternalism in U.S. History," *Journal of Women's History* 5 (Fall 1993): 110–13.

23. Cynthia Eagle Russett, *Sexual Science: The Victorian Construction of Womanhood* (Cambridge, Mass.: Harvard University Press, 1989), pp. 6–7, 4.

24. Much of the following discussion draws on the work of Elizabeth Fee, "Science and the Woman Problem: Historical Perspectives," in *Sex Differences*, ed. Michael C. Teitelbaum (New York: Anchor Books, 1976), pp. 180–220; Russett, *Sexual Science*; and Carl Degler, *In Search of Human Nature: The Decline and Revival of Darwinism in American Social Thought* (New York: Oxford University Press, 1991).

25. Frank Fernseed, "Sexual Distinctions and Resemblances," *Quarterly Journal of Science* 3 (1881): 744.

26. Useful information on Geddes can be found in Philip Boardman, *The Worlds of Patrick Geddes: Biologist, Town Planner, Re-Educator, Peace Warrior* (London: Routledge and Kegan Paul, 1978), and in Philip Mairet, *Pioneer of Sociology: The Life and Letters of Patrick Geddes* (Westport, Conn.: Hyperion Press, 1979).

27. Patrick Geddes and J. Arthur Thomson, *The Evolution of Sex* (London, 1889), pp. 270–71. This book has been considered by historians to be the work that most influenced women's conception of themselves as more committed to peace than men. See particularly Jill Conway, "Stereotypes of Femininity in a Theory of Sexual Evolution," *Victorian Studies* 14 (Sept. 1970): 47–62. Feminist theorist Charlotte Perkins Stetson Gilman held a similar understanding of sex differences. Gilman participated in the Woman's Peace Party initially but later supported President Wilson's decision to intervene in World War I. See Charlotte Perkins Stetson Gilman, *The Man-Made World or Our Androcentric Culture* (1911; reprint, New York: Source Book Press, 1970).

28. Geddes and Thomson, *The Evolution of Sex*, pp. 270–71.

29. Ibid., pp. 270, 280–81.

30. For an excellent analysis of the theory of sexual complementarity in western Europe, see Londa Schiebinger, *The Mind Has No Sex? Women in*

the Origins of Modern Science (Cambridge, Mass.: Harvard University Press, 1989), pp. 217–44.

31. Rosalind Rosenberg, *Beyond Separate Spheres: Intellectual Roots of Modern Feminism* (New Haven, Conn.: Yale University Press, 1982), pp. 120–23.

32. Ibid., pp. 123–27.

33. Helen B. Thompson, *The Mental Traits of Sex* (Chicago: University of Chicago Press, 1908), pp. 172–74. Thompson was also criticizing the work of G. T. W. Patrick, W. K. Brooks, and Havelock Ellis. See Rosenberg, *Beyond Separate Spheres*, pp. 70–71.

34. Thompson, *The Mental Traits of Sex*, pp. 181–82.

35. See also Helen B. Thompson, "A Review of the Recent Literature on the Psychology of Sex," *Psychological Bulletin* 7 (Oct. 1910): 335–42; and Helen B. Thompson Woolley, "The Psychology of Sex," *Psychological Bulletin* 11 (Oct. 1914): 353–79.

36. See Degler, *In Search of Human Nature*, pp. 113–14.

37. Mary W. Calkins, "Community of Ideas of Men and Women," *Psychological Review* 3 (July 1896): 430; quoted in Degler, *In Search of Human Nature*, p. 114.

38. Amy Tanner, "The Community of Ideas of Men and Women," *Psychological Review* 3 (July 1896): 549–50; quoted in Degler, *In Search of Human Nature*, p. 114.

39. Helen Thompson Woolley, "A Review of the Recent Literature on the Psychology of Sex," *Psychological Bulletin* 7 (Oct. 1910): 341–42; quoted in Russett, *Sexual Science*, pp. 173–74.

40. An exception was William I. Thomas, who had begun to doubt the existence of any identifiable differences. See Rosenberg, *Beyond Separate Spheres*, p. 129, and Degler, *In Search of Human Nature*, p. 119.

41. On Addams's connections to the University of Chicago, see Mary Jo Deegan, *Jane Addams and the Men of the Chicago School, 1892–1918* (New Brunswick, N.J.: Transaction Books, 1988); and Kathryn Kish Sklar, *Florence Kelley and the Nation's Work: The Rise of Women's Political Culture, 1980–1900* (New Haven, Conn.: Yale University Press, 1995), chap. 8. Balch's ties to other Wellesley faculty members as well as her personal ties to Calkins are illustrated throughout Palmieri, *In Adamless Eden*.

42 See Degler, *In Search of Human Nature*, chaps. 3, 4, and 7.

43. Minutes of Organizational Conference, WPP Records, box 1, folder 2, reel 12.17, p. 1. Working against racism became an important part of the WIL program in the 1930s; this is examined in Chapter 6.

CHAPTER 3

1. Marie L. Degen, *The History of the Woman's Peace Party* (Baltimore, Md.: Johns Hopkins Press, 1939), p. 41.

2. Addams to Hememway, Jan. 30, 1915, Minutes of Executive Council,

Woman's Peace Party Records, SCPC, microfilm, reel 12.18 (hereafter cited as WPP Records).

3. Platform of New Jersey branch; and Statement of Purpose and Platform, Connecticut branch, WPP Records, reel 12.20.

4. Mrs. Robert C. Hogan to Susan R. Cutts, June 18, 1915, and Minutes of Summer Campaign Committee, June 23, 1915, Correspondence of Washington, D.C., branch, WPP Records, reel 12.20.

5. Minutes of Session 1 of Annual Meeting, 1916, WPP Records, reel 12.17, pp. 28–52.

6. Whitney to Mead, Nov. 20, 1917, WPP Records, reel 12.17.

7. Catt to Addams, Jan. 4, 1915, Catt Papers, LOC, box 4. See also Robert Booth Fowler, *Carrie Catt: Feminist Politician* (Boston, Mass.: Northeastern University Press, 1986), p. 139, and C. Roland Marchand, *The American Peace Movement and Social Reform, 1898–1918* (Princeton, N.J.: Princeton University Press, 1972), chap. 6.

8. Catt to Addams, Jan. 4, 1915, Catt Papers, box 4.

9. Catt to Addams, Nov. 12, 1915, Catt Papers, box 4.

10. Minutes of Executive Board Meeting, Feb. 21, 1917, WPP Records, reel 12.18.

11. Quoted in Mary Gray Peck, *Carrie Chapman Catt, a Biography* (New York: H. W. Wilson, 1941), pp. 267–68. Historian Christine Lunardini believes that although the NAWSA planned to maintain suffrage as its primary goal, events soon demonstrated that it would be impossible to do that and also support the government's war measures. See Christine Lunardini, *From Equal Suffrage to Equal Rights: Alice Paul and the National Woman's Party, 1912–1928* (New York: New York University Press, 1986), pp. 112–13.

12. Fowler, *Carrie Catt*, p. 139.

13. This issue also caused problems for the Women's International League for Peace and Freedom in the 1920s; see Chapter 4. See also Fowler, *Carrie Catt*, pp. 139–40.

14. Roe to Catt, Feb. 25, 1917, Gwyneth King Roe Papers, State Historical Society of Wisconsin, Madison, Wisc., box 6, folder 16.

15. Roe to Belle LaFollette, Dec. 1927, LaFollette Family Papers, LOC, Series D, box 20. Catt and NAWSA were not the only voices speaking for women's suffrage. The National Woman's Party, which had developed out of the Congressional Union and patterned itself after the militant suffragists in England, also had to decide whether to support the government if war was declared. Unlike the NAWSA, the NWP decided to maintain its focus on suffrage only. Because of this decision, no serious conflict developed between the WPP and the NWP, and their leaders worked together more easily in the following decade. See Lunardini, *From Equal Suffrage to Equal Rights*, pp. 110–11.

16. Transcript of oral interview with John C. Board, Aug. 29–30, 1963, Jeannette Rankin Papers, SL, reel 79.11, pp. 29–30.

17. Alice Paul, *Conversations with Alice Paul: Woman Suffrage and the*

Equal Rights Amendment, Suffragists Oral History Project (Berkeley: University of California, Bancroft Library, 1976), p. 175.

18. Minutes of Pennsylvania Branch, Apr. 9, 1917, WPP Records, reel 12.20.

19. Lane to Kate Reely, Apr. 7, 1917, New York WPP correspondence on *Four Lights,* WPP Records, reel 12.21.

20. Interview with John C. Board, Rankin Papers, p. 1.

21. See Charles Chatfield, *For Peace and Justice: Pacifism in America, 1914–1941* (Knoxville: University of Tennessee Press, 1971), p. 7.

22. See Harriet Alonso, *The Women's Peace Union and the Outlawry of War, 1921–1942* (Knoxville: University of Tennessee Press, 1989), pp. 2–6. See also Charles DeBenedetti, *The Peace Reform in American History* (Bloomington: Indiana University Press, 1980), p. 41.

23. For more information on the LEP, see Chatfield, *For Peace and Justice,* pp. 10–11, and DeBenedetti, *Peace Reform in American History,* pp. 92–93.

24. Minutes of Executive and State Chair Meeting, Nov. 19–20, 1915, WPP Records, reel 12.18.

25. Minutes of Session 3 of Annual Meeting, Jan. 9, 1916, WPP Records, reel 12.17.

26. Minutes of Session 4 of Annual Meeting, Jan. 9, 1916, WPP Records, reel 12.17.

27. For a good overview of Dewey's views on pacifism and World War I, see Steven C. Rockefeller, *John Dewey: Religious Faith and Democratic Humanism* (New York: Columbia University Press, 1991), esp. chap. 6; and Robert B. Westbrook, *John Dewey and American Democracy* (Ithaca, N.Y.: Cornell University Press, 1991), esp. chaps. 7 and 8.

28. Emily Greene Balch, "The Great Solution," in *Beyond Nationalism: The Social Thought of Emily Greene Balch,* ed. Mercedes M. Randall (New York: Twayne, 1972), pp. 221–22.

29. Ibid.

30. See Westbrook, *John Dewey and American Democracy,* p. 270, and Rockefeller, *John Dewey,* p. 310.

31. See Chatfield, *For Peace and Justice,* pp. 63–64. Chatfield credits Holmes with contributing to pacifism in wartime the "argument that violence would result in violence; that the means would determine the end; and that, therefore, fighting could not fulfill the high ideals of patriots" (p. 65). Balch appears to have developed these insights before Holmes, and thus the credit for this contribution to pacifist theory should go to her instead.

32. Dewey and Balch knew each other and moved in the same circle of social reformers in New York; furthermore, they were both good friends of Addams. It seems almost impossible, then, that they did not discuss these issues, but I found no record of such discussion in Balch's papers or in any of the secondary works on Dewey. I also found no correspondence between Balch and Holmes, but they too moved in the same circle of social reformers in New York.

33. "The Newer Preparedness," Mar. 3, 1916, Records of the Massachusetts branch, WPP Records, reel 12.22.

34. "Minimum Statement," Nov. 27, 1917, Records of the Massachusetts Branch, WPP Records, reel 12.22.

35. For a more detailed analysis of the positions taken by these organizations, see Chatfield, *For Peace and Justice*, pp. 9–11.

36. "On War Work," Report at Executive and State Chair Meeting, Nov. 19–20, 1915, WPP Records, reel 12.18.

37. Shelley to Florence, May 19, 1917, Rebecca Shelley Papers, Correspondence 1917, Michigan Historical Collections, Bentley Historical Library, University of Michigan, Ann Arbor, Mich., box 1.

38. Balch to President Ellen Pendleton, Apr. 3, 1918, Emily Greene Balch Papers, SCPC, microfilm, reel 129.6.

39. Mead to State Chairs, Apr. 6, 1917, WPP Records, reel 12.18.

40. For comments on this last point, see Minutes of Session 3 of Annual Meeting, 1916, WPP Records, reel 12.17.

41. Ibid.

42. Ibid. See also Forbes, "The Peace Movement and Some Misconceptions," 1915–17, WPP Records, reel 12.17.

43. Committee on Civilian Relief to members of the Massachusetts branch of the WPP, Apr. 20, 1917, WPP Records, reel 12.22.

44. Eastman to the International Committee of Women for Permanent Peace, Apr. 22, 1919, New York branch releases, WPP Records, reel 12.21. In June 1917, the New York branch had urged its members to proclaim themselves as conscientious objectors to "either direct or indirect war service." See press release, June 11, 1917, New York branch, WPP Records, reel 12.21.

45. Diary, June 8, 1917, Ada Lois James Papers, State Historical Society of Wisconsin, Madison, Wisc., box 28, folder 2.

46. Gale to Addams, June 16, 1917, Zona Gale Papers, Correspondence A, State Historical Society of Wisconsin, Madison, Wisc., box 1.

47. For a more detailed description of Addams's activities during the war and the public response to them, see Allen Davis, *American Heroine: The Life and Legend of Jane Addams* (New York: Oxford University Press, 1973), chap. 13.

48. Minutes of Executive Board Meeting, Oct. 25, 1917, WPP Records, reel 12.18.

49. In 1917 the WPP had 166 branches and estimated that each branch had 150 members; that seems a generous estimation. See the Annual Report on Membership, 1916–1917, National Office Secretary Reports, WPP Records, reel 12.18. See also Anne Marie Pois, "The Politics of Organizing for Change: The United States Section of the Women's International League for Peace and Freedom, 1919–1939" (Ph.D. diss., University of Colorado, 1988), p. 96.

50. See Davis, *American Heroine*, chaps. 13 and 14.

51. Addams, *Peace and Bread in Time of War*, excerpted in Christopher

Lasch, *The Social Thought of Jane Addams* (New York: Bobbs-Merrill, 1965), pp. 232–33. In *The Second Twenty Years at Hull House* (New York: Macmillan, 1930), Addams notes that suffrage leaders believed that women gained the vote because of their support of the war. Perhaps in an effort to defend her own position and to cast doubt on the policy of the NAWSA, Addams added: "It has, however, always been true that a change in woman's status has been a by-product of war and that every nation after a war has used woman's strength to recover economic losses as quickly as possible and to help rebuild what war had torn down," pp. 103–4.

52. Addams, *Peace and Bread*, excerpted in Lasch, *Social Thought of Jane Addams*, pp. 239, 246.

53. Balch, "Working for Peace," in Randall, ed., *Beyond Nationalism*, p. 80.

54. For a description of Balch's dismissal and the response of her colleagues and friends, see Randall, *Improper Bostonian*, pp. 246–57; and Patricia Ann Palmieri, *In Adamless Eden: The Community of Women Faculty at Wellesley* (New Haven, Conn.: Yale University Press, 1995), pp. 238–44. Other similar cases attracted far more attention than Balch's: Columbia University dismissed James McKeen Cattell and Henry Wadsworth Longfellow Dana. On the events at Columbia, see Carol Gruber, *Mars and Minerva* (Baton Rouge: Louisiana State University Press, 1975), pp. 187–212; and William Summerscales, *Affirmation and Dissent: Columbia's Response to the Crisis of World War I* (New York: Teachers College Press, 1970).

55. John Craig, *Lucia Ames Mead (1856–1936) and the American Peace Movement* (Lewiston, N.Y.: Mellen Press, 1990), pp. 144–45. Mead believed that American involvement in the war was justified and found attractive Dewey's arguments about using the war to accomplish social change at home. She did not, however, resign from her position as the national secretary of the WPP, so she must have felt some commitment to its program. In the 1920s she transferred her allegiance to the National Council for Prevention of War.

CHAPTER 4

1. For an overview of this congress, see Harriet Hyman Alonso, *Peace as a Women's Issue: A History of the U.S. Movement for World Peace and Women's Rights* (Syracuse, N.Y.: Syracuse University Press, 1993), pp. 81–83.

2. "Shall We Change the Name?" New York City branch, 1918, Woman's Peace Party Records, SCPC, microfilm, reel 12.21. This proposal was signed by Balch, Katherine Devereaux Blake, Dorothy G. Dana, Marilyn Ware Dennett, Madeleine Z. Doty, Crystal Eastman, Emily L. Eaton, Agnes Brown Leach, and Florence Guertin Tuttle.

3. Ibid. Their statement was signed by Laura G. Collins, Jessie Wallace Hughan, Theresa Malkiel, and Lucy Watson.

4. Resignation letter, Sept. 12, 1919, New York WIL, WPP Records, reel

12.21. The women who resigned were Fanny Garrison Villard, Elinor Byrns, Katherine Devereaux Blake, Mary Ware Dennett, Lucy Watson, Rose Hicks, Edna Kearns, Caroline Lexow Babcock, and Gratia Gollar.

5. For an overview of the organization of the WPS, see Harriet Hyman Alonso, *The Women's Peace Union and the Outlawry of War, 1921–1942* (Knoxville: University of Tennessee Press, 1989), pp. 9–15.

6. Balch to Villard, Apr. 1, 1920, Emily Greene Balch Papers, SCPC, microfilm, reel 129.7.

7. Balch to Addams, Sept. 28, 1920, Jane Addams Papers, SCPC, microfilm, reel 1.6.

8. Ibid. Balch enclosed the Palo Alto pledge in her letter to Addams.

9. Minutes, Apr. 29, 1922, Women's International League for Peace and Freedom, United States Section Records, SCPC, microfilm, reel 100.6 (hereafter cited as WIL Records).

10. Villard to Anna Melissa Graves, May 5, 1923, Anna Melissa Graves Papers, SCPC, microfilm, reel 74.2.

11. The following discussion of this issue is condensed from Alonso, *Women's Peace Union*, pp. 14–20.

12. Quoted in ibid., p. 19.

13. See the lists of people testifying on behalf of the WPU amendment in ibid., pp. 187–88.

14. Balch to Anna Garlin Spencer, Dec. 31, 1919, Balch Papers, reel 129.6. Anne Marie Pois sees Balch's advocacy of "unity within diversity" as one of the fundamental bases of the WIL. See Pois, "The Politics of Organizing for Change: The United States Section of the Women's International League for Peace and Freedom, 1919–1939" (Ph.D. diss., University of Colorado, 1988), pp. 111–12.

15. Minutes of National Board Meeting, Nov. 4–5, 1923, WIL Records, reel 100.6.

16. Resolutions Offered, Apr. 1920, WIL Records, reel 100.6.

17. Minutes of Executive Board Meeting, Nov. 5, 1920, WIL Records, reel 100.6; Annual Report, 1921, WIL Records, reel 100.6.

18. Alice Paul, *Conversations with Alice Paul: Woman Suffrage and the Equal Rights Amendment*, Suffragists Oral History Project (Berkeley: University of California, Bancroft Library, 1976), p. 405; Annual Report, 1921, WIL Records, reel 100.6.

19. See Charles Chatfield, *For Peace and Justice: Pacifism in America, 1914–1941* (Knoxville: University of Tennessee Press, 1971), p. 147.

20. Report of Executive Secretary, Aug.–Sept. 1921, WIL Records, reel 100.7.

21. Resolution, 1922, WIL Records, reel 100.6; Notes of Flora B. Surles taken at Meeting of WIL Secretaries, Oct. 9, 1923, WIL Records, reel 100.6.

22. Resolutions passed at Annual Meeting, Mar. 14–16, 1923, WIL Records, reel 100.6. In 1921 the WIL had begun trying to organize women on college campuses, and in 1923 it gave its support to the development of Junior International Leagues. This work was coordinated by Rachel Davis-

Dubois and enlisted the assistance of the Young Friends' Movement, the Fellowship of Reconciliation, the Young People's Socialist Leagues, and the National Student Forum. See Report of the Executive Secretary, Apr. 1921; Minutes of National Board Meeting, Mar. 13–16, 1923; and Final Report of Office and Field Work for the Junior International League, 1923, WIL Records, reel 100.6.

23. Detzer to Hannah Clothier Hull, 1925, Hannah Clothier Hull Papers, SCPC, microfilm, reel 75.1.

24. Moore to Amy Woods, Aug. 26, 1924; Mead to Hull, Sept. 16, 1924; Moore to Woods, Sept. 20, 1924; Moore to Executive Committee of WIL, Nov. 20, 1924; Moore to Hull, Dec. 6, 1924, Hull Papers, reel 75.5. For an overview of this incident, see Nancy Cott, *The Grounding of Modern Feminism* (New Haven, Conn.: Yale University Press, 1987), pp. 254–56.

25. For a good overview of this episode, see Allen F. Davis, *American Heroine: The Life and Legend of Jane Addams* (New York: Oxford University Press, 1973), pp. 260–69.

26. For more information on how charges of communist affiliation affected women's organizations in the 1920s, see Joan M. Jensen, "All Pink Sisters: The War Department and the Feminist Movement in the 1920s," in *Decades of Discontent: The Women's Movement, 1920–1940*, ed. Lois Scharf and Joan M. Jensen (Westport, Conn.: Greenwood Press, 1983), pp. 199–222. See also Cott, *The Grounding of Modern Feminism*, p. 260. For specific examples of charges against the WIL, see R. M. Whitney, *Peace at Any Old Price* (New York: Backwith Press, 1923), Hull Papers, reel 75.5; and Walsh to Balch, Nov. 21, 1924, Hull Papers, reel 75.5.

27. Hull to Moore, Dec. 16, 1924, Hull Papers, reel 75.5.

28. Addams to Hull, Dec. 31, 1924, Hull Papers, reel 75.5.

29. Hull to Addams and Balch, Jan. 21, 1925, Hull papers, reel 75.4.

30. Hull to Moore, Jan. 19, 1925, Hull papers, reel 75.5. The WIL rejoined the National Council of Women in 1929, on the condition that the WIL would not have to change its policies and programs or raise money for the National Council. See National President to Dr. Valerie H. Parker, May 9, 1929, WIL Records, Series C, reel 130.44. Dorothy Detzer told Laura Puffer Morgan of the National Council for Prevention of War that the WIL rejoined the National Council of Women "to be magnanimous and . . . to clear our reputation of being outside the pale in any degree." See Detzer to Morgan, Dec. 10, 1930, WIL Records, series C, reel 130.53.

31. Catt, "The Problem Stated," mss., 1924, p. 13, Carrie Chapman Catt Papers, NYPL, box 5, folder 15.

32. Catt to Allen, Dec. 28, 1923, Catt Papers, box 1, folder 2.

33. Hull to Addams and Balch, Jan. 21, 1925, Hull Papers, reel 75.4.

34. Hamilton to "Dearest Lady" [Jane Addams], Jan. 24, 1925, Addams Papers, reel 1.9.

35. Abbott to Addams, Feb. 8, 1925, Addams Papers, reel 1.8.

36. Quoted in Detzer to Addams, Hull, and Balch, May 19, 1927, Addams Papers, reel 1.11.

37. Catt to Hull, Jan. 30, 1925, Hull Papers, reel 75.5.

38. WIL executive secretary Dorothy Detzer and Frederick Libby were close colleagues who tried to coordinate the efforts of their two organizations whenever possible. Libby evidently reported this conversation to Detzer, who related it to Addams, Hull, and Balch, May 19, 1927, Addams Papers, reel 1.11. For more information on the NCCCW, see Schott, "'Middle-of-the-Road' Activists: Carrie Chapman Catt and the National Committee on the Cause and Cure of War," *Peace and Change: A Journal of Peace Research* (Jan. 1996): 1–21; and Suzan Zeiger, "Finding a Cure for War: Women's Politics and the Peace Movement in the 1920s," *Journal of Social History* (Fall 1990): 69–86.

39. In *The Grounding of Modern Feminism,* Nancy Cott pointed out this change in usage in the early twentieth century; the singular "woman's movement" gave way to "women's movement" and "feminism"; see pp. 3–9.

40. Annual Report, appended to Minutes of Annual Meeting, Apr. 28–30, 1922, WIL Records, reel 100.6; quoted in Pois, "Politics of Organizing for Change," p. 112.

CHAPTER 5

1. Detzer, Report to the National Board, Oct. 18, 1941,Women's International League for Peace and Freedom, United States Section Records, SCPC, microfilm, reel 100.14, p. 3 (hereafter cited as WIL Records).

2. Jane Addams, *The World's Food and World Politics* (National Conference of Social Work, 1918), p. 6.

3. Jane Addams, *Peace and Bread in Time of War* (1922; reprint, New York: King's Crown Press, 1945), p. 81. Addams made a similar observation in *The Second Twenty Years at Hull House* (New York: Macmillan, 1930), noting that women had often been brought into political involvement through club work (pp. 95–96).

4. It is interesting to note that Cynthia Enloe, in her book *Bananas, Beaches and Bases: Making Feminist Sense of International Politics* (Berkeley: University of California Press, 1990), criticizes activists who exhort women to learn more about world affairs. She argues that these activists "are not inviting women to reinterpret international politics by drawing on their own experiences as women." She believes that "if women are asked to join an international campaign . . . but are not allowed to define the problem, it looks to many locally engaged women like abstract do-gooding with minimal connection to the battles for a decent life in their households and in their communities" (p. 15). Addams did in 1922 what Enloe calls for today.

5. See Josephine Donovan, *Feminist Theory: The Intellectual Traditions of American Feminism* (New York: F. Ungar, 1985), chap. 1; and Linda Kerber, *Women of the Republic: Intellect and Ideology in Revolutionary America* (Chapel Hill: University of North Carolina Press, 1980), chap. 1. For an

exploration of women's public roles in the nineteenth century, see Mary P. Ryan, *Women in Public: Between Banners and Ballots, 1825–1880* (Baltimore, Md.: Johns Hopkins University Press, 1990).

6. Addams, *Peace and Bread*, pp. 80–81.

7. Katherine Devereaux Blake, Hearing Before the Subcommittee of the Judiciary Committee on SJR 100, Jan. 22, 1927, Women's Peace Union Records, SCPC, microfilm, reel 88.1. Blake testified as a representative of the WPU, but she was serving on the WIL national board and in subsequent years testified as a representative of the WIL.

8. Minutes of National Board Meeting, Jan. 13–15, 1934, WIL Records, reel 100.8, p. 9.

9. Resolutions on Food, Annual Meeting, May 1–4, 1941, WIL Records, reel 100.11.

10. Report of the National President, Annual Meeting, May 1–4, 1941, WIL Records, reel 100.14, p. 1.

11. Balch, "Economic Imperialism with Special Reference to the United States," reprinted in *Beyond Nationalism: The Social Thought of Emily Greene Balch*, ed. Mercedes M. Randall (New York: Twayne, 1972), p. 143.

12. Hull to Eleanor Morton, Oct. 15,1935, Hannah Clothier Hull Papers, SCPC, microfilm, reel 75.2.

13. Detzer, Report of the Fifth Congress of the WILPF, July 8–15, 1926, Rosika Schwimmer and Lola Maverick Lloyd Papers, NYPL, p. 100.

14. Detzer, "Women and War" [1930s], Dorothy Detzer Papers, Speeches and Releases 1931–40, SCPC, box 1.

15. Hull and Detzer to Roosevelt, Aug. 15, 1936, Hull Papers, reel 75.3.

16. Blake to Hull, Apr. 19, 1938, Hull Papers, reel 75.4.

17. Quoted in "The Nurse and World Peace," editorial in *The Trained Nurse and Hospital Review* (May 1924), Addams Papers, Series 3, box 7.

18. See Crystal Eastman, "To Make War Unthinkable," reprinted in *Crystal Eastman on Women and Revolution*, ed. Blanche Wiesen Cook (New York: Oxford University Press, 1978), pp. 235–37. The revived women's movement of the 1970s and 1980s also emphasized the connection between means and ends; see Jean Grimshaw, *Philosophy and Feminist Thinking* (Minneapolis: University of Minnesota Press, 1986), p. 220, and Donovan, *Feminist Theory*, chap. 3.

19. Balch to Mrs. Cousins, July 31, 1930, Balch Papers, reel 129.8.

20. Balch, "Working for Peace," reprinted in Randall, ed., *Beyond Nationalism*, pp. 77–82.

21. Balch, "A Sketch of Jane Addams' Work for Peace," reprinted in ibid., pp. 208–10. Historian Sondra Herman pointed out Addams's concern for method in *Eleven Against the War: Studies in American Internationalism, 1898–1921* (Stanford, Calif.: Hoover Institution Press, 1969), p. 149.

22. Radio Speech, 1937, Jeannette Rankin Papers, SL, microfilm, reel 78.3; and Transcript of Oral Interview with John C. Board, Aug. 29–30, 1963, Rankin Papers, reel 79.11.

23. Quoted in Charles Chatfield, *For Peace and Justice: Pacifism in*

America, 1914–1941 (Knoxville: University of Tennessee Press), p. 60. Chatfield analyzes the pacifist understanding of the means and ends in chap. 2.

24. Detzer, Radio Address, 1931, Speeches and Releases, 1931–1941, Detzer papers, box 1.

25. Balch to Bertha Mallett, Mar. 14, 1938, Hull Papers, reel 75.5.

26. Bussey to Robert Allen, Jan. 27, 1941, Balch Papers, reel 129.11.

27. Detzer, Interview with Rosemary Rainbolt, June 28, 1974, Detzer Papers, Series 1, box 1, pp. 16–17.

28. See Anne Marie Pois, "The Politics of Organizing for Change: The United States Section of the Women's International League for Peace and Freedom, 1919–1939" (Ph.D. diss., University of Colorado, 1988), pp. 97, 240.

29. Eastman, "Limitation of Armaments," Minutes of Mass Meeting, Jan. 9, 1916, Woman's Peace Party Records, SCPC, microfilm, reel 12.17. See also "A Message to the American People," Minutes of Organizational Conference, Jan. 10–11, 1915, ibid.

30. Statement of Policies Accepted at Annual Meeting, Apr. 24–27, 1929, *Pax International* 4 (June 1929), WIL Records, Series A,2, box 2, folder 6.

31. Katherine Devereaux Blake, Hearing Before the Subcommittee of the Judiciary Committee on SJR 45 (Frazier Amendment), Apr. 12, 1930, p. 48, Women's Peace Union Records, SCPC, microfilm, reel 88.1.

32. For a complete description of this and other disarmament campaigns in the 1930s, see Chatfield, *For Peace and Justice*, chap. 6.

33. Hull to Addams, May 1, 1932, pp. 2–4, Addams Papers, reel 1.15.

34. Addams, Interview with Jim Hard, National Broadcasting Company, June 5, 1932, Balch Papers, reel 129.3. See also Chatfield, *For Peace and Justice*, p. 166.

35. Resolutions Adopted at Annual Convention, May 21, 1933, WIL Records, reel 100.8.

36. Chatfield, *For Peace and Justice*, p. 165.

37. Minutes of National Board Meeting, Nov. 4–5, 1923, WIL Records, reel 100.6.

38. "Statement of Mrs. Hannah Clothier Hull at The White House," May 20, 1933, Hull Papers, reel 75.2.

39. Balch, Tentative Draft, "Policies and Principles, 1934–35," 1933, WIL Records, Series A,2, box 3, folder 4.

40. Detzer to Hull, Aug. 5, 1936, Hull Papers, reel 75.3.

41. Hull to Lloyd, Aug. 15, 1936, Hull Papers, reel 75.3.

42. Principles and Policies Proposed at the Annual Meeting, May 1–4, 1941, WIL Records, Series A,2, box 10, folder 3.

43. For a comprehensive overview of the WPU and its work for this amendment, see Harriet Hyman Alonso, *The Women's Peace Union and the Outlawry of War, 1921–1942* (Knoxville: University of Tennessee Press, 1989).

44. Detzer to Balch, May 29, 1925, Balch Papers, reel 129.7.

45. Mead to Addams, Apr. 29, 1926, Addams Papers, reel 1.10.

46. Blake to Balch, June 9, 1930, Balch Papers, reel 129.8.

47. See Addams to the *Christian Science Monitor*, Aug. 1928, Addams Papers, reel 1.12; and Resolution, National Board Meeting, Dec. 4, 1928, WIL Records, reel 100.7.

48. Balch to Madame Branko, Belgrade, Jan. 22, 1929, Balch Papers, reel 129.8.

49. The most thorough study of the Kellogg-Briand Pact is Robert H. Ferrell, *Peace in Their Time: The Origins of the Kellogg-Briand Pact* (New Haven, Conn.: Yale University Press, 1952). Ferrell analyzed the pact as "the peculiar result of some very shrewd diplomacy and some very unsophisticated popular enthusiasm for peace." He suggested that these origins illustrate the grave problems involved in a democracy's inevitable interaction of foreign policy and public opinion. Ferrell expressed the hope that the American public had become "truly sophisticated" and would support unwaveringly a "realistic" foreign policy (pp. 263–65). Looking back through the lenses of Vietnam and the Cold War, Ferrell's statements themselves seem naive and elitist.

50. Minutes of National Board Meeting, Jan. 15–16, 1938, WIL Records, reel 100.10, p. 6. The WIL had endorsed the general idea of a war referendum in 1935; see Minutes of National Board Meeting, Jan. 19–20, 1935, WIL Records, reel 100.9, p. 6.

51. Hull to Mrs. James W. Elliot, Nov. 20, 1925, Hull Papers, reel 75.1.

52. Balch to WIL Members, Apr. 1927, WIL Records, reel 100.6. Conservative opponents to the league also wanted the United States to be free from the obligation to use military force; their reasons, of course, were very different from those of the WIL.

53. Balch to Addams, Feb. 24, 1932, Addams Papers, reel 1.14.

54. Minutes of Annual Meeting, Mar. 4, 1932, WIL Records, reel 100.8, p. 10.

55. Statement on Sanctions, Mar. 19–20, 1933, Minutes of National Board Meeting, WIL Records, reel 100.8.

56. Hull to Mary, Apr. 22, 1936, Hull Papers, reel 75.3.

57. Hull to Balch, Dec. 30, 1937, Hull Papers, reel 75.3.

58. Olmsted to Balch, Sept. 9, 1937, Mildred Scott Olmsted Papers, Peace Collection, Swarthmore College, Swarthmore, Penn., Correspondence 1930, Series II, box I.

59. See Chatfield, *For Peace and Justice*, pp. 230–31.

60. Detzer to Balch, Jan. 22, 1936, Balch Papers, reel 129.9.

61. Balch to Olmsted, Sept. 3, 1937, Balch Papers, reel 129.10.

62. Balch to Baer, Mar. 1938, Balch Papers, reel 129.10.

63. Hull to the editor of the *New York Times*, Oct. 8, 1937, Hull Papers, reel 75.3.

64. Hull to Balch, Feb. 7, 1938, Hull Papers, reel 75.3.

65. See Pois, "Politics of Organizing for Change," pp. 464–66. Part of the reason for this emphasis was that the WIL was now out of step with the

WILPF, which supported the condemnation of aggressor states. See Hull to Blake, July 20, 1938, Hull Papers, reel 75.4.

66. Balch to Graves, Mar. 30, 1942, Anna Melissa Graves Papers, SCPC, microfilm, Correspondence, reel 74.1. In an interview with her biographer, Mercedes Randall, Balch explained the moral choice that had led to her support for World War II: "It is not possible to have a code of ethics which says this thing is right and this wrong in regards [to] any concrete or specific acts, . . . but the obligation to do right as far as in our power, is an absolute obligation with no exceptions. The rejection of physical violence as always evil, is not possible to maintain." See Interview with Randall, Feb. 22, 1950, Balch Papers, reel 129.18.

CHAPTER 6

1. Draft of Policies and Principles, 1934–35, Women's International League for Peace and Freedom, United States Section Records, SCPC, microfilm, Series A,2, box 3, folder 4 (hereafter cited as WIL Records). This same statement was adopted by the International Congress of the WILPF in 1926 and appeared on WILPF membership cards. See Balch's membership card, Dec. 1930, Emily Greene Balch Papers, SCPC, microfilm, reel 129.8.

2. Tentative Draft of League of Nations Resolutions, 1920, WIL Records, reel 100.6.

3. Action Taken By National Headquarters since the Executive Committee Meeting, Jan. 8–9, 1923, WIL Records, reel 100.6.

4. Detzer to Balch and Hull, July 24, 1932, Balch Papers, Correspondence 1932. See Detzer's comments on the conference in her book *Appointment on the Hill* (New York: Henry Holt, 1948), p. 112. See also Hull to Addams, May 1, 1932, Jane Addams Papers, SCPC, reel 1.15.

5. National Board Resolution re: Inter-American Commission of Women, Oct. 30–Nov. 1, 1940, WIL Records, reel 100.11.

6. Hull to Cordell Hull, July 4, 1936, Hannah Clothier Hull Papers, SCPC, microfilm, reel 75.3.

7. Nancy Cott, *The Grounding of Modern Feminism* (New Haven, Conn.: Yale University Press, 1987), pp. 9, 120–29.

8. Minutes of Annual Meeting, Mar. 8, 1924, WIL Records, reel 100.6; Minutes of Annual Meeting, May 1–4, 1936, WIL Records, reel 100.9; Minutes of Annual Meeting, Apr. 30–May 3, 1937, WIL Records, reel 100.10; and Resolution, n.d., Balch Papers, Writings 1940s, folder 1941.

9. See Blake to Addams, May 18, 1935, Addams Papers, reel 1.17; Lloyd to Hull, July 31, 1934, Hull Papers, reel 75.2; Lloyd, Report on Minorities, 1936, WIL Records, reel 100.9; and Minutes of Annual Meeting, Apr. 30–May 3, 1937, WIL Records, reel 100.10.

10. In 1937, for example, after extended discussion of the ERA, the motion in support of it failed by a vote of 70 to 44. See Minutes of Annual Meeting, Apr. 30–May 3, 1937, WIL Records, reel 100.10.

11. Quoted in Cott, *Grounding of Modern Feminism*, pp. 139–40. Addams decried abstraction as a philosophical principle; see my analysis of her view in "Jane Addams and William James on Alternatives to War," *Journal of the History of Ideas* (Apr. 1993): 241–54.

12. For a few years during the mid 1930s, Detzer's title was changed to national secretary and she shared her responsibilities with Mabel Vernon and Mildred Scott Olmsted. See Margaret Hope Bacon, *One Woman's Passion for Peace and Freedom: The Life of Mildred Scott Olmsted* (Syracuse, N.Y.: Syracuse University Press, 1993), p. 181.

13. Detzer to Addams, Hull, and Balch, May 19, 1927, Addams Papers, reel 1.11.

14. Detzer, Interview with Rosemary Rainbolt, Dorothy Detzer Papers, SCPC, Series 1, p. 13, box 1; ellipses in the original. Evidently the leaders of the WILPF in Europe felt the same; they never admitted men out of fear that the men would take over the organization and force the women out. See Bacon, *One Woman's Passion*, p. 184.

15. Hull to Mary Williams, Feb. 24, 1925, Hull Papers, reel 75.1.

16. See Minutes of National Board Meeting, Jan. 29–30, 1929, WIL Records, reel 100.7; and Minutes of National Board Meeting, Apr. 28, 1932, WIL Records, reel 100.8.

17. Bacon, *One Woman's Passion*, p. 184.

18. Olmsted to Agnes Ryan, Apr. 10, 1935, Agnes Ryan Papers, SL, box 5, folder 60.

19. Minutes of Annual Meeting, May 4–6, 1939, WIL Records, reel 100.13.

20. Report of the Committee to Poll Opinion on Changing Name of WILPF, Jan. 20–21, 1940, WIL Records, Series A,2, box 9, folder 5; Minutes of Annual Meeting, Apr. 27–30, 1940, WIL Records, reel 100.13.

21. Report of the Committee to Poll Opinion on Changing Name of WILPF, Jan. 20–21, 1940, WIL Records, Series A,2, box 9, folder 5; ellipses in the original.

22. See Cott, *Grounding of Modern Feminism*, pp. 269–83; and Estelle Freedman, "Separatism Revisited: Women's Institutions, Social Reform, and the Career of Miriam Van Waters," in *U.S. History as Women's History: New Feminist Essays*, ed. Linda K. Kerber, Alice Kessler-Harris, and Kathryn Kish Sklar (Chapel Hill: University of North Carolina Press, 1995), pp. 170–88. Freedman argues that although the rhetoric of separatism declined, many women reformers still relied on women's support systems (p. 186).

23. See Linda Schott, "Women Against War: Pacifism, Feminism, and Social Justice in the United States, 1915–1941" (Ph.D. diss., Stanford University, 1986), pp. 178–81 and 186–88, for a more detailed description of these activities. For an analysis of women's role in the origins of the civil liberties movement, see Frances Early, "Feminism, Peace, and Civil Liberties: Women's Role in the Origins of the World War I Civil Liberties Movement," *Women's Studies* 18 (1990): 95–115.

24. Minutes of Executive Board Meeting, Jan. 7, 1920, WIL Records, reel 100.6; Resolutions suggested to 1922 convention, WIL Records, reel 100.6.

25. Report of the National President, 1934, WIL Records, reel 100.8.

26. National Board Resolutions re: Civil Rights, 1939, WIL Records, reel 100.11.

27. National Board Resolutions re: Four Freedoms, Jan. 18–19, 1941, WIL Records, reel 100.11.

28. *Rosika Schwimmer: World Patriot* (London: Odhams Press, 1947), pp. 9–10.

29. Detzer, "News of the United States Section," May 1929, WIL Records, reel 100.7.

30. "Statement of Policies," *Pax International* 4, no. 7 (June 1929), WIL Records, Series A,2, box 2, folder 6.

31. See Bill McNitt, "Peace and American Society: Rebecca Shelley and the Peace Movement" (University of Michigan, unpublished paper, 1970); and Shelley to Balch, Dec. 10, 1932, Rebecca Shelley Papers, Correspondence from July to Dec. 1932, Michigan Historical Collections, Bentley Historical Library, University of Michigan, Ann Arbor, Mich., box 1.

32. See Shelley to Balch, Dec. 10, 1932, Shelley Papers, Correspondence from July to Dec. 1932, box 1; Shelley to Witherspoon and Mygatt, Dec. 31, 1939, Shelley Papers, Correspondence, box 2; and Shelley to Doris Stevens, Dec. 15 and Dec. 18, 1939, Shelley Papers, Correspondence, box 2.

33. Report of National President, 1934, WIL Records, reel 100.9; and Hull to Mrs. Reuben Albert Baer, Mar. 7, 1938, Hull Papers, reel 75.3.

34. "Proposed Principles and Policies," May 1–4, 1941, WIL Records, Series A,2, box 10, folder 3.

35. Detzer, *Appointment on the Hill*, pp. 207–8.

36. Ibid.

37. See Jane Addams, "Respect for Law," *The Independent*, Jan. 3, 1901, reprinted in Jane Addams and Ida B. Wells, *Lynching and Rape: An Exchange of Views*, ed. Bettina Aptheker (New York: American Institute for Marxist Studies, 1977); and Allen F. Davis, *Spearheads for Reform: The Social Settlements and the Progressive Movement, 1890–1914* (New York: Oxford University Press, 1967), pp. 101–2.

38. Minutes, 1915–1917, Pennsylvania branch, Woman's Peace Party Records, SCPC, microfilm, reel 12.21.

39. Post to Addams, Dec. 10, 1918; Addams to Post, Dec. 13, 1918; and Post to Addams, Dec. 17, 1918; all in Balch papers, reel 129.6. Apparently there was concern that the delegation from the United States should include a representative of the Jewish community as well. Post also asked Addams about the possibilities of having a Jewish woman in attendance; "Would Miss [Lillian] Wald be so counted? If not, would Miss Alice Lewissohn who was proposed in New York, answer?" See Post to Addams, Dec. 13, 1918, Balch papers, reel 129.6.

40. Post to Addams, Dec. 17, 1918, Balch Papers, reel 129.6.

41. Report on Zurich Conference, 1919, Mary Church Terrell Papers, LOC, microfilm, reel 21.

42. Mary Church Terrell, *A Colored Woman in a White World* (Washington, D.C., Randsdell, 1940), p. 333.

43. Report on Zurich Conference, 1919, Terrell Papers, reel 21.

44. Terrell, *A Colored Woman*, pp. 333–34. I was unable to find an account of this event from Balch's point of view.

45. Report on Zurich Conference, 1919, Terrell Papers, reel 21.

46. Terrell, *A Colored Woman*, pp. 360–63.

47. Ibid, pp. 363–64.

48. Resolution on Race Prejudice, 1922, WIL Records, reel 100.6.

49. The records of the WIL do not explain why Terrell was not reelected. Belle LaFollette did warn WIL leaders that if Terrell was left off the board, "it is certain to be interpreted as due to race prejudice." See LaFollette to Lucy Biddle Lewis, Mar. 27, 1923, LaFollette Family Papers, LOC, Series D, box 26. Mildred Scott Olmsted and Emily Greene Balch later recalled that Terrell had not been reelected because she had been largely inactive. See Olmsted to Balch, Jan. 7, 1929, and Balch to Olmsted, Jan. 11, 1929, Balch Papers, reel 129.8.

50. Paula Giddings, *When and Where I Enter: The Impact of Black Women on Race and Sex in America* (New York: William Morrow, 1984), pp. 140, 153.

51. See Report of Inter-racial Committee, Dec. 1928–Jan. 1929, WIL Records, reel 100.7.

52. See Olmsted to Balch, Jan. 7, 1929, Balch Papers, reel 129.8.

53. Ibid.

54. Balch to Olmsted, Jan. 11, 1929, Balch Papers, reel 129.8.

55. Balch to Hunton, Jan. 11, 1929, Balch Papers, reel 129.8.

56. Hunton to "Lady Mollie" [Terrell], Jan. 19, 1929, Balch Papers, reel 129.8.

57. Balch to Hunton, Jan. 22, 1929, Balch Papers, reel 129.8.

58. Although Terrell did not specify the incident at the 1919 conference, when Balch reputedly reworded Terrell's resolution against racism without Terrell's permission, surely this must have contributed to her negative feeling toward Balch.

59. Terrell to Balch, Feb. 1, 1929, Balch Papers, reel 129.8.

60. Terrell to Hunton, Feb. 1, 1929, Balch Papers, reel 129.9.

61. Olmsted to Balch, Feb. 15, 1929, Balch Papers, reel 129.8; and Note, Feb. 12, 1929, Balch Papers, reel 129.8.

62. "Statement of Policies," reprinted in *Pax International* 4, no. 7 (June 1929), WIL Records, Series A,2, box 2, folder 6.

63. Terrell to Olmsted, Nov. 26, 1930, Balch Papers, reel 129.8; and Olmsted to Balch, Nov. 28, 1930, Balch Papers, reel 128.9.

64. "Colored Women and World Peace," 1932, WIL Records, Series A,2, box 4.

65. Hunton to "friend," Aug. 30, 1932, Bertha McNeill Papers, SCPC, box 1.

66. Annual Report of Interracial Committee, 1932, WIL Records, Series A,2, box 1.

67. Report of Interracial Committee, May 1933, WIL Records, reel 100.8.

68. Report of Interracial Committee, 1934, WIL Records, reel 100.8.

69. Martha Helen Elliott to Addie Hunton, Mar. 18, 1936, sent with accompanying note to McNeill, McNeill Papers, box 1. A similar move was advocated for the New York branch by Caroline Singer; see her memo to Dorothy Hommel and Lyn Smith, Dec. 29, 1937, WIL Records, Series, A,2, box 1.

70. Branch Letter from Chairman of Interracial Committee, 1937, McNeill Papers, box 1.

71. McElwain to McNeill, Apr. 15, 1937, McNeill Papers, box 1.

72. Minutes of Annual Meeting, May 1–4, 1936, WIL Records, reel 100.9. I found no record of a final decision on this matter. Another separatist women's organization, the Young Women's Christian Association, also confronted this issue. The YWCA was less willing than the WIL to integrate African-American women into the organization. See Giddings, *When and Where I Enter*, pp. 155–58.

73. Detzer to Libby, June 26, 1930, WIL Records, Series C, reel 130.53.

74. Report of Executive Secretary, Oct. 1930, WIL Records, reel 100.7. The WIL's action contrasts with the policy of the National Committee on the Cause and Cure of War. When planning its conference for 1924, Carrie Chapman Catt learned that the host hotel excluded African Americans. The hotel manager told her that he considered segregation "a sad thing but that an unalterable rule could not be violated." Catt did not protest the policy but provided lodging in "colored families of good status for any colored delegates who might come." See Catt to Arrangements Committee, Nov. 11, 1924, Josephine Schain Papers, Sophia Smith Collection, Smith College, Northampton, Mass., box 5.

75. Jacquelyn Dowd Hall, *Revolt Against Chivalry: Jessie Daniel Ames and the Women's Campaign Against Lynching* (New York: Columbia University Press, 1979), pp. 165–66. European-American women in the South did not organize to protest lynching until 1930.

76. The WIL Interracial Record, 1933, WIL Records, Series A,2, box 3, folder 4; Statement of Policies, Apr. 24–27, 1929, reprinted in *Pax International* (June 1929), WIL Records, Series A,2, box 2, folder 6.

77. Detzer to White, Feb. 9, 1933, WIL Records, reel 130.53; White to Detzer, Feb. 15, 1933, reel 130.53; and National Board Resolution re Anti-Lynching, Jan. 20–21, 1940, WIL Records, reel 100.8.

78. Report of the Executive Secretary, Aug. 1933, WIL Records, reel 100.8. Detzer's position may have been influenced by the work of Arthur F. Raper. His 1933 book, *The Tragedy of Lynching*, argued that lynchings resulted from economic competition between blacks and whites. Walter White of the

STAFFORDSHIRE
UNIVERSITY
LIBRARY

NAACP made a similar argument. See Daniel Singal, *The War Within: Victorian to Modernist Thought in the South, 1919–1945* (Chapel Hill: University of North Carolina Press, 1982), pp. 332–33.

79. Statement of Policies, Apr. 24–27, 1929, reprinted in *Pax International* (June 1929), WIL Records, Series A,2, box 2, folder 6.

80. Ibid.

81. Hull to Mrs. Harry D. Reed, July 27, 1936, Hull Papers, reel 75.3.

82. Action of WIL on Anti-Semitism, Mar. 19–20, 1933; Resolution at Annual Meeting, May 21–22, 1933; and Minutes of National Board Meeting, Oct. 12–13, 1933; all in WIL Records, reel 100.8.

83. Balch to Addams, Apr. 30, 1933, Addams Papers, reel 1.15.

84. Balch to Mrs. Partridge, Nov. 1938, Balch Papers, reel 129.10; Proposed Principles and Policies, May 1–4, 1941, WIL Records, Series A,2, box 10, folder 3.

85. National Board Resolutions re: Anti-Semitism, Oct. 18–19, 1941, WIL Records, reel 100.11.

86. Walter Lippmann to Balch, Feb. 8, 1916, Balch Papers, reel 129.6; Minutes of Executive Board Meeting, Sept. 28, 1920, WIL Records, reel 100.6.

87. "Social Values in Haiti," reprinted in *Beyond Nationalism: The Social Thought of Emily Greene Balch*, ed. Mercedes M. Randall (New York: Twayne, 1972), p. 145.

88. "Memorandum on Haiti," reprinted in ibid., p. 150.

89. Mercedes M. Randall, *Improper Bostonian: Emily Greene Balch, Nobel Peace laureate, 1946* (New York: Twayne, 1964), pp. 304–5.

90. See Statement of Policies, Apr. 24–27, 1927, reprinted in *Pax International* (June 1929), p. 2; Minutes of Annual Meeting, May 3–5, 1928, WIL Records, reel 100.7; Detzer to Chairmen of State and Local Branches, June 1, 1928, Balch Papers, reel 129.8; National Board Resolution re: Latin America, 1940, WIL Records, reel 100.11; and the Tentative Draft of Policies and Principles, 1934–35, WIL Records, Series A,2, box 3, folder 4.

91. See Balch to James Grafton Rogers, Mar. 16, 1932, Balch Papers, reel 129.9; Press Release from the Department of State, Sept. 27, 1932, Balch Papers, reel 129.8; and Detzer to Anna Melissa Graves, July 18, 1933, Balch Papers, reel 129.9.

92. Notes for speech, n.d., Detzer Papers, box 1, Speeches and Releases, 1931–40, pp. 1–2.

93. Balch to Graves, 1941, Anna Melissa Graves Papers, SCPC, microfilm, reel 74.1.

94. "Report to Tenth International Congress of WILPF," 1946, McNeill Papers, box 2.

95. Detzer, *Appointment on the Hill*, p. 208.

96. See Minutes of Organizational Conference, Jan. 10–11, 1915, WPP Records, reel 12.17; Platform of the WPP, reprinted in Marie L. Degen, *The History of the Woman's Peace Party* (Baltimore, Md.: Johns Hopkins Press, 1939), p. 41; and the statement of principles expressed on the membership card of the WILPF, Dec. 1930, Balch Papers, reel 129.8.

97. Note from Addams, enclosed in letter from Camille Drevet, Apr. 1932, Addams Papers, reel 1.15.

98. "Women and War," [n.d.], Detzer Papers, Speeches and Releases, 1931–40, box 1.

99. Radio Address for Pittsburg WCAE, [n.d.], Detzer Papers, Speeches and Releases 1931–40, box 1.

100. Hull to Mrs. Harry D. Reed, July 27, 1936, Hull Papers, reel 75.3. As early as 1923, the Women's Peace Union had opposed the use of violence to settle labor disputes. See Press Release, n.d. [1920–23], Women's Peace Union Records, SCPC, microfilm, reel 88.2.

101. Annual Report of Labor Secretary, Apr. 30, 1937, WIL Records, reel 100.10.

102. "Principles of Our Labor Work," 1937, WIL Records, reel 100.10.

103. Ibid.

104. Ibid.

105. Annual Report of Dorothy Detzer, Apr. 30, 1937, WIL Records, Series A,2, box 2, p. 12.

106. Annual Report of Labor Committee, Apr. 1938, WIL Records, reel 100.10.

107. Hull to Mrs. W. C. Paxson, June 17, 1937, Hull Papers, reel 75.3. See also National Board Resolutions re: Four Freedoms, Jan. 18–19, 1941, and National Board Resolutions re: Labor, Oct. 18–19, 1941; both in WIL Records, reel 100.11.

108. Charles Chatfield, *For Peace and Justice: Pacifism in America, 1914–1941* (Knoxville: University of Tennessee Press, 1971), p. 257.

109. Draft of Policies and Principles for 1934–35, 1933, WIL Records, Series A,2, box 2, folder 4.

110. See, for example, Hull to Miss Rufus Adams, May 13, 1936, Hull Papers, reel 75.3; and Hull to Mr. Noel Spannagel, Feb. 2, 1939, Hull Papers, reel 75.4. The New York City branch of the WIL also opposed the decision by the WIL national board to affiliate with the American League. See Harriet Alonso, *Peace as a Women's Issue: A History of the U.S. Movement for World Peace and Women's Rights* (Syracuse, N.Y.: Syracuse University Press, 1993), pp. 130–33.

111. Chatfield, *For Peace and Justice*, p. 261, and Anne Marie Pois, "The Politics of Organizing for Change," pp. 403–4.

112. Proposed Principles and Policies, May 1–4, 1941, WIL Records, Series A,2, box 10, folder 3.

113. Jane Addams, *The Second Twenty Years at Hull House* (New York: Macmillan, 1930), p. 37.

CHAPTER 7

1. National Board Resolutions re: War with Japan, Dec. 10, 1941, Women's International League for Peace and Freedom, United States Branch Records, SCPC, microfilm, reel 100.11.

STAFFORDSHIRE UNIVERSITY LIBRARY

2. See Susan Lynn, *Progressive Women in Conservative Times: Racial Justice, Peace, and Feminism, 1945 to the 1960s* (New Brunswick, N.J.: Rutgers University Press, 1992). Lynn argues that "the mixed-sex composition of the AFSC led it to ignore feminist issues altogether." Lynn contrasts the American Friends Service Committee to the YWCA, the "all-female nature" of which led it "to advocate measures to increase women's status" (p. 5).

3. For an excellent critique of this kind of formulation, see Nancy Cott, "What's in a Name? The Limits of 'Social Feminism'; or Expanding the Vocabulary of Women's History," *Journal of American History* 76 (Dec. 1989): 809–29.

4. Gerda Lerner argues that "feminist consciousness is a prerequisite for the formulation of the kind of abstract thought needed to conceptualize a society in which differences do not connote dominance." See Gerda Lerner, *The Creation of Feminist Consciousness: From the Middle Ages to Eighteen-Seventy* (New York: Oxford University Press, 1993), p. 281.

5. Both Lori Ginzberg, in her study of women's benevolent work in the nineteenth century, and Peggy Pascoe, in her study of women's mission homes in the late nineteenth and early twentieth centuries, explicitly compare the arguments about the differences between men and women made by their historical subjects with the arguments made by cultural feminists today. See Lori Ginzberg, *Women and the Work of Benevolence: Morality, Politics, and Class in the Nineteenth-Century United States* (New Haven, Conn.: Yale University Press, 1990), afterword; and Peggy Pascoe, *Relations of Rescue: The Search for Female Moral Authority in the American West, 1874–1939* (New York: Oxford University Press, 1990), epilogue.

6. I have relied here on the insights of Gerda Lerner. In *The Creation of Feminist Consciousness*, Lerner notes her belief that "all human beings develop ideas based, at least in part, on their own experience. Women, because of educational deprivation and the absence of a usable past, tended to rely more heavily on their own experience in developing their ideas than did men" (p. 119).

7. See, for example, Barbara Epstein, *The Politics of Domesticity: Women, Evangelism, and Temperance in Nineteenth-Century America* (Middletown, Conn.: Wesleyan University Press, 1981); Ruth Rosen, *The Lost Sisterhood: Prostitution in America, 1900–1918* (Baltimore, Md.: Johns Hopkins University Press, 1982); and Ginzberg, *Women and the Work of Benevolence.*

8. In her book *Relations of Rescue*, Peggy Pascoe persuasively challenged the view that Victorian women considered themselves, and were considered by others, to be morally superior to men. Pascoe argues that this interpretation has two faults: it conjures up an unfair image of the dour, self-righteous Victorian prude, and it overestimates the degree of power actually available to women. Pascoe believes that it is more accurate to portray Victorian women as in search of "female moral authority"—influence in certain areas based on women's supposed traits of piety, purity, and morality. See pp. xvi–xvii and 208.

9. See, for example, Daniel Joseph Singal, "Towards a Definition of Amer-

ican Modernism," in *Modernist Culture in America* (Belmont, Calif.: Wadsworth, 1991), p. 11.

10. See Lerner, *The Creation of Feminist Consciousness*, pp. 281–82, 275.

11. Ibid., p. 283.

12. See Lewis Perry, *Intellectual Life in America* (New York: Franklin Watts, 1984), pp. 371–36; see also Singal's discussion of Tate's admiration of Emily Dickinson's ability to "function at that exact level of integrated perception where thought and emotion are miraculously fused," in *The War Within: From Victorian to Modernist Thought in the South, 1919–1945* (Chapel Hill: University of North Carolina Press, 1982), p. 253.

13. Lerner, *The Creation of Feminist Consciousness*, pp. 11–12.

14. For an example of similar ideas among Mexican workers, see Emilio Zamora, *The World of the Mexican Worker in Texas* (College Station: Texas A & M University Press, 1993), esp. chap. 4.

Index

In this index an "f" after a number indicates a separate reference on the next page, and an "ff" indicates separate references on the next two pages. A continuous discussion over two or more pages is indicated by a span of page numbers, e.g., "57–59." *Passim* is used for a cluster of references in close but not consecutive sequence.

STAFFORDSHIRE
UNIVERSITY
LIBRARY

Library of Congress Cataloging-in-Publication Data

Schott, Linda K.
   Reconstructing women's thoughts : The Women's
International League for Peace and Freedom before
World War II / Linda K. Schott.
     p.   cm. — (Modern America)
Includes index.
ISBN 0-8047-2746-5 (cloth)
   1. Women's International League for Peace and Freedom.
U.S. Section—History. 2. Women and peace—History.
3. Women—United States—History. I. Series: Modern
America (Stanford, Calif.)
JX1965.S36   1997
327.1'72'082—dc20   96-20604
                                       CIP

∞ This book is printed on acid-free, recycled paper.

Original printing 1997

Last figure below indicates year of this printing:

06 05 04 03 02 01 00 99 98 97